# *Music Cataloging*

# MUSIC CATALOGING

## The Bibliographic Control of Printed and Recorded Music in Libraries

RICHARD P. SMIRAGLIA

1989

**Libraries Unlimited, Inc.** • Englewood, Colorado

LIBRARIES UNLIMITED, INC.
P.O. Box 3988
Englewood, CO 80155-3988

---

**Library of Congress Cataloging-in-Publication Data**

Smiraglia, Richard P., 1952-
  Music cataloging.

  Bibliography: p. 203.
  Includes index.
  1. Cataloging of music.  2. Cataloging of sound
recordings.  3. Classification--Music.  4. Classifi-
cation--Sound recordings.  I. Title.
ML111.S635  1989      025.3'48      88-27222
ISBN 0-87287-425-7

#19/29028

*To ggb*

# CONTENTS

# *PREFACE*

---

*Manifesto = a public declaration of motives and intentions; treatise = a formal, systematic essay; textbook = a book giving instruction in the principles of a subject of study.*[1]

This book is all three of these things. Primarily, it is a textbook designed to introduce the field of music cataloging to students of music librarianship, students of cataloging, and/or music librarians or general catalogers who find themselves in need of a basic explanation of the prevalent practices in the bibliographic control of music materials.

Accordingly, I have taken a narrow definition of music materials, limiting this text to the practice of cataloging, classification, and control of scores and musical sound recordings, because I strongly believe that the bibliographic control of music books is no different than that of other kinds of textual materials. Readers should have a good grounding in bibliographic control before they approach this volume, and are referred in particular to Arlene Taylor's text of Bohdan Wynar's *Introduction to Cataloging and Classification.*[2]

This text is further limited in that it does not attempt to cover the managerial aspects of music technical services. Practices such as binding, shelving, copy cataloging, cataloging workflow, staffing patterns, and the design of online systems, to name a few, are influenced by the broader demands of music library administration. For background in managerial techniques readers are referred to the Music Library Association's Technical Reports Series, where many of these topics receive monographic treatment, and to the two historical collections of essays on music librarianship edited by Carol Bradley.[3]

A final limitation is musical background. Readers should approach this text with an understanding of the history, theory, and performance of Western art music, and it will be helpful if the reader is informed and open-minded about other musics as well.

The book opens with an introduction to bibliographic control, for it is against this broad conceptual backdrop that I view the practice and study of music cataloging. This introduction also demonstrates the tortoiselike progress of true theory building in the bibliographic control of music materials. It is in this sense that I regard this book as my *manifesto.* Empirical understanding and testable theories will be increasingly important if music librarians are to design appropriate computer-based retrieval systems. Throughout the book, areas for further research and development are noted.

Chapter 1 is an introduction to music materials. In this chapter the various kinds of scores and recordings that are common in libraries are defined and some of their bibliographic characteristics are highlighted. Photographs are used to show the physical differences among various formats of musical presentation.

Following is a series of three chapters on descriptive cataloging. The first of these chapters is a historical examination of the development of descriptive conventions in music cataloging. The two chapters that follow, one on description of musical items and one on access to musical works, explain current practices against that historical backdrop.

The next series of three chapters is devoted to subject analysis of musical works. This time the introductory chapter presents a conceptual overview of subject analysis, followed by chapters on verbal subject systems (subject headings) and classification. Each of these chapters includes a historical examination of the development of what have become de facto standards for subject cataloging and classification of music materials.

The final group of four chapters treats issues that deal with record manipulation and retrieval. The development of the music format for machine-readable cataloging is described along with an introduction to content designation of music bibliographic records. This is followed by a chapter on authority control, in which the machine-readable authority record is presented and prospects for its future examined. Next is a chapter on filing practices, which includes a historical examination of the development of pseudo-classified arrangements of music uniform titles. Finally, a chapter on sources of music cataloging describes the most common printed union catalogs and online bibliographic databases.

As an aid to students of music cataloging, most chapters include brief lists of suggested readings. These are, for the most part, historical or otherwise significant documents in music librarianship, or they are general texts that will provide further or more detailed instruction. Following the final chapter is a glossary that defines terms used throughout this book. At the end is a selected bibliography of articles and books with which beginning music catalogers ought to be familiar.

Writing this book has been a fascinating experience. Among the more interesting observations that occurred to me in the process were those associated with the literature. A glance at the selected bibliography will show the richness and breadth of the literature of music cataloging. A century of developments and local practices is described in a variety of articles and a very few books. It occurs to me that a field so rich in literature is ripe for further academic development. There is significant potential for historical research as well as empirical study.

A related observation is that there has been some difficulty with the dissemination of techniques. New generations of music catalogers often seem to be unaware of (or at least fail to cite) developments reported by preceding generations. Bradley's historical work has helped somewhat to alleviate this,[4] and I hope this book will also help new music catalogers to enter the field with a solid overview of historical developments and traditional techniques.

There is also a noticeable division in the literature between music catalogers and general catalogers who deal with music. It was particularly intriguing to note the difference between the development of rules for description of scores, which took place under the aegis of the American Library Association with the cooperation of music specialists, and the development of similar rules for description of sound recordings. The many reports of techniques developed by generalists indicated that the two "camps" seemed to be largely unaware of each other.

It is interesting to muse about this situation and it is important for music catalogers to remain aware of it. I suspect that the forms of literature developed by music catalogers have been insufficient in many ways, not the least of which has been a failure to reach general catalogers who also work with music materials. Perhaps another problem has been the small number of full-time library science professors working in music librarianship. At any rate it behooves us to become as familiar with our past as music librarians as we must become with our present as music information managers in the information age.

# Notes

[1]Derived from definitions in *Webster's New World Dictionary of the American Language*, concise ed., ed. David B. Guralnik (Cleveland, Ohio: World Publishing Co., 1962).

[2]Bohdan S. Wynar, *Introduction to Cataloging and Classification*, 7th ed. by Arlene G. Taylor (Littleton, Colo.: Libraries Unlimited, 1985).

[3]Carol June Bradley, *Manual of Music Librarianship* (Ann Arbor, Mich.: Music Library Association, 1966); and *Reader in Music Librarianship* (Washington, D.C.: NCR Microcard Books, 1973).

[4]See particularly Carol June Bradley, "Notes of Some Pioneers: America's First Music Librarians," *Notes* 43 (1986): 272-91; and Carol June Bradley, "The Genesis of American Music Librarianship, 1902-1942" (Ph.D. diss., Florida State University, 1978).

# ACKNOWLEDGMENTS

This book represents the most complex project I have undertaken to date, and I must express my thanks to the many people and institutions who have had a part in its genesis.

A prime indicator of the strength and autonomy of a profession is the existence of a professional literature. I am happy to report that music cataloging is a healthy profession with a vast literature. Credit for this revelation goes to all those who played a role in compiling and manipulating the comprehensive bibliography from which I worked. The University of Illinois Library Research and Publication Committee supported a proposal to employ research assistants to compile this bibliography and for that I and the graduate assistants named in the next sentences are most grateful. During my time at Illinois, David Hunter compiled the original retrospective bibliography, which was updated, exceptionally well organized, and thoroughly automated by Virginia Danielson. Dean Jensen updated the recordings and popular music sections of the bibliography, and Char Kneevers retrieved the majority of the material. At Columbia, Robert Cianchette has been calm when I haven't; and he has played an important role in completing the final manuscript.

The book owes its genesis to Heather Cameron, formerly of Libraries Unlimited, who patiently encouraged me to proceed when there were many other demands on my time. As always, my friend, mentor, and colleague Dr. Arlene Taylor has been there for me, listening to the outline of each chapter and delighting in my discoveries. My students at Columbia have read the majority of the manuscript and offered tactful advice on the text; in particular, Charles Whitlow and David Thomas both plodded through the first manuscript and offered helpful advice. Perhaps the most sensitive review of the manuscript (and most tactful response) was provided by my colleague Deborah Campana of Northwestern University.

The legacy of excellent librarians is excellent library collections, three of which have been of tremendous assistance to me in this research. I owe a great debt to the collections and staff of the libraries at the University of Illinois at Urbana-Champaign. Not only were the library science and music collections of tremendous help in the research and planning stages of this book, but more important, for thirteen years my professional practice and opinions were shaped through increasing intimacy with those collections. Also, my thanks to Dr. Olha Della Cava, Librarian at the School of Library Service Library at Columbia University, and Dr. John Roberts, then Librarian at the Otto E. Albrecht Music Library at the University of Pennsylvania. Both have maintained and continued to build excellent collections in this field, and more important, both were exceedingly patient and helpful during the last summer of writing when I was frantic for assistance. As always, my colleague and friend Brad Young, also at Penn, has helped shape this text.

I am grateful to Barbara Tillett for helping me to acquire a copy of the Library of Congress rules on cards. Brad Young graciously allowed me to scrutinize his copy of the PRECIS manual for the *British Catalogue of Music*. Glenn Patton of OCLC helped me acquire technical information about videorecordings. As often before, David Sommerfield of the Music Section, Special Materials Cataloging Division at the Library of Congress has been willing to answer my questions about many policies and practices of his section.

Authors of books about cataloging face many challenges, but one of the greatest is that of finding good examples. Early in the preparation of this manuscript (when I had access only to OCLC) Richard Griscom and Ralph Papakhian helped me find many of the examples from RLIN and LC-MUMS that appear in chapter 8. I am especially grateful to OCLC and RLG for permission to include printed screen displays from their systems throughout this book. For the photographs that appear in chapter 1, I am indebted to Richard Pardo, Media Coordinator at the School of Library Service, Columbia University.

Finally, this text would not have come to be had it not been for the inquisitiveness of all the students over the past decade of instruction in music cataloging, who have challenged me to tell them, *why*?

# INTRODUCTION
## *Bibliographic Control, Theory, and Music Cataloging*

## Introduction

Just as music librarianship must be viewed as a subset of librarianship, music cataloging must be viewed as a subset of its parent field, bibliographic control. The processes of bibliographic control, though not format-dependent, are affected by the physical and intellectual characteristics of the items and works controlled. Principles govern bibliographic control and provide a framework for theoretically grounded research. In order to introduce music cataloging as an element of bibliographic control, this chapter examines these issues with attention to the functional requirements of music materials.

## Bibliographic Control

Bibliographic control is the process by which bibliographic data are created, stored, manipulated, and retrieved. Because it is a process, it is not format sensitive, which is to say that bibliographic control is the same process regardless of the type of material to which it is applied. Further, bibliographic control is a two-way communicative process that allows an information service (such as a library or archive) to serve as a sort of middleman between creators of information (such as authors or composers) and consumers of information (such as readers, researchers, scholars, musicians, etc.). The process is circular, because the consumers of recorded information often become the creators of new information, which is used in turn to create still other new information.[1]

The concept space wherein bibliographic control operates is often referred to as the *bibliographic universe*. The bibliographic universe is a subset of all knowledge. In this particular subset all instances of *recorded* knowledge can be found. Knowledge that is not in some way recorded (written down, printed, taped, etc.) is beyond control, and is dependent on frail human abilities such as memory for communication and subsequent utilization. On the other hand, recorded knowledge can be easily communicated. Its containers (books, tapes, maps, scores, etc.) may be held, owned, loaned, and otherwise passed from person to person, facilitating communication of information. The creation of tools that can be used to retrieve these items, which in turn facilitate communicating the knowledge they contain, is bibliographic control.

There are many types of these retrieval tools, usually referred to collectively as bibliographic sources. Among the more common are sources such as abstracting and indexing services or enumerative bibliographies, which seek to provide bibliographic control over a literature or a significant portion of it, and catalogs, which are bibliographic sources that seek to provide bibliographic control over specific collections of bibliographic items.

## FUNCTIONS

There are three functions that are common to all kinds of bibliographic sources.[2] The first is the *identifying function*, sometimes called the finding function, which allows a user to recognize a particular bibliographic item in a catalog. A known-item search, in which a user matches a citation to a bibliographic record, is the most straightforward example of the identifying function.

The second is the *collocating function*. Collocating is defined as "the arranging of elements in certain positions, particularly side-by-side."[3] In the collocating function a bibliographic source gathers similar access terms together and displays them side-by-side, allowing the user to approach the representation for a work as a member of a larger class of works. Thus the collocating function allows a work by Mozart to be seen as one of many works by Mozart, or a recording of Mozart's *Requiem* to be seen as one of many manifestations (scores, recordings, etc.) of the *Requiem*. The collocating function also works in files arranged by subject terms, so that the Mozart *Requiem* may be found among all works in the form "Requiem."

The third function is the *evaluating function*. This function, sometimes called the selecting function, allows the user to choose one from among many bibliographic records as being the record that might best correspond to the desired information carrier. Thus, a catalog user looking at bibliographic records for sound recordings of Mozart's *Requiem* may specifically choose a compact disc recording because that is the playback mechanism available for listening. The presence in the bibliographic record of information about playback allows the user to evaluate the bibliographic data and make a successful selection.

## DOMAINS

Patrick Wilson has shown that bibliographic control functions in two conceptual domains.[4] The first domain is the *descriptive domain*, in which routine bibliographic activity takes place. This is the domain in which bibliographic sources are constructed. The second domain is the *exploitative domain*. In the exploitative domain the user attempts to make the best possible use of a body of knowledge.

Exploitative control is achieved only as a result of descriptive control. Bibliographic sources, in particular the arrangement of access points, provide pathways to understanding the works and items described. The three functions—identifying, collocating, and evaluating—all operate in the descriptive domain. The third function, however, is the user's gateway to exploitative control. To the extent that a bibliographic source provides a user with the opportunity to exploit information, that source can be said to have successfully provided bibliographic control.

The processes that are used to fulfill the functions of the descriptive domain are descriptive cataloging; subject analysis; classification; and record manipulation, arrangement, and retrieval. As noted earlier, these processes are not format-specific. However, differences in the ways bibliographic items are produced and distributed affect significantly the effectiveness of these processes, when measured against the functions of bibliographic sources. In the next segment of this chapter, the areas of bibliographic control that are unique to music materials (scores and recordings) will be explored.

# Descriptive Cataloging

Descriptive cataloging is the act of transcribing and annotating the inherent bibliographic data from a bibliographic item in such a way that the item itself can be identified by reference to its description. Inherent bibliographic data are statements appearing on bibliographic items (such as title, composer, publisher, etc.) that uniquely identify them. In most cases these statements also uniquely identify the works contained in the items. In descriptive cataloging, *description* is the process of transcribing data to identify an item, and *access* is the process used to identify and index the work. Both activities are served by the bibliographic record, which stands in the bibliographic source as a surrogate for the item and the work. The inability to approach these two functions in distinctly different ways has plagued music catalogers throughout the history of music librarianship.

## DESCRIPTION

Transcription of inherent bibliographic data from music materials is often more complex than its textual parallel. Different historical patterns in music and music publishing have yielded substantial differences in the physical formats of even printed music materials, as well as differences in the presentation of inherent bibliographic data.

These differences derive for the most part from different patterns of use. As commercial products, most bibliographic items are defined by the demands of the end users. It can be stated that books are designed to record and convey ideas through text for both leisure and scholarship. The same is true of printed music, and even of recorded music. But music materials offer other dimensions. D.W. Krummel has pointed out the functional necessities that shaped musical documents.[5] The physical requirements for musical documents are derived from their primary use by performing musicians, scholarly uses being clearly secondary in the main. Documents to be used in performance had to have stiff paper that would lie flat on a music stand, and notation that was both easily legible at a distance and conveniently arranged to facilitate page turning. Further, the process of publication has been historically different as well. James Young has shown that "any musical document may be viewed as a product of a shifting confluence of art, commerce, and technology."[6] Thus variant physical characteristics exist, and these affect the transcription of inherent bibliographic data into the standard areas of the description.

## ACCESS

Access to works in bibliographic sources has been commonly provided by entry under the name of the author, with specific works identified using their transcribed titles. In a bibliographic universe in which each work has only one physical manifestation and each item contains only one work, this approach can be successful. While it is doubtful that such a universe exists for any kind of material, it is clear that the universe of musical works differs radically from this model.

Musical works exist in a multitude of physical manifestations. Performing editions are intended to be used by performers to make music. Study editions are lap-sized or pocket-sized for use by students and scholars. Simplified versions are used in teaching. Arranged versions are used to widen the appeal of popular works by making them available for use in a variety of performing media. Popular excerpts from lengthy works are issued separately. Any or all of the above may have been recorded by a variety of performers. Each recording may be issued in a variety of playback media. All of these manifestations, alike because they contain the same musical idea, must collocate in a bibliographic source. Likewise, each manifestation, different because each communicates a variation of the original musical idea, must be simultaneously differentiated in a bibliographic source.

This challenge has been the driving force behind the development of music cataloging. Mere transcription and juxtaposition under the names of composers, satisfactory for the identifying function, was never sufficient to fulfill the collocating or evaluating functions. Artificial devices have been required to adequately control musical works in bibliographic sources. Name-uniform title headings are used to uniquely identify each manifestation of a work, simultaneously collocating all versions under a common entry point. Once the desired work has been located through use of these headings, the descriptions of the items are examined to choose the appropriate item. The separation of description and access functions, increasingly understood in general bibliographic control, is a historical reality in music cataloging.

# Subject Analysis and Classification

Subject analysis, or the determination of topical and form descriptors, is likewise more complex in music because of the nature of musical composition. The domination of Western art music and the triumph of form throughout much of its history have meant that the most easily categorized aspects of musical works have been their intellectual forms, the forces required to perform them, and the physical formats. Topicality has been avoided and cultural influences disregarded.

In recent years music collections have broadened to include both non-art musics and non-Western musics, and Western art music has increasingly abandoned the regularity that characterized its development for centuries. A result has been the breakdown of traditional music indexes that are dependent on form and medium access points. Faceted approaches to classification and indexing offer the most satisfactory solutions for the future, particularly given the increasing power of machine-indexing systems.

# Authority Control

Authority control is the process of maintaining consistent use of headings in a bibliographic source through the use of an *authority file*. An authority file, in essence a type of thesaurus, records forms of headings authorized for use in the bibliographic source, and for each records variants that may be used as references. A sophisticated authority file also records the sources of information used to formulate authorized access points.

Music authority control utilizes the same processes as general authority control. However, two factors—fewer names and more works per person—have been important in developing different traditions for the authority control of musical headings. In music cataloging, because of the prevalence of name-uniform title headings, the authority file has become the locus of information about musical works, as distinct from information about their physical manifestations. A hierarchy of headings for variant manifestations of musical ideas exists in the authority file, where the cataloger creates links among the versions of a work, or among works with similar characteristics. These links form a syndetic structure that helps provide powerful searching pathways for users of bibliographic sources, satisfying both the collocating and evaluating functions.

# Theory

*Theory* can have two meanings. In colloquial speech the word is often used to mean *idea* or *principle*. In science, it is used to denote a body of systematically organized knowledge, derived from the results of empirical research and therefore subject to refutation. Theory, in the latter sense, allows researchers to analyze, explain, and even predict certain observed phenomena.

There is little such theory in librarianship, or in bibliographic control, and consequently there is exceedingly little in music librarianship. However, there has been a great deal of conceptual thought and writing about the bibliographic control of music materials. Much of this could serve as background for empirical research in the bibliographic control of music materials.

An example is seen in recent work in music authority control. Arsen Papakhian, responding to a study of the frequency of occurrence of name headings in general catalogs, discovered that a different pattern could be observed in a catalog that included music materials.[7] Papakhian's premise, which could have been stated as a theory, was that fewer names would occur with greater frequency in a music catalog. His results supported that contention.

Richard Smiraglia, attempting to describe the requirements for uniform title headings for musical works, found further evidence that multiple manifestations of musical works are commonplace.[8] An earlier study of multiple manifestations of textual works had found that only a small number of works existed in more than one manifestation. Smiraglia studied musical works and found that multiple manifestations existed for virtually every work, and that the majority of the manifestations had titles that differed from those of the original editions.

These two findings together illustrate the slow but certain generation of a theory. It can be stated (likewise it can be tested and potentially refuted) that different frequencies of occurrence of headings occur in music catalogs, that one important factor is the incidence of multiple physical manifestations, and that authority control is required to relate the variant titles found on these multiple manifestations.

# Conclusion

The conceptual framework for bibliographic control clearly envelopes the bibliographic control of musical works. The chapters that follow present the various aspects of music cataloging within this framework. It is also clear that different functional requirements and different commercial histories affected the physical and intellectual characteristics of musical works. These differences, also noted throughout the remainder of this book, provide opportunities for research and theoretical development. Music cataloging is a challenging field that offers many opportunities for research.

# Notes

[1]See the discussion in Donald B. Cleveland and Ana D. Cleveland, *Introduction to Indexing and Abstracting* (Littleton, Colo.: Libraries Unlimited, 1983).

[2]Richard P. Smiraglia, "Theoretical Considerations in the Bibliographic Control of Music Materials in Libraries," *Cataloging & Classification Quarterly* 5 (1985): 1-16.

[3]Sally H. McCallum, "Some Implications of De-Superimposition," *Library Quarterly* 47 (1977): 113.

[4]Patrick Wilson, *Two Kinds of Power: An Essay on Bibliographical Control* (Berkeley: University of California Press, 1968).

[5]D. W. Krummel, "Musical Functions and Bibliographical Forms," *The Library* (5th scr.) 31 (1976): 345.

[6]James Bradford Young, "An Account of Printed Musick ca. 1724," *Fontes artis Musicae* 29 (1982): 130.

[7]Arsen R. Papakhian, "The Frequency of Personal Name Headings in the Indiana University Music Library Card Catalogs," *Library Resources & Technical Services* 29 (1983): 273-85.

[8]Richard P. Smiraglia, "Uniform Titles for Music: An Exercise in Collocating Works," *Cataloging & Classification Quarterly* 9(3) (1989): 97-114.

# 1
# *BIBLIOGRAPHIC CONTROL OF MUSIC MATERIALS*

*The cataloguer must be a music cataloguer, the latter being defined as a person who can read music (i.e., can identify the key, meter, medium, period, style and form when looking at a composition) and have in addition some background in music history and bibliography, as well as considerable ability with languages. The music cataloguer must also have a firm grasp of the general principles of descriptive and subject cataloguing, and of the classification system.*[1]

## Introduction

Thus the noted music scholar and librarian Rita Benton outlined the qualifications required for a cataloger of music materials in 1976. It is true that the proper bibliographic control of music materials, that is, control that will make possible the use of music and sound recordings for study, performance, and entertainment, requires understanding of not only the tools of bibliographic control but also the nature of music, the origins and uses of music materials, and the traditions of music bibliography.

Music materials, that is, manuscript, printed, and recorded music, are records of an art form that has been practiced and enjoyed by nearly every human being in every age. Western art music (i.e., what is frequently referred to as "classical" music) has evolved from certain Mediterranean folk traditions through the practices of Christian liturgies in the Roman Church, into modern Western European sensibility. In the centuries before electronic communication media, house music was a common form of entertainment. Like poetry, literature, or a fine meal, good music was a way of freeing the soul from the doldrums of everyday living. Music is passion, music is salve for the wounded psyche, music expresses the tensions of life itself.

Music libraries and music librarians collect, preserve, and transmit the records of these instances of musical expression. Some of our musical past is recorded for study, some for recreation, some for entertainment. Like the library of texts, a music library requires bibliographic control to facilitate retrieval, use, and further collection of the records of our musical heritage.

In this opening chapter music materials frequently found in libraries are described, their functional uses are enumerated, something of their history is mentioned, and their bibliographic control is introduced. In subsequent chapters these materials are analyzed bibliographically, their forms are documented, and means of indexing and retrieving the resulting bibliographic records are discussed.

# Music Materials

Music materials—manuscript, printed, and recorded music—take a variety of forms that have a variety of uses. Within the three broad categories some variation is possible. Bibliographers have struggled to grasp the details of the process of musical creation and its resultant records, the physical manifestations of score and recording that form the core of a library collection. Obviously, a composer whose intention is to communicate a musical idea will write it down in a notation that will be understandable to at least his peers if not also to future generations. First, manuscript (or holograph, if in the composer's hand) sketches reveal the earliest origins of many musical ideas. Once conceived and outlined, a musical work may then be turned over to a copyist for a fair copy: a legible manuscript that can be used for a trial performance.

Published music is issued with commercial as well as artistic considerations in mind. Thus letterpress music printing, which was too cumbersome a process, gave to way to printing from engraved plates, a process that was more flexible. This meant that music publishing was less expensive and therefore that the music itself could be made more widely available to the consuming public. This in turn fueled the publication of music that was more secular and that had a wider popular appeal. This convergence of artistic and commercial priorities continues today with the receding of music printing into electronic forms, with scores provided on demand to reduce stocks. Obviously the major form of personal music consumption today is recorded music. Clearly, as electronic media have become widely available this evolutionary process has repeated itself. At the time of this writing the long-time staple of recorded music, the 33⅓ rpm grooved LP disc, is being replaced in popularity by the digitally encoded, laser-read compact audio disc.

## PRINTED MUSIC MATERIALS

As noted above, many factors affect the physical manifestations of various music materials. One of the most important, obviously, is the intended use of the item. Will this representation be used for performance, rehearsal, or study? If the first, will it be used by a conductor, a soloist, an accompanist, or the members of an ensemble? These musical considerations play the most important role in shaping the physical formats of printed music materials. Of course, any or all of these formats may also be acquired by a library in microform.

## TYPES OF SCORES

A score is a representation that shows all voices arranged vertically on a single set of staves. In most instances a score shows the parts of an ensemble in a way that allows simultaneous comprehension of all the parts. A basic division in bibliographic format exists between scores, which represent all voices, and parts, which represent only one.

### Scores, Full Scores

A score represents all of the parts of an ensemble, such as an orchestra or band, or less commonly a chamber ensemble such as a piano trio, string quartet, or wind quintet. A *full* score, so designated to distinguish it from a *condensed* score or a *miniature* score (see below), contains all the parts, each separately notated. The format is large enough to be easily read by a conductor in rehearsal or performance.

### Condensed Scores

A condensed score is also used for conducting, but contains only harmonic representation of the parts. For instance, if the flutes and clarinets are doubling a chordal accompaniment, this will be represented as a single chord on one stave, usually with an abbreviation called a *cue* (e.g., "Fl" = flute; "Cl" = clarinet) to indicate the instrumentation.

### Miniature Scores

A miniature score is a small, pocket-sized full score with notation that has been reduced visually so as to fit in a small space. Miniature scores are used to study works, sometimes carried to concerts to be followed in performance, more often in the library followed while listening to a recording. Some libraries separate miniature scores from other printed music formats so that they can be easily retrieved for use in listening centers. Also, it is important to prevent miniature scores from slipping behind larger full scores or falling between shelves. Figure 1 shows two orchestral scores, one a full score, the other a miniature score.

Figure 1. Full score, and miniature score.

Some full scores for modern orchestral ensembles are produced with miniature type. This is to accommodate all of the instruments on a single page. Although these are usually described in cataloging as miniature scores, they are often shelved and used as full scores.

### Close Scores

Close score is the designation used to describe music for vocal ensembles represented on two staves. This process is often used for hymnals, in which case the upper voices appear on the top stave and the lower voices appear on the bottom stave with words printed between the lines. Were it not for the presence of the interlinear text, a close score might give the appearance of keyboard music. Note that music for choral performance is usually printed in full score format.

### Instrumental/Conductor/Score/Part

This curious combination is descended from an era when it was commonplace for the leader of an ensemble to also play one of the lead parts. A common occurrence of this format is in music for chamber orchestra, where the continuo part includes miniature notation (also referred to as *cues*) showing the entrance of other instruments so that the harpsichordist can also conduct. This format is also common among music for jazz ensembles, where the lead part includes cues showing the entrance of other instruments.

### Vocal Score

The vocal score is used primarily to rehearse dramatic works. It is a score for a dramatic work (such as an opera, or a musical) with all the voice parts represented in full score, but with the accompaniment arranged for piano (or some other keyboard instrument).

Figure 2 shows two common formats for music that includes voices contrasting the score of a popular song with a vocal score of a mass. The song (nominally a *full* score, but usually referred to as a *song sheet*, or *sheet music*) is for voice and keyboard with chord symbols and guitar chord diagrams.

Figure 2. Song sheet and vocal score.

### Chorus Score

Chorus scores, similarly, are scores that give only the chorus parts and the keyboard accompaniment of a dramatic work. These scores are used to rehearse the chorus, and sometimes used by chorus members in performance.

### Piano Scores

A piano score is an arrangement (usually referred to as reduction) of an orchestral work to a version on two staves resembling piano music. This type of arrangement is called reduction because it is not intended for pianistic performance, but rather is used to illustrate an orchestral work in the classroom, or to teach harmonization, analysis, etc., of such works.

## TYPES OF PARTS

A part is simply the music notation for only one instrument or voice in an ensemble. Libraries may acquire parts in sets for chamber music performance (see figure 3), which usually include only one of each part, or in multiple copies for orchestral and band performance.

Figure 3. Score and parts.

Most printed music materials resemble books or pamphlets in their structure. Bibliographic data such as composer and title appear at the top of the first page of music (the *caption*) or less frequently on title pages or covers.

## RECORDED MUSIC MATERIALS

Sound recordings are simply mechanical representations for reproducing sound, usually music in performance. Figure 4 illustrates a variety of recorded music. More recent than printed formats, the earliest sound recordings collected by libraries were piano and organ rolls for player pianos, etc. These were punched paper scrolls that were used to reproduce music on a mechanical keyboard instrument, usually a piano. Piano rolls usually came with title-page-like bibliographic data on their leaders. Often produced by famous pianists, many of these recordings still exist in libraries.

Figure 4. Rock-videocassette, LP disc, 45 rpm disc, compact disc, audiocassette tape.

## Sound Discs

The earliest phonograph records were wire cylinders, later wax discs, used with needles to cause sound vibrations that were then amplified for the human ear. These were eventually replaced by plastic discs (78 rpm), then in the 1950s by vinyl long-playing discs (33⅓ rpm). Small discs (45 rpm) with only one selection per side were produced mostly for children. All of these recordings are termed *analog recordings* because they produce vibrations that are said to be "analogous" to the original sound vibrations in the way they are perceived by the human ear. Since the late 1970s digital recording technology has been used to produce the master recordings from which analog discs were produced.

Since 1982 the compact digital audio disc, read by lasers with digital computerized sound reproduction, have taken the market by storm. Compact discs can hold more music, and take more wear and tear because playing them does not cause deterioration, and thus may be a perfect library musical storage medium. These recordings are referred to as digital because of the means of sound playback. Figure 5 contrasts two analog discs with a compact digital disc.

Figure 5. Digitally-recorded analog disc, analog disc, compact disc.

## Sound Tapes

Original magnetic tape recordings were made on ½-inch tape on large spools or reels. These were largely replaced in the 1970s by cassettes containing ⅛-inch tape. Tapes are more inexpensively produced (as are tape players) but tended to be less popular than discs among music aficionados because of the amount of background noise produced during playback. New digital tape technology (called DAT, for digital audio tape) promises to eliminate the background noise problem, thus providing the flexibility of tape with the high quality sound reproduction currently associated with compact discs. All of these formats are likely to find their way into library collections.

### Music Videorecordings

Another recent innovation in music is the growing popularity of music videorecordings. The introduction of this medium shows the convergence of not only commercial and artistic influences in the music industry, but also the increasing influence of visual media for home entertainment (most notably television and the videorecording industry) on the music industry. Filmed (or videotaped) performances that would once have been the province of motion picture theaters or public television are now readily available for home use through purchase or rental. Video discs were introduced in the early 1980s in two playback formats, the now obsolete RCA electronic format and a twelve-inch digital format similar technologically to compact audio discs. Half-inch videotape cassettes were also introduced in two playback formats (Sony Corporation's Beta format and the more popular, less expensive VHS format). Primarily the province of opera and rock music, videorecordings of all types of concerts as well as the short, film-like rock videos are now widely available. These items require treatment as videorecordings in description in order to identify playback characteristics, but also require careful attention to the structure of musical access points.

All sound recordings present special bibliographic problems because of their physical characteristics. The discs are usually sold in protective containers. Primary information about the music and the performers is printed on a permanently affixed paper label found on each side of analog discs, but often more extensive information is printed on the cardboard containers or in accompanying booklets. Cassette tapes are sold in plastic boxes with decorative paper inserts and with permanently affixed labels on each side. Compact discs are sold in clear plastic protective cases known as "jewel-boxes." Label information is impressed on the clear plastic lacquered disc. Paper inserts at the bottom of the jewel-box identify some bibliographic data, but the accompanying booklet is inserted in the clear plastic cover to serve double duty as a decorative cover, analogous to the jacket of an LP disc. Figures 6-9 (see pages 9-10) show the variety of these sources of bibliographic data for an LP disc, a compact disc, a cassette tape, and a music videotape.

(Text continues on page 11.)

Figure 6. LP disc and container.

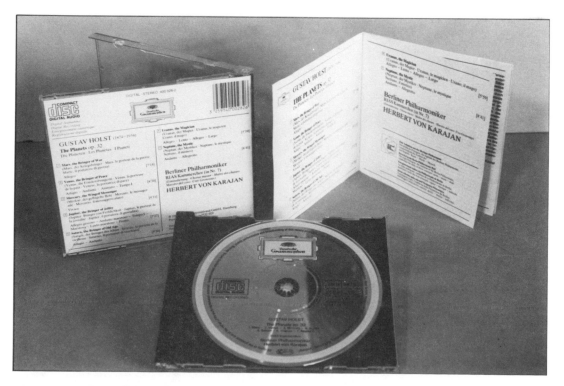

Figure 7. Compact disc, container, and booklet.

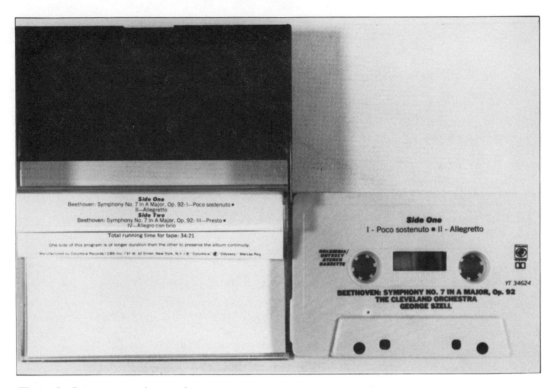

Figure 8. Cassette container and tape.

Figure 9. Videocassette container and tape.

# Bibliographic Control Techniques
# for Music Materials

Music bibliographic sources are produced by the same means as all others. That is, materials are described in a uniform manner, headings are created that represent musical works, creative persons or bodies, topics and genres; materials are arranged in a sequence; and records are manipulated, stored, and retrieved for maintenance and retrieval purposes.

Music catalogs, then, are very much like other kinds of catalogs. Dictionary catalogs are popular because they allow the substitution of subject headings based on forms of composition for title added entries for musical works with generic titles. Many music collections have what they call "divided" catalogs. These tend to be catalogs that are divided by format, so in reality they represent a series of dictionary catalogs. A typical division is to have one catalog for scores and books (i.e., all printed materials), and another for recordings.

Another peculiarity of music catalogs is the traditional file for publisher's number. Particularly useful for sound recordings, these numbers tend to be unique and therefore function as quick known-item retrieval devices much the way ISBNs do for book materials.

In the chapters that follow, traditional means of bibliographic control are discussed in light of their application to music materials. Historical background information illuminates the development of current practices. Tools and current approaches are outlined, and examples are given in each case.

# Notes

[1]Rita Benton, "The Nature of Music and Some Implications for the University Music Library," *Fontes Artis Musicae* 23 (1976): 54.

# 2
# *DESCRIPTIVE*
# *CATALOGING*

*Music cataloging and book cataloging are essentially the same. The differences between the two are few and do not really affect the principles of bibliographical description. They either find their explanation in musical terminology or in traditional peculiarities of composers and publishers.*[1]

## Introduction

These words by Oscar Sonneck, the opening lines to the earliest statement of rules for music cataloging, stand in stark contrast to the constant pleadings of music librarians everywhere, who are well known to protest that "music is different." While it is true that music materials (scores and recordings) are different kinds of bibliographic entities than books, it is also true that descriptive cataloging is based on a series of evolving but universal principles.

Descriptive cataloging is the more carefully codified aspect of the bibliographic control of library materials. Involving a dual series of processes that ultimately reflect the physical characteristics of items and the intellectual characteristics of works, descriptive cataloging is an aid to all three functions of bibliographic control. Both works and the objects that convey them may be identified through carefully composed descriptions. Headings for works are collocated and shown to relate to one another through the careful and authoritative establishment and use of name and title access points. These processes are essentially the same for any materials that are collected by libraries as records of knowledge and made accessible to users through library catalogs.

As Sonneck was aware, music materials and musical works have unique characteristics that must be accounted for in both description and access processes. This chapter examines those characteristics and the development of cataloging practices that incorporate them. Subsequent chapters cover the current rules for description of music materials and access to musical works.

## Rules for Cataloging
## Music Materials

A general observation about the development of rules for cataloging music materials is that the history of the development of catalogs and cataloging rules in general is of overriding importance. Music has almost always been collected in libraries but has received careful bibliographic treatment only since the late nineteenth century, when procedures for bibliographic description of book materials began to be stated as principles that could be extended from books to all kinds of materials. Further, the technologies of book and later card catalogs, enhanced by the introduction of means for mechanical reproduction of unit entries, and finally the employment of computers for maintaining and searching bibliographic databases, have all played critical roles in the development of music catalogs as well. A second observation is that many difficulties in descriptive cataloging, particularly the distinction between description of objects and access to works, are more acute in music and therefore more easily perceived by music librarians. Many solutions devised for the organization of music catalogs have later found application in general situations as well.

## PRINTED MUSIC

The first recognized codification of practices for cataloging printed music was the appendix by Oscar Sonneck (quoted at the head of this chapter) prepared for the fourth edition of Charles Ammi Cutter's widely accepted *Rules for a Dictionary Catalog*. This edition appeared in 1904. Sonneck's Music Division at the Library of Congress was at this time engaged in the compilation of several book catalogs, which were designed to communicate the holdings of the Music Division to musical scholars. It may be important to recall that the introduction and growth of academic music libraries from the end of the nineteenth century coincide with or follows naturally from the development of musicology as an academic discipline, which seems to date from about 1885.[2] Of course, performance, composition, and conservatory education have a centuries long history. Public circulating collections also first appeared in U. S. cities in the late 1880s.[3] Like many other aspects of librarianship, the influence of the higher education movement was critical in the development of bibliographic control for music materials. It was now important for catalogs to indicate not only the items held by a library, but also the variety of potential relationships, subject and otherwise, among multiple manifestations of musical works.

As did other librarians of his day, Sonneck refers to a process known as *bibliographical description* or *bibliographic cataloging*. The underlying intellectual principle of bibliographic cataloging was the arrangement of works, entries for which had also to carry details of distribution to distinguish editions, and sufficient indication of physical details to enable the user to retrieve the items that contained them. The functioning of this principle was dependent on an assumed one-to-one correspondence between physical objects and intellectual entities. In other words, for each work one book, and for each book one work. This principle, tenuous at best for books, was never applicable to musical works, for each of which a variety of different scores might have to coexist in the catalog. Nevertheless, this approach influenced the development of all cataloging rules, which inevitably turned on the choice of main entry, until the *Anglo-American Cataloguing Rules, Second Edition* (*AACR2*) appeared in 1978.

Sonneck's three-page discussion covered issues in music bibliography that continue to dominate catalog code development to the present day. This appendix, too short to constitute a "code" in itself, was to be used in conjunction with Cutter's *Rules*; therefore, only musical exceptions were discussed. The first consideration was choice of main entry. To organize musical works, entries were to be under composer, the recognized *author* of a musical work, with added entries for authors of words. Librettos were to be entered under the librettist with an added entry under the corresponding composer. Descriptive details were added beginning with the title of the work to subarrange compositions under the heading for the composer.

Consequently, choice among title pages, captions, and covers to provide the best title was the next problem. Publication details foundered on the common practice of music publishers to omit a date of publication. Sonneck gives advice on determining a date or approximate date, ending with a discussion of the utility of publisher's plate numbers. Notes were to include source of title, key, medium of performance, and printed format (score, parts, and combinations thereof).

Codification, as it is known in general cataloging circles, was not to come until the 1940s. The prevalent practices in the United States regarding choice of main entry were recorded in the 1908 Anglo-American code and the LC rules issued on cards from 1903 through the 1930s.[4] Musical materials are mentioned only briefly in each. The 1908 rules include rules for entry of music under composer, with added entries for editors, arrangers, and authors of words. A special instruction is included for variations, which are to be entered under the composer of the variations. Subsequent rules are for librettos (under librettist) and thematic catalogs (under composer cataloged). The rules on cards incorporate rules for main entry of librettos and collation of works with musical illustrations. In 1915 *Library Journal* devoted an entire issue to music collections. Reports from individual libraries indicate a variety of methods for dealing with the presence of music in dictionary card catalogs. An article by Otto Kinkeldey describes in glowing terms the printed catalogs of major music collections, including those prepared by LC under Sonneck's guidance. Of particular value, according to Kinkeldey, are the conscientiously recorded plate numbers, which "should become a matter of convention in all future music catalogs."[5]

An early attempt at codification appears in draft form in a 1920 American Library Association *Bulletin*.[6] This report presents for public comment greatly expanded rules for printed music. The rules are presented in three sections: Author, Title, and Plate Number. The rules for entry are those previously mentioned for scores, variations, and librettos. Title rules indicate use of alternatives when "title page is insufficient or misleading."[7] A special rule for dramatic vocal works introduces a concept known as *common title*. For works whose many editions have appeared with titles and texts in different languages the cataloger is to "choose a common title ... giv[ing] preference to the language used by the composer."[8] This common title is to be enclosed in square brackets and followed by the title page title. Cross references from the variant forms of the title are specified. Arrangement, key, and opus number are elements that are to be included in the title area. Language of text and number of parts are to be given in a note. The plate numbers are also to be given in a note, and specific instructions for interpreting and transcribing them are included. These rules, simultaneously submitted to the ALA and the British for consideration, were to have been included in an updated Anglo-American code that was never to materialize. However, they might have been influential in the formulation of the similar, but more detailed rules that were published by ALA in 1927 as part of a manual called *The Care and Treatment of Music in a Library*.[9]

As music collections grew and proliferated, so did procedures for cataloging them. Four treatises of the 1930s by Kay Schmidt-Phiseldeck, Øyvind Anker, E. Weiss-Reychser, and Lionel McColvin stand out for their discussions of problems of title transcription.[10] Schmidt-Phiseldeck, Anker, and Weiss-Reychser were all writing for German and Danish music libraries, collections that were by now being heavily used for musicological research. McColvin's treatise is a chapter in his classic book on music libraries, chronicling the growth of public circulating music libraries in Britain. All four authors decry the difficulties of identifying musical works—in particular identifying specific manifestations of those works—from the title transcriptions that would be derived according to standard cataloging practice. This problem is critical in the bibliographic control of music materials. If the catalog is to collocate works and their editions, some artificial device, beyond simple title transcription, would be required because of the variety of titles that appear on manifestations of even a single work. Further, a new function, differentiating different works with similar titles, also required the same type of device.

Several solutions were attempted. Schmidt-Phiseldeck, Anker, and Weiss-Reychser provided detailed schemes for transcribing and supplying terms, thus ensuring a systematic record of musical data that would satisfy various collocating and differentiating functions. McColvin, expanding on the work of the ALA subcommittee, had two suggestions. When the work had a descriptive title he recommended beginning always with the composer's original title, followed by an English language title, both in square brackets. If the title page title differed it was to be transcribed (i.e., without brackets) between the original and the

English versions. For other works whose titles indicate a form of composition he abandons transcription entirely, suggesting always giving the information in English.

A 1938 article by John Russell presented the rules for cataloging music that were in use at the Henry Watson Music Library, a department of the Manchester Central Library.[11] These rules expand on the 1920 draft rules in several ways. First, they reflect the diversity of creative roles inherent in musical works as well as the variety of manifestations of works that can be collected in a library. Detailed rules for entry specify added entries for editors, revisers, arrangers, translators, transcribers, and authors of words. Special rules are provided for cadenzas, librettos, variations, and transcriptions. Form of entry is addressed with two special provisions for pseudonyms (to be preferred as the best known form) and Russian names (to be entered as found in a popular English language music dictionary).

Following these instructions for entry a series of rules for title is presented. By now the provisions have grown quite detailed. A *common title* consisting of the original title, preferably in the language of the composer unless another version is better known, is used to group together manifestations of works with words, whenever two or more entries are present. The common title is enclosed in square brackets, and followed by the title page title. In other circumstances, the rules prescribe transposition of title page elements to achieve the best collocating device. Consequently, the presence of parallel titles requires transcription of the more familiar language version first, best known titles of overtures are given first (supplied in square brackets if necessary) even when the title of the work from which they were taken is present, titles and numbers of symphonies are to be given in brackets when not present on the title page, and the title of the work from which an excerpt is drawn is given first in brackets if necessary. These instructions are then followed by rules for title transcription that are the same as those in the 1920 draft, including date of composition along with opus number as critical elements of the title, and less specific information about plate numbers, which are still required. A sequence of details, like those used by Anker and others, is given. Two important principles are illustrated here. First, the collocating and differentiating functions of the *common title* are clearly codified by the acceptance of its use as an entry element to be supplied in square brackets when necessary. Second, the rules for entry of musical works are now definitely distinct from those for description of published scores.

## SOUND RECORDINGS

By the 1930s the sound recording had become a staple of many archival collections and not a few circulating collections. The earliest collection of circulating recordings seems to have been at the St. Paul (Minnesota) Public Library.[12] The development of rules for cataloging sound recordings has much in common with that of rules for printed music. The first rules were issued by libraries with large circulating collections. Primary consideration was given to the musical content of the recordings. Beginning in 1933 the Music Library Association attempted to compile a report on the collection maintenance and cataloging practices of major collections. The results of that effort were reported to a joint meeting of ALA and MLA and subsequently published in 1937.[13] Adhering to the principle of bibliographic cataloging, the report introduces the concept of analysis as a standard practice:

> Unlike books or music, records should be cataloged [by] the music they contain, without regard to their physical form. Thus, if there are two or more selections [on one] disc, each should be cataloged separately, since [often] there is little or no connection between them.[14]

Given the tradition of entry of the work, it was natural that catalogers would devise this approach for access to recorded musical works. The same principles observed for printed music were followed. Main entry was to be under composer; added entries were to be made under performers. The *standardized title* system was to be used, including the original title in the original language, which was to be supplied in brackets if it did not appear on the label. An exception was allowed if the language was obscure: titles in Russian, or Greek, or in Czech or Scandinavian languages were to be replaced with English language versions. This exception was to remain in the U.S. rules until *AACR2*. The imprint was replaced by the name of the issuing company, without place (which was considered to be either too well known or irrelevant) and the serial number of the recording. The date given would be the year of issue unless it differed from the date of recording, in which case both were given. The first note was an indication of the recording method and type of groove, information that was essential for playback of the recordings. Notes naming performers and referring to a published score (a one-to-one correspondence was assumed by these rules) were considered desirable.

Individualism was still possible in music cataloging. Unlike books, for which LC had been issuing printed cards since 1901, card distribution for music was extremely limited until the late 1940s, and cards would not be available for recordings until 1958. This meant that all cataloging for sound recordings was original cataloging, and many schemes were published in the literature of general librarianship. One recurring theme could be found in the procedures of public libraries. Recordings that contained several musical works were frequently entered under a collective title or, if appropriate, the name of a featured performer. This practice reflected the commercial success of the recording industry and the growing demand for recorded music of many kinds. Where the music libraries had collected recorded versions of their scores, the public libraries had collected the popular records of performances. This rift would persist until *AACR2*.

## CODIFICATION, DISSEMINATION, STANDARDIZATION

In 1941 and 1942 the Music Library Association issued mimeographed drafts of its *Code for Cataloging Music* and its *Code for Cataloging Phonograph Records*.[15] These drafts taken together represented nearly a decade of effort at standardizing the principles and procedures for cataloging music materials. Intended to be used in conjunction with standard cataloging practices, the code was rich in detail concerning sources of musical information, without which the general cataloger would be at sea attempting to establish the now commonplace *conventional title*. Rules for conventional titles were now substantially complete, including provisions for collective titles and for terms indicating the particular musical manifestation of a work (e.g., the arranged medium), and would not change substantially. The distinction between entry under a version of the title that would serve a collocating *and* differentiating function, and transcription of the title page title for purposes of identification was now codified. Nevertheless, the treatment of recordings as musical versions of scores stood in opposition to this principle, for the unit of entry was to be the musical work so as to collocate the scores and the recordings. The effect of this rule was to neglect the identification function for sound recordings and in many cases to obscure the identification of performances as creative entities.

The MLA code was never published in a single volume, but parts of it were incorporated in regular codes (which underwent a developmental crisis in the 1940s) and thus evolved over the next three decades. The MLA rules for entry and heading were incorporated in the *A.L.A. Cataloging Rules for Author and Title Entries*, published in 1949.[16] The rules for description of music and recordings were adopted by LC and published in the LC *Rules for Descriptive Cataloging in the Library of Congress*.[17] In this guise these rules received wide dissemination and were accepted for use by many U.S. libraries.

In 1958, responding to a desire to have music rules in a single volume, MLA and ALA jointly published the *Code for Cataloging Music and Phonorecords*.[18] Minor rule revisions that had been adopted since the 1949 publications were incorporated. In addition to the material from the 1949 codes, the LC filing rules for conventional titles and rules for "simplified" cataloging of music were incorporated. The rules for simplified cataloging (sometimes referred to as *brief cataloging*) were an early attempt to allow for less expensive and less permanent cataloging of music materials. A curious juxtaposition ensued in the rules for conventional title, however, because the simplified rules required use of the best known title of the work, while the main text required use of the original.

With few exceptions (one being the simplified rules) and revisions to provide for the by now standard 33⅓ rpm long-play recording, these rules were incorporated into the 1967 editions of the *Anglo-American Cataloging Rules*.[19]

### IAML Code

In 1951 the International Association of Music Libraries (IAML) undertook the massive project of producing a joint, international code for cataloging music materials. As previously noted, this was a time of crisis and debate in the field of bibliographic control. Just as the influential studies of Seymour Lubetzky and Eva Verona led to the understanding of principles for descriptive cataloging generally,[20] the IAML code provided a detailed background on which to base principles for cataloging of music collections. Destined to take thirty years to complete, the five volume multilingual *Code International de Catalogage de la Musique* documented practices that found their way into the ISBD (International Standard Bibliographic Description) and ultimately into catalog codes worldwide.[21]

IAML's International Cataloguing Code Commission was chaired by Kay Schmidt-Phiseldeck, and had members from nine nations. The first volume published, *Der Autoren-Katalog der Musikdrücke*, appeared in 1957. This volume was a comparative study of the music cataloging practices in thirty-one European and North American libraries. The text is in German and English. Practices are described and comparative tables of practices in North American libraries are provided. An especially valuable part of this volume is a set of twelve title page surrogates, each of which is accompanied by reproductions of the catalog entries of several of the participating libraries.

Volume 2 of the IAML code is the 1961 *Code restraint* or simplified rules, this time in French, German, and English, side-by-side. This volume is addressed to the experienced catalog librarian who has little or no music background and is designed for use in a new library or for the music collected by a general library.

The third volume, the *Rules for Full Cataloging*, was drafted twice by Virginia Cunningham, then the head of the Music Section of the Descriptive Cataloging Division of LC, and the committee's U.S. representative. In a 1967 article Cunningham described her experience as a participant at the 1961 International Conference on Cataloging Principles (ICCP) and her subsequent redrafting of the detailed provisions to incorporate those principles.[22] Published in 1971 with text in English, French, and German, the full code incorporates agreements on musical issues beyond those that are addressed by ICCP. In particular, provisions for the now required *filing title* are precursors of changes to come in Anglo-American practice. Required whenever variant titles occur, filing titles for works with distinctive titles are to be based on the original title, which is defined as that of the first edition, the holograph titles being too difficult to determine. For works with non-distinctive titles, the basis is to be the name of the musical form in the language of the cataloging agency, in the plural form when appropriate. Identifying elements are added to uniquely identify the work, usually only an opus number is required, and medium of performance is a frequently chosen alternative. Description is now a completely separate function, based entirely on data transcribed from the publication and recorded in its language. An extensive glossary of terms useful in music cataloging is also included.

The final volumes, *Rules for Cataloging Music Manuscripts* and *Le Catalogage des Enregistrements Sonores* (*The Cataloging of Sound Recordings*) appeared in 1975 and 1983 respectively. The latter, in particular, is a very modern code despite its use of the term *catalog card* where *bibliographic record* is intended. Many ISBD provisions are incorporated, the principle of the unit record divorced from choice of entry is endorsed, and filing titles (to be established using volume III) are required for musical works recorded under different titles. Alternative practices are offered for entry under performers (not recommended for main entry) and recording performers' names in statements of responsibility or in notes. Examples are provided according to the practices of the Bibliothèque Nationale, LC, Deutsche Bibliographie, USSR libraries, and the Swedish Radio Grammophone Record Library. The LC and Deutsche Bibliographie examples employ *AACR2* and *Regeln für Alphabetische Katalogisierung* (*RAK*), both post-ISBD codes.

### ISBD and AACR2

The ISBD movement has coincided with the continuous development of *AACR2*. ISBD (PM) and ISBD (NBM), the International Standard Bibliographic Description documents for printed music and nonbook materials, were published in the late 1970s. While ISBD (NBM) was available for consultation in the preparation of *AACR2*, ISBD(PM) existed only in draft form at that time. In the intervening years thorough ongoing revision of both ISBD and *AACR2* have seen increasing conformity. It should be remembered that *AACR2* represents one set of choices for use in the Anglo-American library community from among the options presented within the ISBD framework.

*AACR2* appeared initially in 1978 and was implemented on a large scale in the United States in 1981. It incorporates the ICCP principles and the ISBD framework for bibliographic description. (The content-designating punctuation devised for use in the original ISBD document had been incorporated into *AACR* in 1974.) Thereby *AACR2* abandons the long-held principle of bibliographic cataloging in favor of a dual approach to fulfilling the functions of the catalog. Identifying functions are fulfilled with complete descriptions of bibliographic objects based on the cardinal principle that a description should reflect the item in hand. Collocating functions are fulfilled with a complex system of uniform headings representing works as intellectual entities. The two systems are interposed one on the other to create a multifunction bibliographic source (a catalog) that can serve to identify and locate *both* works and objects that contain them. Description of each kind of material reflects the material-specific characteristics within the broad ISBD framework. Entry of works is based on principles of attribution of creativity that are universal in scope. Thus *AACR2* is truly able to integrate cataloging of all types of objects.

For music materials this has been of great benefit, allowing music materials to enter the mainstream of bibliographic control of library materials. Thus, for example, the *uniform title* is now recognized in the general cataloging community as a device that both collocates and differentiates. The unique creative contributions of performers have also been codified in the rules for entry. At the same time, bibliographic peculiarities of music and recordings have been adequately provided for in the provisions for description of each kind of material.

As first published in 1978, *AACR2*'s rules for music and sound recordings were less than perfect. Attempts to carry out the integration of nonbook materials into the ISBD framework in part I of *AACR2* had succeeded at the cost of necessary detail in the chapters for printed music and sound recordings. Attempts to approach the entry of sound recordings from the perspective of the performance had yielded confusing formulations and undesirable results. Rules for uniform titles, derived historically to satisfy a variety of collocating and differentiating functions, were published in a sequence that was confusing and invited misapplication. Attempts to reconcile the British and North American approaches to the basis of uniform titles resulted in a compromise unsatisfactory to all. Continuous revision of the code has corrected most of these difficulties. When the revision of *AACR2* appears in 1988 it will contain provisions that reflect nearly a century of development in the bibliographic control of music materials. The ease with which the entirely new technology of digital compact disc recordings was incorporated into the code is a tribute to its flexible provisions and sound principles.

# Issues in Descriptive Cataloging

In the preceding discussion several issues that still perplex music catalogers were raised. In each instance a departure from regular library practice is considered necessary to produce results that satisfactorily index music materials. In the remainder of this chapter these issues are explored in greater detail. Discussion of specific applications can be found in chapters 3 and 4.

## DESCRIPTION OF MUSIC MATERIALS

### Chief Source of Information

The choice of a chief source of information for both printed music and sound recordings has always been a matter of difficulty for music catalogers. There are several potential problems. Title page analogies notwithstanding, different, more commercial traditions of music publishing and recording come into consideration, making this a less easily resolved problem than is the case with printed books.

In printed music, the usual locus of title information is, naturally enough, at the top of the first staves. The tradition in book publishing that led to the authoritative use of a title page and its verso for titles, names of responsible parties, and details of publication has no uniform parallel in music. Title pages exist that are purely decorative and intended to encourage sale of the music. The infamous *passe partout* or list title pages give information about several pieces, only one of which is actually contained in the item in hand. Often no title page is present at all, but a cover of sturdier stock mimics the presentation of data on a title page. Sometimes a score and parts will have separate covers, each with different information but neither with complete data. Music issued by publishing houses with a tradition of book publishing might have standard title pages, with the traditional title, authorship, and publication data in the usual locations on the recto and verso. Title and statements of responsibility traditionally appear in a caption, above the first measures of music. Publication details usually appear at the foot of the first page of music (the copyright symbol and date must appear in this location by law). Any or all of these sources might be present and when more than one is present they might give conflicting or just different data.

Sound recordings have slightly different problems. There is no integral source of data for a sound recording. The title, responsibility, and publication data might be printed on the object but are not presented as part of the recorded performance (as they are for other kinds of nonbook materials such as film). Cassettes and traditional grooved discs have labels that are more or less permanently glued to them. Digital discs have these details imprinted on their faces. Obviously, the small space available constricts the presentation of data, small type notwithstanding. Containers and accompanying booklets have more space and can therefore hold more information, but have the disadvantage of being easily discarded. Like printed materials, the information appearing in different locations might be different or conflicting.

Choice of an appropriate data source should be dependent on the purpose of the transcription, but this too has been an issue for contention historically. In the old tradition of bibliographic cataloging, the purpose of recording the author's name and title was to create a unique heading (or entry) for a *work* through their juxtaposition. This was easily accomplished by giving the author's name first, followed by the title, thus allowing collocation of the works of a single author, subarranged in filing alphabetically by title. This tradition was based on an understanding of book publishing that assumed a fairly ordered universe in which a one-to-one correspondence existed between a work and a book, subsequent editions had the same title, and translations were infrequent. Further, because of the idea of this one-to-one correspondence it was thought that the goal of a library catalog, as distinct from descriptive bibliography, was to organize the works, not the books; thus physical details of the books could be disregarded or recorded in a sketchy manner.

This was never an appropriate approach to music, because of the traditional variety of manifestations of any given musical work. Full scores, miniature scores, parts, and various arrangements were commonplace, as were competing editions employing different phrasing or fingerings, or translations of vocal works. Attempts to create functionally collocating headings for musical works by recording composer and title data from printed music were unsuccessful for this reason. In the beginning catalogers tried substituting whatever data source provided the most authoritative data in the hope that this would create the best heading. Ultimately, two traditions developed to solve the problem: in Europe the systematized supplying (not transcribing) of musical data to create order, in the United States the uniform title (at first *standard*, then *common*, later *conventional* or *filing* titles). But these were problems of access, not description.

In the modern approach to descriptive cataloging more pragmatic solutions are possible. The cardinal principle in *AACR2* is to describe the item in hand. The function this fulfills is an identifying function that allows the user to match the description with the object, or the description in the catalog with a description in another bibliographic source. Thus the cataloger is allowed to choose the information source that has the most complete data, so as to provide the fullest description of the item. For printed music a title page is preferred, a list title page may be disregarded if another source has fuller information, and in the absence of a title page the fullest source is used. For recordings, the labels are preferred unless the item is a collection and the container provides a collective title that the labels do not. In either case, necessary data that appear prominently in the item may be interpolated as appropriate using square brackets as an editorial device to indicate supplied data.

### Edition

The concept of *edition* is another instance where the tradition of music publishing is at variance with that of book publishing. Further, the international use of the terms involved is confounded in different languages. Fortunately, the term is so little used with recordings that the concept is only an issue for printed music.

The term edition is often defined as all copies produced from the same typeface, so that all copies printed from one setting of type, or all copies printed from one set of engraved plates, or all copies photographically reproduced from one camera ready copy constitute an edition. If the type or plates or master copy are significantly changed, the copies produced constitute a subsequent edition. This phenomenon is universal and these terms, if stated somewhat broadly, are agreed to by all catalogers.

Another common usage of the term edition is to mean the subsequent form (usually revised) of a work that has been issued by its author or an editor. Thus the phrase "Second edition, revised and enlarged" appearing on a chief source of information indicates that the original work issued under the same title is presented here (reset, "Second edition"), with corrections ("revised") and new materials ("enlarged"). It is this usage that presents problems for music catalogers.

In book publishing the definitions have become blurred enough that catalogers simply transcribe all statements including the word edition. Publishers use the word loosely to mean product, so that "bicentennial edition" (indicating a commemorative printing) or "large-print edition" (meaning a different physical form) are fairly typical examples of the kinds of expressions found in modern books. Because a new edition means that a new item has been acquired, which occasions a new bibliographic record, the terms are considered valid edition statements regardless of their meaning.

In music, however, the term edition and its foreign equivalents are frequently used to mean *version*. Thus a statement such as "Piano edition" or "Edition for keyboard" does not indicate a subsequent printing or reformulation of the text. Rather, statements of this kind indicate a new intellectual effort, an alteration of the original work here offered for sale. Consequently, these statements must be included as statements of responsibility because they indicate a new work, rather than statements of edition, indicating a new item.[23]

## Material Specific Details

In the ISBD the third area of description is reserved for details that are of value to the identification function, but that are specific to a particular type of object and that do not conveniently fit into any of the traditional areas of description. Thus this area is used for serials to indicate the numbering and chronological designation, for maps to indicate the scale and coordinates, and for computer files to indicate the type of file (program or data).

For printed music the ISBD (PM) makes use of this area for transcribing statements that indicate the particular musical manifestation of the piece in hand. Statements such as "Score and Parts" or "Partitur" often appear on title pages or covers of printed music. In the era of bibliographic cataloging such statements were disregarded in lieu of a cataloger's authoritative statement of the type of musical format. Confusion resulted when *AACR2* appeared because no provision had been made for such statements, even though they were prominent parts of the inherent bibliographic data for many musical items. In 1983 a version of these provisions was added to *AACR2*.

## Dates

Dates of publication have traditionally been recorded to help identify a work as to its edition. In music this has always been a difficult task. Kinkeldey's praise of Sonneck's systematic recording of plate numbers was largely a reflection of his own understanding that these numbers could be used to date printed music, which only rarely was published with an indication of its date. Probably for commercial reasons, publishers of music almost never included a date of publication until very recent times. Even now, copyright dates are commonplace because of the requirements of the copyright law, but actual dates of publication remain rare in printed music.

Sound recordings, perhaps for the same commercial reasons, also rarely indicate a date of release (the equivalent of publication). Like printed music, recordings are now required by copyright law to display a date of phonograph copyright (preceded by the symbol "Ⓟ") and often they also display dates of copyright of accompanying text or artwork. Increasingly dates of recording are indicated in the accompanying textual matter, and these are probably the more significant dates discographically, for it is the date of recording that would uniquely identify a particular performance.

In either case it is possible through time consuming (and therefore expensive) detective work to arrive at accurate dates in most instances. It is unlikely, however, that the expense is justified given the typical use of the average library catalog, and good estimates may be satisfactory in most cases.[24]

## Publisher's/Manufacturer's Numbers

Plate numbers, publisher's numbers, and record manufacturer's serial numbers are devices that are critical in the description of music materials. Not only do these numbers uniquely identify particular bibliographic manifestations, they also provide fast access to bibliographic data in known-item searches, and when collocated in indexes they provide valuable snapshots of the output of a particular publisher or manufacturer.

*Plate numbers*, which were originally found near the imprint on the title page and at the bottom of each page printed from a plate, were probably used to keep engraved plates in order in the publisher's warehouse, to keep the plates and the printed sheets together during production, and possibly for inventory of the printed copies. The term *publisher's number* is more generic, and is usually used to mean a sequential number assigned by a publisher and seemingly used for ordering and inventory control. Publisher's numbers are usually found only on the cover or title page. Edition numbers are a type of publisher's number that closely resemble series numbers, but can be distinguished by their tendency to appear with the name of the publisher (e.g., Edition Breitkopf). Given a detailed knowledge of the practices of individual publishers at particular times, these numbers may be used to identify particular impressions, to estimate probable dates of publication, and to systematically arrange the output of a particular publisher.

*Manufacturer's numbers* are similar catalog numbers that appear in conjunction with label names on sound recordings and have similar discographical uses. Matrix numbers are a type of manufacturer's number that appear on the matrix (the ungrooved band at the center of a phonograph disc) of a recording. Matrix numbers are analogous to plate numbers and appear to be used to organize masters for impressing discs. Sometimes matrix numbers also appear on labels, usually in parentheses near the label number, and are distinguishable because they usually differ for each side.

Originally these numbers were included in the imprint area of the bibliographic record because they were considered necessary for the identification of edition, and therefore served the same function as the transcription of place, publisher, and date for a book. In *AACR* plate and publisher's numbers were transcribed only in the event that no date of publication was available, and manufacturer's numbers were transcribed with the label name in the imprint for sound recordings. The ISBD format, however, recognizes no material-specific use of the fourth area of the description, which is reserved for the location and name of the publisher and the date of release of the item in hand. Consequently, in codes currently in use all such numbers are transcribed as notes (matrix numbers are only transcribed in the absence of a manufacturer's number). MARC field 028 is used in machine-readable cataloging to generate both notes and index entries for these numbers. Because of the importance of these numbers for musical research and bibliographic control, debate continues over the appropriate location for them in bibliographic records and over means for authority control of their alphabetical designations.

## ACCESS TO MUSICAL WORKS

### Main Entry

Because of the widespread use of unit record systems and particularly online catalogs, the concept of main entry is seriously dated and therefore should not be troublesome. However, *AACR2* continues to present rules for entry of various responsible persons and/or bodies, and titles as either "main" or "added" thus debate continues over choice of main entry for some types of music materials.

Since the beginning of music catalogs, the concept of personal authorship has been extended to composers of music, with added entry always provided under authors of words and others (arrangers, editors, translators) who have contributed to the intellectual content of a work. *AACR2* not only continued this tradition, but extended the concept to performers of sound recordings in certain instances. Recordings that contain more than one musical work by more than one composer may be entered under the heading for a principal (i.e., featured) performer when there is a collective title, or in the absence of a collective title when the music is in a popular idiom.

This approach is clearly a compromise. A dichotomy exists such that recordings that present the music of one composer are treated as though they were audio versions of scores, while their counterparts are approached as performances. It is believed that this approach mimics the forms in which these recordings are presented. That is, recordings that contain music by one composer tend to feature that composer's name more prominently in the accompanying textual matter than the names of performers. The opposite is true of collective recordings, which seem usually to feature performers and occasionally feature a subject or genre of music.

On the other hand, printed music is approached from the book tradition so that a score is entered under the heading for its composer, or its title in the event that there are four or more composers. This approach causes discollocation of printed versions and recordings of music in the popular idiom. While a recording may be entered under the name of the performer, the corresponding printed manifestation would have to be entered under its title because the intellectual origin of the music is diverse. This approach fails to recognize the very different tradition of creation of music in popular idioms. The anticipated consolidated reprinting of *AACR2* will provide solutions to some of these problems by allowing printed transcriptions of performances to be entered as though they were recordings.

### Basis of Uniform Titles

Much of the history of descriptive cataloging of music is the history of the music uniform title. Originally devised as a *common* title (later termed *distinctive*), used to collocate editions of vocal works in translation, later a *standard* or *conventional* title was developed with the additional goal of distinguishing and differentiating among works known by the name of a type of composition or a medium of performance. Both functions have been subsumed under the broad category of uniform title in current rules.

Historically the distinctive uniform titles were based on the title of the first edition in the composer's language. Two exceptions were possible. First, if a later title had become better known it could be substituted. Second, if the original title were in a language not commonly understood by a library's clientele (usually in the United States this meant Russian, Czech, or Scandinavian) then the title of a well-known translation could be used. In some quarters, popular titles as determined from standard reference sources were always preferred to original titles, especially for recordings. In *AACR2* the unfortunate requirement is that the original title as formulated by the composer be preferred, unless a later title in the same language can be shown to be better known. This has led to some unfortunate results, particularly with titles by well-known Russian composers. A related issue is whether the titles of excerpts, entered under the title of the whole work, should be in the same language as the title of the work from which they were drawn.

Many solutions have been offered but no consensus has developed among catalogers in the Anglo-American community about how to resolve this problem.[25] The IAML code specifies the use of the title from the original edition, unless a later title (presumably in any language) is better known, and alternatively, if the original language is not common to a library's users a translation may be preferred. In cases of doubt a thematic catalog is suggested.[26] Others have suggested using English language reference sources to determine the best known titles.[27] Though major revision of the order of rules for constructing music uniform titles will be apparent in the 1988 version of *AACR2*, this problem remains unresolved.

# Notes

[1]O. G. Sonneck, "Music," in Charles Ammi Cutter, *Rules for a Dictionary Catalog*, 4th ed., rewritten (Washington, D.C.: U.S. Government Printing Office, 1904), 138.

[2]"Musicology," in *The New Harvard Dictionary of Music*, ed. Don Randel (Cambridge, Mass.: Belknap Press, 1986), 520-22.

[3]"Symposium on Music in Libraries," *Library Journal* 40 (1915): 563. The Brooklyn Public Library claims to have begun the first circulating collection in 1882.

[4]*Catalog Rules; Author and Title Entries*, American ed., comp. by committees of the American Library Association and the (British) Library Association (Chicago: ALA Publishing Board, 1908). Library of Congress, [*Rules on Cards*] [1907?-1939?].

[5]Otto Kinkeldey, "American Music Catalogs," *Library Journal* 40 (1915): 575.

[6]"Rules for Cataloging of Musical Scores," in "Report of the Committee on Catalog Rules," American Library Association *Bulletin* 14 (1920?): 295-96.

[7]Ibid., 295.

[8]Ibid., 296.

[9]"Chapter III, Cataloging Rules," in Ruth Wallace, ed., *The Care and Treatment of Music in a Library*, American Library Association, Committee on Cataloging, Contribution No. 1 (Chicago: American Library Association, 1927), 15-31.

[10]The most formal presentation including sample cards was in Kay Schmidt-Phiseldeck, *Musikkatalogisierung: ein Beiträg zur Lösung ihrer Probleme* (Leipzig, Germany: Breitkopf & Härtel, 1926). These provisions were used at the State Library in Aarhus, Denmark. A compilation of procedures used in several German libraries was E. Weiss-Reychser, *Anweisung zur Titelaufnahme von Musikalien* (Leipzig, Germany: Einkaufshaus für Bucherein, 1938). Rules (largely translated from Schmidt-Phiseldeck) for use in Norwegian libraries are found in Øyvind Anker, "Katalogisering av Musikalier," *Bok og Bibliotek* 6 (1939): 37-43. The English provisions are recorded in "Chapter Two: Cataloguing" in *Music Libraries, Volume 1*, ed. Lionel R. McColvin and Harold Reeves (London: Grafton, 1937).

[11]John F. Russell, "The Cataloguing of Music," *Library Association Record* 40 (1938): 247-50.

[12]"Symposium on Music in Libraries," 573-74. This report of the St. Paul Public Library's purchase of phonograph records, accompanied by the curious note that the collection was "destroyed in the fire April 27, 1915," is often referred to as the first circulating collection of phonograph records. In the same issue of *Library Journal* on page 570 is a report of a circulating collection of piano rolls (referred to as "music records") in the Public Library at Richmond, Indiana in 1911.

[13]Philip L. Miller, "Cataloging and Filing of Phonograph Records," *Library Journal* 62 (1937): 544.

14Ibid., 545.

15Music Library Association, *Code for Cataloging Music*, preliminary version. "Chapter 2: Title," "Chapter 3: Imprint" (1941). "Chapter 4-5: Collation-Notes" (1942, Mimeographed). The first chapter was published as part of the ill-fated ALA draft code: *Music: Entry and Heading*. Reprinted from *A.L.A. Catalog Rules*, preliminary 2nd American ed. (Chicago: American Library Association, 1941); Music Library Association, *Code for Cataloging Phonograph Records* (Music Library Association, *n.p.* 1942, Mimeographed).

16*A.L.A. Cataloging Rules for Author and Title Entries* (Chicago: American Library Association, 1949).

17Library of Congress. Descriptive Cataloging Division, *Rules for Descriptive Cataloging in the Library of Congress: (Adopted by the American Library Association)* (Washington, D.C.: Library of Congress, 1949).

18*Code for Cataloging Music and Phonorecords.* Prepared by a Joint Committee of the Music Library Association and the American Library Association, 1958).

19*Anglo-American Cataloging Rules*, North American Text (Chicago: American Library Association, 1967).

20The most influential of these were Seymour Lubetzky, *Cataloging Rules and Principles: A Critique of the ALA Rules for Entry and a Proposed Design for Their Revision* (Washington, D.C.: Processing Department, Library of Congress, 1953); his unattributed work, *Studies of Descriptive Cataloging* (Washington, D.C.: Processing Department, Library of Congress, 1946); and Eva Verona, "Literary Unit versus Bibliographical Unit," *Libri* 9 (1959): 79-104.

21International Association of Music Libraries. International Cataloging Code Commission, *Code International de Catalogage de la Musique* (Frankfurt, West Germany; New York: C. F. Peters, 1957-1983).

22Virginia Cunningham, "From Schmidt-Phiseldeck to Zanetti," *Notes* 23 (1967): 449-52. In the editor's footnote Cunningham is described as "Mrs. Music Cataloguer of the United States."

23It should be pointed out that current Library of Congress practice is to transcribe statements such as "Edition for high voice" in the edition area because such statements tend to indicate the availability of the item in several transposed versions. See Richard P. Smiraglia, *Cataloging Music: A Manual for Use with AACR2*, 2nd ed. (Lake Crystal, Minn.: Soldier Creek Press, 1986), 14.

24Techniques for dating early music are described in D. W. Krummel, *Guide for Dating Early Published Music: A Manual of Bibliographical Practices* (Hackensack, N.J.: J. Boonin, 1974). Techniques for dating recent music and recordings are discussed in Smiraglia, *Cataloging Music*, 19-21.

25One remarkable suggestion, that several be formulated in different languages and applied selectively by libraries, appears in Don C. Seibert and Charles M. Herrold, "Uniform Titles for Music under AACR2 and Its Predecessors: The Problems and Possibilities of Developing a User-Friendly Repertoire," in *Cataloging Special Materials: Critiques and Innovations*, ed. Sanford Berman (Phoenix, Ariz.: Oryx Press, 1986), 133-50.

[26]Virginia Cunningham, comp., *Rules for Full Cataloging*, Code International de Catalogage de la Musique, Vol. III (Frankfurt, West Germany; New York: C. F. Peters, 1971), 30.

[27]"Report from Louisville," *Music Cataloging Bulletin* 16, no. 5 (1985): 5.

# Suggested Reading

International Association of Music Libraries. International Cataloging Code Commission. *Code International de Catalogage de la Musique.* Frankfurt, West Germany; New York: C. F. Peters, 1957-1983.

Kinkeldey, Otto. "American Music Catalogs." *Library Journal* 40 (1915): 575.

Music Library Association. *Code for Cataloging Music. Music: Entry and Heading.* Reprinted from *A.L.A. Catalog Rules*, preliminary 2nd American ed. Chicago: American Library Association, 1941. "Chapter 2: Title," "Chapter 3: Imprint," 1941. "Chapter 4-5: Collation-Notes," 1942, Mimeographed. *Code for Cataloging Phonograph Records*, 1942, Mimeographed.

Sonneck, O. G. "Music." In *Rules for a Dictionary Catalog*, by Charles Ammi Cutter, 138. 4th ed., rewritten. Washington, D.C.: U.S. Government Printing Office, 1904.

# 3
# *DESCRIPTION OF MUSIC AND RECORDINGS*

## Introduction

This chapter discusses creating the descriptive portion of the bibliographic record for printed and manuscript music and for sound recordings. Choice and form of access points, including uniform titles, are outlined in the next chapter. The provisions discussed in these two chapters are those of the Anglo-American Cataloguing Rules, Second Edition (*AACR2*) as practiced by the Library of Congress.[1] LC policies for music cataloging are disseminated in two ways. Rule Interpretations (LCRIs) are official policy statements issued by LC's Office for Descriptive Cataloging Policy. LCRIs appear quarterly in *Cataloging Service Bulletin*.[2] In addition, clarifications of specific practices known as Music Cataloging Decisions (MCDs) are issued by LC's Music Section, Special Materials Cataloging Division. MCDs and LCRIs are both announced in the monthly *Music Cataloging Bulletin*.[3] Detailed guidance for the application of these rules and policies to music cataloging can be found in *Cataloging Music*.[4]

The two parts of *AACR2* reflect its approach to descriptive cataloging. Part I contains rules for description; part II has rules for choice and form of access points. As already noted, the cardinal principle is that description should reflect the physical and bibliographic characteristics of the item in hand. Once the item has been carefully described, entries are developed to provide access to the intellectual entities contained.

One result of this descriptive principle is a preference for unit description of sound recordings. In earlier codes the entries were based on the musical works. If a recording had several musical works, several separate sets of entries (i.e., cards) were made, each linked to the others using "with" notes. But, if the principle is that the item in hand should provide the basis of description, then the logical result is that a bibliographic (or discographic) description should reflect the characteristics of the recording. Entries may still be created for each musical work, but the description is a representation of the disc or tape as a bibliographic entity.[5]

Part I of *AACR2* is structured in a general-specific pattern. Chapter 1 contains all general provisions for creating bibliographic descriptions. Chapters 5 and 6 contain the specific rules for printed music and sound recordings, respectively. Certain provisions of other chapters may be utilized where appropriate. For example, rules from "Chapter 2: Books" are applicable in the choice of a title-page substitute. Likewise, provisions of chapters 4, 12, and 13 for manuscripts, serials, and analysis respectively, may all be applied to music materials that are unpublished, serial, and/or anthologies, as appropriate. Chapter 6 provides rules for description of all sound recordings, musical or not; therefore, musical recordings must be described in conjunction with the provisions of chapter 5. Likewise, videorecordings are described according to the provisions of chapter 7, but must take into account provisions of chapters 5 and 6. Thus this presentation approaches description of both music and recordings in a single sequence.

The sequence of descriptive data is that of the ISBD's eight areas:

1   Title and statement of responsibility

2   Edition

3   Material specific details — Musical presentation statement

4   Publication, distribution, etc.

5   Physical description

6   Series

7   Notes

8   Standard number, Terms of availability

Data are transcribed or supplied as instructed in the rules. Prescribed punctuation is also derived from the practice of the ISBD. When printed or otherwise displayed, a frequently followed format that closely resembles that of LC printed cards is:

```
      Area 1. -- Area 2. -- Area 3. --
Area 4.
      Area 5. -- (Area 6)
Area 7.
Area 8.
```

This format is used for examples in this book. Because this chapter focuses on creation of the descriptive portion of the bibliographic record, all examples in this chapter show only the areas applicable to description of particular items.[6]

In the next section of this chapter, partial examples are used to illustrate specific descriptive techniques for printed music and sound recordings. At the end of the chapter several examples of complete descriptions of printed music, sound recordings, and music videorecordings are given, along with an explanation of the features of each.

# Bibliographic Description of Music and Recordings

## CHIEF SOURCE OF INFORMATION

The chief source of information is that part of the item from which title and statement of responsibility will be transcribed. As such it is the chief locus of inherent bibliographic data. As discussed in the previous chapter, music and recordings provide data in ways that differ from printed books.

If printed or manuscript music has a title page it is used as the chief source of information. If not, whichever of the caption or cover provides the fullest information is chosen as chief source. The caption is the information appearing above the first measures on the first page of the music. A cover should not be confused with a decorative title page (which should be preferred). A cover must be made of substantially heavier material than the paper on which the music is printed, and in general a cover will not have music printed on its verso.

When a title page is present but consists of a list of works with the title information for the item in hand underlined or otherwise indicated, this is what is known as a *passe partout* or *list* title page. Preference is given to whichever of the list, the cover, or the caption furnishes the more complete information. Whichever source is chosen, if it is not a title page it must be indicated in a note.

For sound recordings, the labels on the recordings serve collectively as the chief source of information, whether printed on paper (as with phonograph records) or imprinted on the disc itself (as with digital discs). Piano and organ rolls have bibliographic data printed on their leaders, usually in the style of a title page. This "label" is preferred to any data appearing on the container. However, when the recording is an anthology, and the container provides a collective title that the labels themselves do not, the container may be preferred as the chief source of information. It is important to remember that the name of a performer, if presented prominently, can be considered to be the collective title of a sound recording.

## AREA 1 – TITLE AND STATEMENT OF RESPONSIBILITY

Elements to be transcribed into area 1 include the title proper, other title information, statements of responsibility, and for recordings, general material designation (GMD).[7] For printed and recorded music these data are transcribed. If data do not appear in the chief source of information, they may be supplied in square brackets if they appear prominently in the item. For instance, popular music folios usually have the name of a featured performer on their covers and title pages, but the names of the people who wrote the words and music appear in the captions of the individual songs. If the words and music for all the selections are by the same person (or persons) who is named in all the captions, then that is considered a prominent statement and may be supplied in square brackets. Likewise, for other kinds of printed music editors, arrangers, and translators may be named in a caption but not on a chief source. These statements may be transcribed in square brackets in area 1. For sound recordings it is uncommon to supply any information that has not appeared in the chief source. Of course, for manuscripts the entire description may be supplied if necessary.

Transcription of musical titles is dependent on the presence of terms denoting a type of composition. If the title consists of the name of a type of composition (i.e., if it is "generic"), then numbering, key or tonal center, date of composition, and medium of performance may be transcribed as part of the title proper. If the title is not the name of a type of composition (i.e., if it is distinctive) or if it includes a modifier (such as "Symphonie espagnole"), then all such statements are transcribed as other title information.

For example, in the title-page title *Trio No. 2 in D Major for Two Flutes and Piano* the key word is *Trio*, which is the name of a type of composition. Thus the statements of number, key, and medium of performance are included as part of the title proper in the bibliographic record:

Trio no. 2 in D major for two flutes and piano ...

However, in the title-page title *La Mer, Three Symphonic Sketches for Orchestra* the title is *La Mer* (French for *the sea*), which is not the name of a type of composition. This is a distinctive title. Thus the subtitle "Three Symphonic Sketches for Orchestra" is transcribed as other title information:

La mer : three symphonic sketches for orchestra ...

The title-page title *Trio pathétique for clarinet, bassoon/cello & piano* includes the word *trio* but here it is modified by the word *pathétique*, which makes it distinctive. Thus the statement of medium of performance is transcribed as other title information:

Trio pathétique : for clarinet, bassoon/cello & piano ...

This distinction between distinctive and generic titles is important because the addition of medium and numbering statements to generic titles aids machine retrieval by creating an access point that is likely to be unique. When it is not clear whether or not a term is the name of a type of composition, a source such as *The New Harvard Dictionary of Music* can be consulted.[8] If the term is defined there it is safe to assume that it is the name of a type of composition and should be treated accordingly.

Statements of responsibility are transcribed according to *AACR2*'s general provisions. Composers of music; authors of words; and arrangers, translators, editors, etc., are considered to be performing different functions and should be transcribed in subsequent statements. In this example, the names of Haydn (the composer) and Robbins Landon (the editor) are transcribed in subsequent statements of responsibility because each has performed a different function:

> Symphony no. 8, G major : Le soir / by Joseph Haydn ;
> edited and with a foreword by Robbins Landon ...

Statements in the chief source indicating arrangement or version (such as "piano score") are statements of responsibility and should be transcribed in area 1 even when no name is associated with them. For example:

> Violin concerto no. 5 in A major, K219 / Mozart ; violin and
> piano ...

For sound recordings, the names of persons responsible for creating the music (composers, lyricists, etc.) are routinely transcribed in the statement of responsibility. Performers' names are transcribed only when the music is in a popular idiom and it can be assumed that their participation has been more than "performance, execution, or interpretation of the musical work."[9] In this example, Hancock is a performer whose contribution meets the criterion of participation beyond mere performance, so his name is transcribed in the statement of responsibility area:

> Feets don't fail me now [sound recording] / Herbie Hancock ...

Other performer's names are given in a note.

Often printed music is intended for international consumption and its chief sources will present some or all of the information in more than one language. These are called parallel statements and are transcribed in the order in which they occur, even when one or more is incomplete. Each parallel statement is preceded by an equals sign. For example:

> 9 sinfonie = 9 symphonies = 9 Symphonien / Ludwig van
> Beethoven ...

A more complex example illustrates how to transcribe complete parallel statements. Each statement includes both title proper and other title information:

> Fürwahr, er trug unsere Krankheit : Kantate für Sopran, Bass,
> fünfstimmigen Chor, zwei Violinen, zwei Gamben, Violone (Fagott)
> und Generalbass = Behold, he bore all our infirmities : Cantata for
> soprano, bass, five-part chorus, two violins, two violas da gamba,
> violone (bassoon) and thorough-bass / Dietrich Buxtehude ...

The GMD (general material designation) is used for recordings but not for music. Placement of the GMD is dependent on the number of works represented in area 1. When only one work is named in the title area (or when a collective title appears) the GMD appears at the end of the title proper. When two or more works by the same author or composer are recorded in the title area, the GMD falls at the end of area 1, following the last statement of responsibility. This placement is different from that in the ISBD (NBM), which stipulates always placing the GMD after the first title proper. The GMD for recordings is "sound recording." The following examples illustrate these three possible placements for the GMD:

> One work by one composer:

> The well-tempered clavier [sound recording] = Das
> Wohltemperierte Klavier = Le clavier bien temperé / J.S. Bach ...

> Two works by one composer:

> Sonata no. 12 in A-flat major, op. 26 ; Sonata no. 13 in E-flat
> major, op. 27, no. 1 : Sonata quasi una Fantasia [sound recording] /
> Beethoven ...

> Works by different composers:

> Sonata for piano, op. 1 / Alban Berg. Three piano pieces,
> op. 11 / Arnold Schönberg. Sonata, piano, no. 3, op. 92, no. 4 /
> Ernst Krenek [sound recording] ...

## AREAS 2 AND 3 — EDITION AND MUSICAL PRESENTATION STATEMENT

Area 2 contains edition statements and names of those responsible for subsequent editions. Area 3 contains musical presentation statements. The two may be easily confused in musical publications. Edition statements indicating a routine updating or reimpression (e.g., 3rd ed.) are actually uncommon on musical publications (see discussion in chapter 2). If they do appear they are transcribed in area 2. Statements of responsibility ("piano edition") that indicate a version or arrangement, or musical presentation statements ("Score and parts," "Study score," etc.) that indicate the physical format of the printed music, are more common. Musical presentation statements that appear in the chief source are transcribed in area 3. When no edition or musical presentation statement is available, the area is not used.

In this example, no edition statement is present, but the word *Stimmen* (German for *parts*) is a musical presentation statement.

> Quartett für Flöte, Klarinette, Horn und Fagott, op. 41 /
> Gebauer ; herausgegeben von Gyorgy Balassa, Imre Sulyok. --
> Stimmen ...

Here, the word *Partitur* (German for *score*) is a musical presentation statement:

> Symphonie no. 8, F dur, op. 93 / von L. van Beethoven.
> -- Partitur ...

In the following example, the word *edition* is found on the chief source, but the word is used here to mean *version*, so the statement is transcribed appropriately as a statement of responsibility:

> L'heure espagnole : Trio sur l'opéra / Maurice Ravel ;
> edition [pour] piano, flute et violoncelle avec contrebass et
> clarinette ad libitum ... [par] H. Mouton ...

The next example is more complex. The statement "for voice and piano" is a statement that implies the *version* of the work, so it is transcribed in the statement of responsibility even though no arranger is named. The phrase "edited by" is also treated as a statement of responsibility because it means that the music has been somehow altered (probably by the addition of phrasing). It is another example of the use of the word *edited* in a non-bibliographic sense. The word *High* means that the music has been transposed for high voice. The Library of Congress treats such statements as edition statements (see discussion in chapter 2):

> 45 arias from operas and oratorios / Handel ; selected and edited by Sergius Kagen ; English translations by Nicholas Grannitto and Waldo Lyman ; for voice and piano. -- High ...

## AREA 4 — DETAILS OF PUBLICATION, DISTRIBUTION, ETC.

Elements in area 4 include place of publication, name of publisher, and date of publication. The Library of Congress includes the publisher's address as well for printed music.[10] Otherwise, area 4 is constructed in the same way it would be for a book.

For sound recordings, the name given in area 4 must be the *label-name*, transcribed from the label of the recording. Often a single publisher (such as EMI) will own more than one label. The label-name ("His Master's Voice") should be given in area 4 in such cases.

Dates of publication are rarely provided on either music or recordings, though a variety of copyright dates may be present. Copyright dates found on the first page of a printed music item may be transcribed in lieu of a date of publication. These are transcribed without square brackets because the first page of music is one of the prescribed sources for this information. When the copyright date gives a misleading impression of the date of publication (i.e., if it is obviously very old) it may be advisable to add a printing date as well, if it can be determined from a colophon, or through various musicological means (see discussion of dates in chapter 2). East European publications indicate the date of publication in their license numbers. Uncertainty about a date supplied by the cataloger may be indicated with a question mark within the square brackets.

For sound recordings the phonogram copyright date (preceded by the symbol Ⓟ ) is the date sought, for it is the date of copyright of the *sound*. A Ⓒ copyright date on a sound recording produced after 1971 indicates the date of copyright of the artwork or the notes on the container. These can be used to *estimate* a date of release for the recording, which should be given in brackets. The date of a recording session may be considered but care should be exercised, for commercial considerations very often cause major time lapses between the date of the recording session and the release of the recording. Also it is not uncommon for a recorded performance to be rereleased several times in different physical formats.

One or more of these dates may be present on any given recording. The latest Ⓟ date that applies to the entire recording should be transcribed. When separate Ⓟ dates appear for each work recorded, the cataloger should use the latest date to infer the date of release, giving this date in square brackets (because it has been supplied) and without the Ⓟ (because it is now an estimated date of release and therefore no longer represents an official date of copyright). A question mark may be supplied to indicate uncertainty.

## AREA 5 — PHYSICAL DESCRIPTION

The physical description area consists of three elements: extent of item (an arabic numeral and a specific material designation), other physical details (for printed materials the presence of illustration, for recordings the playback characteristics), and the size of the item.

For printed music the cataloger must determine the type of score in hand. Several terms are listed in the rules at 5.5B1, each of which is carefully defined in the glossary of *AACR2*. An important distinction is made between scores and pages of music. A *score* is notation for an ensemble "presented in such a way that simultaneous moments in all voices or parts are aligned vertically."[11] If the music is only for one performer it is not called a score and is described as "p. of music." The extent of a score is given in parentheses: "1 score (34 p.)."

Parts are similarly represented by an arabic numeral: "3 parts." When both score and parts are present, the parts designation is preceded by a plus sign: "1 score (18 p.) + 1 part (3 p.)." Only bibliographically unique parts are counted. Multiple copies are indicated in a note. Designation of extent (i.e., pagination) is only given when there is only one part.

Sound recordings are described as "1 sound disc," "1 sound cassette," etc. The extent of the item is indicated by supplying an approximate duration in parentheses if it appears on the item. Other physical details include designation of the playback characteristics (analog or digital), the playing speed for analog discs (or cassettes when the speed is not the standard 1⅞ ips), and the number of sound channels (mono., stereo., quad., etc.) when given on the item.[12]

> Virtuoso music in 18th-century France [sound recording]. --
> Ocean, N.J. : Musical Heritage Society, p1981.
>     1 sound disc (44 min.) : analog, 33⅓ rpm, stereo. ; 12 in. ...

## *AREA 6 – SERIES*

Area 6 is the series area and is used to indicate bibliographic level by transcribing the title and statement of responsibility of a series or larger work of which the item in hand is a part. Publisher's numbers that contain the name of the publisher should not be confused with series statements. For example, "Kalmus orchestra library" is a series, but "Edition Peters" is a type of publisher's number.

Likewise, a label-name on a sound recording should not be confused with the name of a series. For instance, when the label says: "Odyssey Great Performances," "Great performances" is a series; "Odyssey" is the label-name.

## *AREA 7 – NOTES*

Notes are made to amplify or clarify bibliographic characteristics noted in the first six areas. Of particular importance for music are notes on the form of composition and medium of performance, variations in the title proper, bibliographic relationships, and plate and publisher's number.

**Scores**

Notes for scores are given in this order as appropriate:

1. Form of composition and medium of performance;

2. Language of sung or spoken text;

3. The source of the title proper;

4. Variations in the title proper;

5. Parallel titles and other title information;

6. Statements of responsibility;

7. Edition and history;

8. Notation of the score;

9. Publication, distribution;

10. Duration of performance;

11. Accompanying material;

12. Series;

13. Dissertation;

14. Audience;

15. Contents;

16. Plate and publisher's numbers;

17. Copy described and library's holdings.

The following examples illustrate the notes that are most commonly made for printed music. More detailed examples can be found at the end of this chapter.

In the first example the form of composition is not apparent from the description:

> Tod und Verklärung : Op. 24 / Richard Strauss. -- Wien :
> Universal-Edition, Wiener Philharmonischer Verlag, c1904.
>     1 miniature score (123 p.) : ill. ; 19 cm.
> ⟶     Symphonic poem ...

Likewise, in the next example, the medium of performance and language of sung text are not apparent from the description. Also, the title has been transcribed from a title-page substitute:

> Oberto conte si S. Bonifacio : cavatina : D'innocenza i
> cari inganni / eseglita dalla Signora Jenny Lind ; Verdi. --
> New York (706 Broadway, New York) : S.T. Gordon, [ca. 1860]
>     1 vocal score (9 p.) ; 34 cm. -- (Bouquet of operatic
> songs)
> ⟶     For voice and piano.
> ⟶     English and Italian words.
> ⟶     Caption title ...

In the following example, the title proper was transcribed from the title page, but a variation of the title appears in the caption (the top of the first page of music) and is given in a note:

> Symphony no. 3 in E flat ("Eroica") op. 55 / Ludwig van
> Beethoven. -- Miami, Fla. : Kalmus, [19--]
> 1 score (96 p.) ; 33 cm. -- (Kalmus orchestra library)
> Caption title: Symphonie nr. 3 (Eroica) Es-dur ...

In the next example no statement of responsibility appears prominently in the chief source, so none is transcribed in area 1. However, statements found elsewhere in the item are given in a note.

> Joan Jett & the Blackhearts. -- [United States] : Jett
> Pack Music Co. : New York, N.Y. : Exclusive selling agent
> for the United States and Canada, Warner Bros. Publications, c1982.
> 1 score (79 p.) : ill. (some col.) ; 31 cm.
> Rock music, as performed by Joan Jett and the Blackhearts; for
> voice and piano with chord symbols.
> Words and music by Joan Jett and others; "transcribed and
> arranged by Marco Swados" ...

Information about the source of the edition should be given in an edition and history note:

> The Fitzwilliam virginal book / edited from the original
> manuscript, with an introduction and notes by J.A. Fuller
> Maitland and W. Barclay Squire -- Rev. Dover ed. / corrected,
> edited and with a preface by Blanche Winogron -- New
> York : Dover Publications, c1980.
> 2 v. of music : facsims. ; 29 cm.
> "An unabridged and unaltered republication of the work
> published at Breitkopf and Härtel in 1899" ...

Whenever the musical notation is unusual or irregular a note is made identifying the type of notation used. In the following example, the note "graphic notation" is made, because some of Cage's works utilize standard notation:

> Ryoanji : for bass, with percussion or orchestral obbligato
> and ad libitum with other pieces of the same title / John
> Cage. -- New York : Henmar Prss : Sole selling agent, Peters,
> c1984.
> 17 p. of music ; 22 x 28 cm.
> Graphic notation ...

Often, important information about the distribution of an item is found on a stamp or label that has been added subsequent to publication. This information should be transcribed in a publication, distribution, etc., note:

> Tho' love is warm awhile / composed & sung by Mr. Braham. --
> New York : Wm. Dubois, [ca. 1817]
> 1 vocal score ([2] p.) ; 33 cm.
> For voice and piano; from the opera The devil's bridge,
> composed by Braham and Charles Horn, libretto by Samuel Arnold.
> Caption title.
> Library copy has distributor's stamp: Franklin Music
> Warehouse, No. 6 Milk St., Boston.

If a particular audience is specified in the item, a note should be made to that effect:

> Edward and Emma : a favorite ballad for the piano forte or
> harp / composed by Thomas Costillow. -- [London] : Printed for
> the Author ... and sold by Messrs. Longman and Broadrip, [178-?]
> 3 p. of music ; 33 cm.
> For piano with interlinear words; German flute part on p. 3.
> Caption title.
> "This ballad composed for juvenile performers being within the
> compass of an octave" ...

When the duration of the work is given in the item, it is included in a note:[13]

> Serenade for solo flute / by Philip Glass. -- Bryn Mawr,
> Pa. : Elkan-Vogel, c1969.
> 7 p. of music ; 31 cm.
> Cover title.
> Duration: 9:00 ...

Contents notes are made for musical works whenever the parts of the work have distinctive titles, as is often the case with suites:

> Un jour à la campagne / Paul Bonneau. -- Berlin : Ahn
> & Simrock, c1960.
> 1 miniature score (73 p.) ; 22 cm.
> Suite for orchestra.
> Contents: Chant du coq -- La pluie s'amuse --
> Tourbillon -- Crepuscule.

Contents notes are also made for items that include more than one work, or parts of a work. When the works in the collection all have the same title as the title proper of the collection, only the other title information is given in the contents note:

> 6 Sonaten für Violine (Flöte), Violoncello und Cembalo
> (Klavier), op. 2 / Johann Christian Bach ; [herausgegeben
> von] Erik Smith. -- Wien : Doblinger, 1976-
> 1 score (6v.) + 2 parts (6v.) ; 30 cm. -- (Diletto
> musicale ; Nr. 571-576)
> Contents: No. 1, F-Dur -- No. 2, G-Dur -- No. 3, D-Dur
> -- No. 4, C-Dur -- No. 5, A-Dur -- No. 6, Es-Dur.

Notes on plate numbers and publisher's numbers are very important for bibliographic purposes (see discussion in chapter 2). Plate numbers are found at the bottom of each page of printed music (originally at the bottom of each page printed from an engraved plate). They are transcribed exactly as they appear, unless digits following a hyphen at the end of the number correspond exactly to the number of pages in the item (i.e., the number of plates), in which case these digits are disregarded:

> Kleines Klavierkonzert für die Jugend / Peter Herrmann. --
> Partitur. -- Leipzig : DVfM, c1973.
> 1 score (74 p.) -- (Concertare)
> Pl. no.: DVfM 1425.

Publisher's numbers serve a similar purpose, but are usually found only on the cover, in the preliminaries, or on the first page of music. Often publisher's numbers contain an epithet identifying the publisher. The entire statement is transcribed exactly as it appears:

> Konzert No. 1, F-Dur, für Klarinette (C oder B) und Streicher,
> zwei Oboen und zwei Hörner ad lib. / Karl Stamitz ; herausgegeben
> und mit Kadenzen versehen von Walter Lebermann. -- Mainz :
> B. Schott's Söhne ; New York : Schott Music Corp., c1971.
> 1 score (62 p.) ; 31 cm. -- (Concertino)
> Publisher's no.: Edition Schott, 6130 ...

When both a plate number and a publisher's number are present, both are transcribed, with the publisher's number given first:

> Symphonie No. 6 : Paukenschlag, G dur / Joseph Haydn. --
> Partitur mit unterlegtem Klavierauszug. -- Bruxelles : Cranz,
> [19  ]
> 1 score (51 p.) ; 28 cm.
> Cover title.
> Publisher's no.: Edition Cranz 2043.
> Pl. no.: C. 45167 ...

## Sound Recordings

Notes for sound recordings tend to be lengthier because of the number of discographical characteristics that must be described (e.g., the performance, the music, and the disc). In addition to those listed for scores, notes of particular importance for recordings are notes on statements of responsibility, data on recording sessions, edition history, and contents of anthologies. Notes are given in the following order as applicable:

1. Manufacturer's number;[14]

2. Artistic form and medium of performance;

3. Language of sung or spoken text;

4. Source of title proper;

5. Variations in title;

6. Parallel titles and other title information;

7. Statements of responsibility;

8.  Edition and history;

9.  Publication, distribution;

10.  Physical description;

11.  Accompanying material;

12.  Series;

13.  Dissertation;

14.  Audience;

15.  Other formats available;

16.  Contents

17.  Copy described and library's holdings.

Expanding on the preceding examples of notes commonly made for music, the following examples illustrate the additional notes that are most commonly made for sound recordings. More detailed examples can be found at the end of this chapter.

The first note given for every sound recording is the note that contains a transcription of the manufacturer's label-name and serial number. The label-name should be given exactly as it was transcribed in area 4 of the description, and the number should be transcribed exactly as it appears on the label:

> Scriabin, Schoenberg, Berg, Prokofiev, Hindemith,
> Krenek [sound recording]. -- New York, N.Y. : CBS Masterworks,
> [1986], p1959-1969.
>    3 sound discs : digital, stereo. ; 4¾ in. -- (Glenn Gould
> legacy ; v. 4)
>    CBS Masterworks: M3K 42150.

Occasionally each disc in a multidisc set will have a different number. When these numbers are sequential they can be given in a single note, with the numbers separated by a dash:

> The 25-year retrospective concert of the music of John Cage [sound
> recording]. -- New York, N.Y. : G. Avakian, c1959.
>    3 sound discs : analog, 33⅓ rpm, mono. ; 12 in.
>    G. Avakian: K08P-1493--K08P-1498 ...

It is fairly common for a variety of different numbers to be associated with one recording. It is not unusual for a boxed set to have sequential numbers on the disc, but a completely different number on the container (this practice allows the manufacturer more versatility in marketing the recordings). When this happens, transcribe the numbers on the disc first. If the number on the container is a variation of the number on the disc, give it in parentheses along with a word indicating its location on the item:

> Mass no. 3 in B flat, D. 324 ; German Mass : D. 872 [sound
> recording] / Schubert. -- Hollywood, Calif. : Angel, 1983, p1982.
>    1 sound disc (54 min.) : analog, 33⅓ rpm, stereo. ; 12 in.
>    Angel: S-37793 (on container: DS-37793) ...

When the number on the container is altogether different from that on the disc, give the number on the disc first, and give the number from the container in a second note, again giving in parentheses the location of the second number):[15]

Symphonie Nr. 5 cis-moll ; Frühe Orchesterlieder [sound
recording] / Gustav Mahler. -- Hamburg : Deutsche
Grammophon, p1985.
  2 sound discs : analog, stereo. ; 12 in. + 1 booklet.
  Deutsche Grammophon: 415 477-1--415 478-1.
  Deutsche Grammophon: 415 476-1 (on container) ...

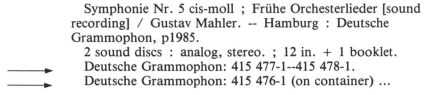

Because the statement of responsibility in area 1 is limited to the names of composers, authors, and improvisatory performers, the note that records the names of the principal performers is very important. This note is structured like a statement of responsibility in area 1, with the names of persons performing different functions given in subsequent statements:

Le nozze di Figaro [sound recording] / Wolfgang Amadeus
Mozart ; [parole di Lorenzo da Ponte] -- West Germany :
Deutsche Grammophon, p1968.
  3 sound discs : digital, stereo. ; 4¾ in.
  Deutsche Grammophon: 415 520-2 (415 521-2--415 523-2).
  Opera buffa in 4 acts.
  Edith Mathis, Gundula Janowitz, sopranos ; Tatiana Troyanos,
mezzo-soprano ; Hermann Prey, Dietrich Fischer-Dieskau,
baritones ; other soloists ; Chor und Orchester der Deutschen
Oper Berlin ; Karl Böhm, conductor ...

However, for an anthology with a collective title in which each work is performed by a different performer, do not use a statement of responsibility note, but give the names of the performers in the contents note (see below).

Notes on edition and history include statements found in the item that identify the particular recording. Such statements may include the location and date of the performance as well as names of engineers and studios associated with the recording.

The four temperaments ; Nobilissima visione [sound recording] /
Hindemith. -- Santa Monica, Calif. : Delos, p1986.
  1 sound disc (52 min.) : digital, stereo. ; 4¾ in.
  Delos: D/CD 1006.
  The 1st work is a ballet in the form of variations for piano and
string orchestra; the 2nd work is a suite from a ballet.
  Carol Rosenberger, piano (1st work) ; Royal Philharmonic
Orchestra ; James DePreist, conductor.
  Recorded June 1976 at Abbey Road, London ...

Important notes that elaborate the physical description of the recording include those that indicate the presence of significant accompanying material, the durations of individual works, and phrases such as "compact disc."

Eine kleine Nachtmusik KV 525 ; Divertimento KV 252
(240a) ; Divertimento KV 131 [sound recording] / Wolfgang
Amadeus Mozart. -- Hamburg : Deutsche Grammophon, p1986.
  1 sound disc (63 min.) : digital, stereo. ; 4¾ in.
  Deutsche Grammophon: 419 192-2.
  Orpheus Chamber Orchestra.
  Recorded Dec. 1985 at the Performing Arts Center, State
University of New York at Purchase.
  Compact disc.
  Durations: 17:13; 12:33; 32:57
  Program notes by Anthony Burton in English with French
translation and by Hans-Gunter Klein in German with Italian
translation ([12] p. : ill., port.) inserted ...

If the recording is an anthology with a collective title, however, do not record the durations in a physical description note, but record them in the contents note (see below).

It is also useful to make a note about other formats in which the recording has been issued, if the information is readily available:

> 7800 Fahrenheit [sound recording] / Bon Jovi. -- New
> York : Mercury, 1985.
> 1 sound disc (47 min.) : analog, 33⅓ rpm, stereo. ; 12 in.
> Mercury: 422-824 509-1 M-1.
> Rock music.
> Song texts on inner sleeve.
> Issued also as compact disc (Mercury: 824509-2 M-1) and
> cassette (Mercury: 422 824-509-4 M-1) ...

Finally, contents notes are very important for sound recordings that have collective titles because these recordings are anthologies. Often, library users will be seeking a specific work (frequently a specific song title) and the presence of a contents note can be critical. Contents for sound recordings are given in the same manner as for scores, except that durations of the individual works (if indicated in the item) are included parenthetically in the contents note:

> The Jimi Hendrix concerts [sound recording] -- Burbank,
> Calif. : Reprise, p1982.
> 2 sound discs (70 min.) : analog, 33⅓ rpm. ; 12 in.
> Reprise: 1-22306.
> Jimi Hendrix, guitar, vocals ; Mitch Mitchell, drums ; Noel
> Redding, bass, vocals ; Billy Cox, bass (on Red house and Hey
> Joe).
> "Contains previously unreleased performances" --
> container.
> Contents: Fire (3:47) -- I don't live today (6:26) -- Red
> house (8:01) -- Stone free (10.18) -- Are you experienced (6:11) --
> Little wing (3:48) -- Voodoo chile (6:49) -- Bleeding heart (7:14) --
> Hey Joe (4:42) -- Wild thing (3:12) -- Hear my train a comin'
> (8:04).

When the recording is a multiperformer anthology, the performers' names are also given parenthetically in the contents note:

The early twentieth century [sound recording]. -- New York :
Time-Life Records, 1967.
4 discs : analog, 33⅓ rpm, stereo. ; 12 in. + 2 booklets -- (The
story of great music)
Time-Life Records: STL 146.
Instrumental and vocal works, most originally issued on Angel
records.
Automatic sequence.
"A listener's guide to the recordings" (28 p. ; 30 cm.) and booklet
(58 p. : ill. (some col.) ; 30 cm.) by Frederic V. Grunfeld and the
editors of Time-Life Records in container.
Contents: Verklärte Nacht, op. 4 / Schoenberg (Leipzig
Gewandhaus Orchestra ; George Sebastian, conductor) -- Four
pieces for clarinet and piano / Berg (John Neufeld, clarinet ; Peter
Hewitt, piano) -- Le sacre du printemps / Stravinsky (Philharmonia
Orchestra ; Igor Markevitch, conductor) -- Concerto for
orchestra / Bartok (Royal Philharmonic Orchestra ; Rafael
Kubelik, conductor) -- Classical symphony / Prokofiev
(Philharmonia Orchestra ; Efrem Kurtz) -- Concerto in D major for
string orchestra / Stravinsky (Bath Festival Orchestra ; Yehudi
Menuhin, conductor) -- Piano pieces, op. 33A and 33B /
Schoenberg (Leonard Stein, piano) -- Three songs, op. 23 /
Webern (Marni Nixon, soprano ; Leonard Stein, piano) -- La
creation du monde / Milhaud (Orchestre de la Societe des Concerts
du Conservatoire ; Georges Prêtre, conductor) -- An American in
Paris / Gershwin (Hollywood Bowl Symphony Orchestra ; Felix
Slatkin, conductor) -- Bachianas brasileiras no. 5 / Villa-Lobos
(Marni Nixon, soprano ; Concert Arts Cello Ensemble ; Felix
Slatkin, conductor) -- Piano concerto no. 3 in C major, op. 26 /
Prokofiev (John Browning, piano ; Philharmonia Orchestra ; Erich
Leinsdorf, conductor)

If both durations and performers' names are available in the item, both may be given:

Musik der Gegenwart [sound recording]. -- Köln : Deutsche
Harmonia Mundi, p1984.
1 sound disc : analog, 33⅓ rpm, stereo. ; 12 in. -- (Anthologie
ostdeutscher Musik. Bereich Schlesien)
Deutsche Harmonia Mundi: HM/IOM 693.
Recorded Oct. 31, 1980, Apr. 20, 1983, Jan. 14, 1983, and
Mar. 10, 1982, respectively, WDR, Cologne.
Digital recording.
Program notes in English, French, and German by Rudolf Luck
(5 p. : ill.) bound in container.
Contents: Der Weg nach Eisenstadt : Haydn-Fantasien für kleines
Orchester / Gunter Bialas (Kölner Rundfunk-Sinfonie-Orchester ;
Jiri Belohlavek, conductor) (16:20) -- Einsamkeit : in memorian
W. Buchebner : für kleines Orchester / Michael Denhoff (Ensemble
Köln ; Robert HP Platz, conductor) (10:25) -- Traumtanz : für
Schlagzeug und Streicher op. 30 / Martin Christoph Redel (Martin
Christoph Redel, percussion ; Südwestdeutsches Kammerorchester
Pforzheim ; Alberto Blancafort, conductor) (15:05) -- Gesänge der
Frühe : op. 13, für Klarinette, Fagott, Horn, Violine, Viola,
Violoncello und Kontrabass / Peter Kiesewetter (Kölner
Nonett) (18:33).

# Examples

In this final section, several complete descriptions are presented, along with explanations of the features of each description. Because this chapter focuses on the description of items, only the descriptive portion of the bibliographic record is shown in these examples (i.e., no access points are present).

> Quintett G-dur für 2 Violinen, 2 Bratschen und Violoncello /
> Michael Haydn ; [bearbeitet von Hans Albrecht]. -- Lippstadt :
> Kistner & Siegel ; St. Louis : sole agent for the USA, Concordia
> Pub. House, [1950]
>   1 score (23 p.) + 5 parts ; 30 cm. -- (Organum. 3. Reihe.
> Kammermusik ; Nr. 40)
>     Pl. no.: 30050.

In this first example, the medium of performance and key are transcribed as part of the title proper because the title is generic, that is, it consists of the name of a type of composition. Albrecht, who probably edited the music, is named in the caption. Since that is a prominent location for descriptive data the name is interpolated into the statement of responsibility.

The item consists of a score and five parts, one for each performer. The score and parts are the same height. The number appearing at the foot of each page of music is transcribed as a plate number. No other notes are required to amplify the transcribed data.

> Impromptu for Roger : piano solo / Donald Martino. --
> Newton, Mass. : Dantalian, c1978.
>   3 p. of music ; 28 cm. -- (Dantalian signature edition ;
> no. 601)
>     Reproduced from holograph.
>     For Roger Sessions.

In this example the title is distinctive, because the genre term *impromptu* is not used alone but is part of the prepositional phrase *Impromptu for Roger*. Consequently, the medium of performance is transcribed as other title information. Because this is music for one solo instrument, piano, it is not described as "score" but rather, as pages of music. Notes point out that the music is reproduced from a holograph, meaning it is in Martino's manuscript, and that the "Roger" from the title is composer Roger Sessions.

> Here's to the women : 100 songs for and about American
> women / [compiled by] Hilda E. Wenner, Elizabeth Freilicher.
> -- 1st ed. -- Syracuse, N.Y. : Syracuse University Press, c1987.
>   313 p. of music ; 28 cm.
>     Unacc. melodies; includes chord symbols.
>     Bibliography: p. 297-302.
>     Discography: p. 283-287.
>     Includes indexes.
>     Contents: Friends and lovers -- Activism -- Labor --
> Contemporary issues -- Growing up -- Role models -- Women
> emerging.
>     ISBN 081560209X (pbk. : alk. paper) : $19.95.

This is a collection of songs by various composers. The phrase "compiled by" has been added to the statement of responsibility in square brackets to indicate that Wenner and Freilicher are not the composers. A true edition statement has been transcribed in area 2.

The music is simple melody notation. Chord symbols (i.e., letters denoting the chords) appear above the melodies. The volume is described as pages of music, because it is not in score format. Notes indicate the presence of bibliography, discography, and index. The contents note gives the chapter heads to indicate the kinds of songs included.

> The trial of Lucullus : opera in one act for radio or stage
> performance (1947) / Roger Sessions ; [words by] Bertholt
> Brecht ; translated by H.R. Hayes. -- 1947.
> 1 ms. score (278 p.) ; 38 cm.
> Ms. (photocopy).

This is a photocopy of a manuscript of Roger Sessions' opera *The Trial of Lucullus.* The title is distinctive, much like the title of a book, so the secondary statements appear as other title information. Note that for a manuscript area 4 includes only a date. Area 5 is constructed as normal, except that the designation 'ms.' is inserted to show that the score is handwritten. Because it is not certain in whose hand the notation appears, the manuscript note gives only the information that this is a photocopy.

> Spring of Chosroes : for violin and piano / Morton Feldman. --
> London : Universal, c1979.
> 2 scores (23 p. each) ; 31 cm.
> Duration: ca. 12:00.
> Pl. no.: UE 16530.

This recent work for violin and piano consists of identical scores so that each performer can follow both parts during a performance. This is indicated in area 5. The duration is expressed as an approximation (i.e., ca.) because it appears that way in the score.

> A hard day's night [sound recording] / The Beatles. --
> [S.l.] : Parlophone, [1987?], p1964.
> 1 sound disc : digital ; 4¾ in.
> Parlophone: CDP 7 46437 2.
> Songs; principally written by J. Lennon, P. McCartney.
> Original sound recording made by EMI Records Ltd.
> Compact disc.
> Digitally remastered.
> Contents: A hard day's night -- I should have known better --
> If I fell -- I'm happy just to dance with you -- And I love her --
> Tell me why -- Can't buy me love -- Any time at all -- I'll cry
> instead -- Things we said to day -- When I get home -- You
> can't do that -- I'll be back.

This description identifies a compact disc re-release of the Beatles' movie sound track. The GMD appears at the end of the title proper. The statement of responsibility includes the name of the performers, as it appeared on the label. The date of release is estimated and supplied in square brackets next to the date of the phonogram copyright. Complete contents are given, but only the song titles are included since the composers were identified in a statement of responsibility note.

> Turandot [sound recording] / Puccini. -- [New York] : CBS,
> p1984.
> 2 sound discs (127 min.) : digital ; 4¾ in.
> CBS Masterworks: M2K 39160.
> Opera.
> Libretto by Giuseppe Adami and Renato Simoni based on the play
> by Carlo Gozzi.
> Eva Marton, Katia Ricciarelli, sopranos; Jose Carreras, tenor;
> other soloists; Chor und Orchester der Wiener Staatsoper;
> Wiener Sangerknaben; Lorin Maazel, conductor.
> Recorded live in Vienna.
> Compact disc.
> Program notes in English, French, and German and Italian
> libretto with English, French, and German translations (188 p. :
> ill.) in container.
> Issued also on phonodisc (I3M 39160 : IM 39161--IM 39163).

This description expresses the extent of the recording with a rounded indication of the duration of the two compact discs. The relationship to the original Gozzi work and the names of the librettists are given in a statement of responsibility note. The names of the principal performers, which are not transcribed in area 1 because they are Western art musicians, are also given in a statement of responsibility note. Notes are also made on the recording session, the substantial libretto accompanying the discs, and the availability of the recording in an LP disc format.

> Streichquartett no. 12, op. 96, B 179 ; Zypressen / Antonín
> Dvôrák. Streichquartett no. 2, op. 10 / Zoltan Kodaly [sound
> recording]. -- West Germany : Deutsche Grammophon, p1987.
> 1 sound disc (60 min.) : digital, stereo. ; 4¾ in.
> Deutsche Grammophon: 419 601.
> Hagan Quartett.
> Recorded in February 1986, Salzburg, Austria (1st work) and in
> June 1986 in Bamburg, West Germany.
> Compact disc.
> Program notes by Michael Stegemann in German, English,
> French, and Italian with biographical notes about the performers in
> German, English, French, and Italian (16 p. ; ill.) in container.

Because this recording has no collective title the titles and composer statements of responsibility for both works are transcribed in area 1. The GMD follows both transcriptions. Notes give the details of the recording, including the name of the performing ensemble and the details of the recording sessions. The pamphlet with program notes is noted here because of the biographical information it provides about the performers, which is not likely to be available elsewhere.

Richard Strauss dirigiert Richard Strauss [sound recording]. --
West Germany : Deutsche Grammophon, [1976]
    5 sound discs : analog, 33⅓ rpm, stereo. ; 12 in.
    Deutsche Grammophon: 2740 160 (2563 633-2563 637).
    Title from container.
    The composer conducting the Orchester der Staatsoper Berlin (the
1st-7th works), the Berliner Philharmoniker (the 8th work), or the
Bayerisches Staatsorchester (the remainder).
    Recorded 1926-1941.
    In container; manual sequence.
    Program notes by G. Vadas, with English translation by J. Coombs
and French translation by A. Wahls, discographical information,
and durations (11 p. ; ill.) in container.
    Contents: Don Quixote -- Tod und Verklärung -- Don Juan --
Intermezzo, op. 72, Symphonic interludes -- Suite from the music
to Der Burger als Edelmann -- Der Rosenkavalier, Waltzes from
Act 2 -- Till Eulenspiegel -- Salome, Salome's dance -- Japanische
Festmusik -- Der Rosenkavalier, Waltzes from Act 3 -- Ein
Heldenleben.

This collection is on the old standard 33⅓ rpm LP discs. These discs are described as analog, in area 5. In the first note the label-name and manufacturer's number for both the collection and the individual discs are given. The sequential numbers for the discs are given in parentheses. Notice, too, that in the statement of responsibility note, the conjunction "or" is used to indicate non-simultaneous events. Because this set comes in a box, the note "in container" is added. "Manual sequence" means that the discs will have to be turned at the end of each side if the entire collection is to be played in one session (i.e., side 2 is on the verso of side 1, rather than on the next disc).

Finally, the next two examples illustrate how musical videorecordings make use of some of the provisions used to describe musical sound recordings.

Cyndi Lauper in Paris [videorecording]. -- Livonia, Mich. :
CBS/FOX Video Music, c1987.
    1 videocassette (ca. 90 min.) : sd., col. ; ½ in.
    Cyndi Lauper, vocals, with vocal and instrumental acc.
    Concert filmed at Le Zenith in Paris during "True Colors" tour.
    VHS format; hi-fi stereo., digital sound (mono compatible).
    Contents: Change of heart -- The goonies 'r' good enough -- Boy
blue -- All through the night -- What's going on -- Iko iko -- She
bop -- Calm inside the storm -- 911 -- One track mind -- True
colors -- Maybe he'll know -- Time after time -- Money changes
everything -- Girls just want to have fun -- Baby workout --
True colors (a capella version).
    CBS/FOX Video Music: 3570.

Notice that the running time (duration) is used as the statement of extent in area 5. In the notes area similarities can be observed where the performers are named in a statement of responsibility note, an edition and history note gives the details of the filming, a physical description note amplifies the information given in area 5, and the song titles are included in a complete contents note. The manufacturer's catalog number is given in area 8 (Standard numbering) for videorecordings.

> The Nutcracker [videorecording] / Jodav Productions and
> Kroyt-Brandt Productions. -- New York : MGM/UA Home Video,
> 1982, c1977.
>> 1 videocassette (78 min.) : sd., col. ; ½ in.
>> Cast: Mikhail Baryshnikov, Gelsey Kirkland, Alexander
> Minz ; National Philharmonic Orchestra, Kenneth Schermerhorn,
> conductor.
>> Credits: producer-writer, Yanna Kroyt Brandt ; director, Tony
> Charmoli.
>> The American Ballet Theatre and Mikhail Baryshnikov produc-
> tion, music by Tchaikovsky.
>> Videocassette release of the production originally broadcast by the
> Columbia Broadcasting System on Dec. 16, 1977.
>> VHS format.

This videorecording of a ballet shows some different features. Notice that the production companies are named in the statement of responsibility in area 1, and that the performers and other credits are given in a subsequent statement of responsibility note. Again, an edition and history note indicates the source of the performance recorded.[16]

# Notes

[1]The basic rules are contained in *Anglo-American Cataloguing Rules, Second Edition*, ed. Michael Gorman and Paul W. Winkler (Chicago: American Library Association, 1978). Three sets of revisions, many of which apply to music materials, have been issued by the Joint Steering Committee for Revision of AACR: *Revisions* (Chicago: American Library Association, 1982); *Revisions 1983* (Chicago: American Library Association, 1984); *Revisions 1985* (Chicago: American Library Association, 1986).

[2]*Cataloging Service Bulletin* (Washington, D.C.: Cataloging Distribution Service, 1978- ), quarterly.

[3]*Music Cataloging Bulletin* (Canton, Mass.: Music Library Association, 1969- ), monthly.

[4]Richard P. Smiraglia, *Cataloging Music: A Manual for Use with AACR2*, 2nd ed. (Lake Crystal, Minn.: Soldier Creek Press, 1986).

[5]*AACR2* rule 6.1G1 allows the option of creating separate descriptions for portions of a recording, which may be linked with "with" notes, as before. LC has chosen not to exercise this option.

[6]*AACR2* does not specify a format beyond the sequence of the eight areas for the presentation of bibliographic data, allowing individual libraries to design their own. Traditional "card" format is described in Arlene Taylor's edition of B. S. Wynar, *Introduction to Cataloging and Classification*, 7th ed. (Littleton, Colo.: Libraries Unlimited, 1985), 28-38.

[7]It is the policy of the Library of Congress not to use the GMD for maps, manuscripts, music, and text. Compare 1.1C, *Cataloging Service Bulletin* 11 (Winter 1981): 6-7.

[8]*The New Harvard Dictionary of Music*, ed. Don Michael Randel (Cambridge, Mass.: Belknap Press, 1986).

[9]*AACR2*, 149.

[10]LCRI 1.4C7, *Cataloging Service Bulletin* 13 (1981): 39. The address is included if it appears on the item, if the music was issued by a U.S. publisher in the current three years, and if no ISBN is present.

[11]*New Harvard Dictionary*, 735.

[12]Use the duration as a statement of extent if stated on the item, rounded up to the next whole minute. Detailed instructions appear in 6.5B2, *Cataloging Service Bulletin* 33 (Summer 1986): 36-37.

[13]Durations are given in notes in the form HH:MM:SS (H = hours; M = minutes; S = seconds). See *Music Cataloging Bulletin* 15, no. 7 (July 1984): 3.

[14]The Library of Congress routinely places this note first. See 6.7B19, *Cataloging Service Bulletin* 14 (Fall 1981): 17.

[15]See 6.7B19, *Music Cataloging Bulletin* 16, no. 3 (March 1985): 4.

[16]For more detailed instruction on describing film and videorecordings see Sheila S. Intner, "Cataloging Motion Pictures and Videorecordings Using AACR2," in *Policy and Practice in the Bibliographic Control of Nonbook Media*, ed. Sheila S. Intner and Richard P. Smiraglia (Chicago: American Library Association, 1987), 128-37.

## Suggested Reading

*Music Cataloging Bulletin*. Canton, Mass.: Music Library Association, 1969- . Monthly.

Smiraglia, Richard P. *Cataloging Music: A Manual for Use with AACR2*. 2nd ed. "Chapter 1: Description." Lake Crystal, Minn.: Soldier Creek Press, 1986.

# 4
# *ACCESS TO*
# *MUSICAL WORKS*

## Introduction

Following the thorough bibliographic description of a musical item, attention is turned to problems of providing access to the intellectual entity or entities the musical work(s) contained by that item. Initial considerations must focus on the nature and origin of the creative entities, musical compositions, and/or performances, regardless of the particular physical manifestation in hand. Physical characteristics such as the format of the score are considered only after the work has been identified, responsibility attributed, and uniform titles constructed. Philosophically the musical work must be perceived by the cataloger as separate and distinct from its physical manifestation.

However, like all other occurrences of recorded knowledge collected in libraries, bibliographical (or discographical) considerations affect the identification of musical works, and thereby also influence the access points through which they will be retrieved.

A critical issue is the definition of the phrase "musical work." The broadest possible definition must be embraced for the purposes of bibliographic control. In cataloging, a musical work is considered to be any instance of recorded knowledge that is realized musically. A musical performance and a printed score are both musical works.

The next question might well be which, then, is the original work, the performance or the score? The answer is dependent on the type of music and the cultural traditions and economic influences that shape its realization and subsequent manifestations. Musical works might better be conceptualized as continuous sequences of events that shape a musical idea, which in turn comes to be commonly understood in a particular way. A common sequence in traditional Western art music begins with the composer's sketch and extends through such events as the generation of a perfect copy, a trial performance, and/or subsequent published editions, which in turn generate performances. In other traditions the events occur in a different sequence, usually beginning with a musical expression which is followed by a transcription in musical notation. Thus the musical work is never exactly fixed in any particular manifestation but may continue to evolve at every occurrence of its realization.[1] It is the whole sequence of recordings of these evolving musical ideas that must be collocated through the use of uniform headings, then, and not just a corresponding score and sound recording. Neither is it appropriate, therefore, to consider a recording to be a version of a score. Rather, both are expressions of a musical idea.

In practical application *AACR2* refers to a broad spectrum of published manifestations as "musical works." Access points are based on the inherent bibliographic characteristics of the original published manifestation, with consideration given to subsequent versions if they become popularly recognized and thus replace the original characteristics in still subsequent manifestations. Because only some of the possible manifestations are considered in the creation of access points, it is important for the music cataloger to be aware of other manifestations, details of which may occur to library users as possible points of access to the works.

Access points consist of names and titles in various combinations. Three steps are common in the creation of access points for musical works: choosing main and added entries, establishing the forms of names, and constructing a uniform title. This chapter addresses the provisions of *AACR2* that are applicable to this process. A provision of many rules is to enter "under the heading for the work." This expression usually means to make a composer/uniform title heading.

Partial examples are used in this chapter to illustrate the provisions for choice of access points and construction of uniform titles. No subject headings or classifications appear in these examples. Main entry headings appear at the top of each description, and added entries will be found at the bottom, enumerated with Roman numerals. At the end of the chapter several examples of complete descriptions and their access points appear with explanations of the features of each.

# Choice of Access

## *PRINTED MUSIC*

The choice of main and added entry access points for printed music follows the traditions observed since Sonneck's appendix to Cutter's *Rules*. That is, the composer of music is the personal author and is therefore assigned main entry:

Brahms, Johannes, 1833-1897.
[Quartets, strings, no. 3, op. 67, Bb major]
Streichquartett B dur, Op. 67. -- Wien : Wiener Philharmonischer
Verlag, [1938]
1 miniature score (40 p.) : ill. ; 18 cm. -- (Philharmonia
Partituren ; Nr. 374)
Duration: 29 min.

For musical works that include words, the composer is the principal personal author and is assigned main entry. Added entries are made under the heading for the author of the words:

Rorem, Ned, 1923-
To Jane / words by Percy B. Shelley ; music by Ned
Rorem. -- [New York] : Boosey & Hawkes, [c1976]
4 p. of music ; 31 cm.
For medium voice and piano.
Pl. no. 2688.

I. Shelley, Percy Bysshe, 1792-1822. II. Title.

When the text of a musical work is based on another textual work, this fact is recorded in the description, and an added entry is made under the heading for the textual work:

Verdi, Giuseppe, 1813-1901.
Otello : dramma lirico in quattro atti / Giuseppe Verdi ; versi
di Arrigo Boito. Partitura d'orchestra. -- Milano ; New York :
G. Ricordi, c1913.
1 miniature score (572 p.) ; 24 cm.
Based on Shakespeare's play Othello.

I. Boito, Arrigo, 1842-1918. II. Shakespeare,
William, 1564-1616. Othello. III. Title.

Librettos are entered according to an optional rule.[2] When the publication makes reference to a musical setting, the libretto is entered under the heading for the musical work, with added entries for the librettist and any text on which the libretto may have been based:

     Giordano, Umberto, 1867-1948.
      [Andrea Chenier. Libretto. English & Italian]
      Andrea Chenier : an opera in four acts / music by Umberto
     Giordano ; libretto by Luigi Illica ; English translation by Charles
     and Mary Jane Matz ; arias translated in collaboration with Mary
     Ellis Pelt. -- New York : F. Rullman, c1954.
      47 p. ; 26 cm.

      I. Illica, Luigi, 1857-1919. II. Matz, Charles. III. Matz, Mary
     Jane. IV. Peltz, Mary Ellis.

There are special subrules for ballad operas, ballets, added accompaniments, and liturgical music. In each case deliberately composed music is entered under the heading for the composer as personal author. Ballad-operas that consist of songs drawn from several sources are treated as collections, and entered under their titles. Music to which an accompaniment has been added is treated as an arrangement, and entered under the original composer. Music that is part of an officially prescribed liturgy is entered according to the general *AACR2* provisions for liturgies.[3]

Arrangements, musical works that have been rewritten for a different medium of performance, are entered under the heading for the original composition.[4] An added entry is made under the heading for the arranger:

     Debussy, Claude, 1862-1918.
      [Beau soir; arr.]
      Beau soir : for cello (or viola) and piano / Debussy ;
     [transcribed by] Alexandre Gretchaninoff ; [viola part edited by
     Milton Katims]. -- New York : International Music, c1946.
      1 score (4 p.) + 1 part (1 leaf) ; 31 cm.
      Cover title.
      Score for cello or viola and piano; part for viola.
      Originally for voice.
      Pl. no.: 696, 759.

      I. Grechaninov, Aleksandr Tikhonovich, 1864-1956. II. Title.

The term *arrangement* as used with music in popular idioms must not be confused with the use of the term in Western art music. When the term is used with popular music it should be understood to mean "composition," or "orchestration." This usage is found often on jazz "arrangements":

     Albam, Manny.
      Rose bowl / composed and arranged by Manny Albam. -- New
     York : Belwin, c1966.
      6 p. of music +    parts ; 31 cm. -- (The Manny Albam
     originals) (Relda's stage band series)
      Caption title.
      For jazz ensemble.
      Pl. no.: RSB 4.

      I. Title.

Adaptations (paraphrases, variations, etc.) are entered under the heading for the composer of the adaptation. An added entry is made under the heading for the music on which the adaptation is based:

———➤    Liszt, Franz, 1811-1886.
    [Chants polonais]
    Chants polonais de Frédéric Chopin / transcrits pour piano par
François Liszt. -- Nouv. éd. / revisée par Eugen d'Albert. --
Berlin : Schlesinger, c1907.
    26 p. of music ; 35 cm.
    Caption title.

———➤    I. Chopin, Frédéric, 1810-1849. Spiewy polskie. Selections.
   II. Title.

Anthologies of popular music, referred to as "pop-folios," are often written transcriptions of sound recordings. Usually the chief source of information includes the title of the corresponding record album and the name of the featured performer. According to a recent LC policy decision these publications may be treated like their corresponding recordings and entered under the heading for the featured performer:[5]

———➤    Air Supply (Musical group).
    Hearts in motion / Air Supply. -- Miami, Fla. : Columbia
Pictures Publications, c1986.
    1 score (54, [1] p.) : ports. ; 31 cm.
    Rock music, from the record album of the same title.
    "Piano/vocal/chords."
    "Includes professional fake book arrangements."
    Discography: p [55].
    Contents: It's not too late / Graham Russell -- Lonely is the
night / Albert Hammond and Diane Warren -- Put love in your
life / Graham Russell -- One more chance / John Lang, Richard
Page and Steve George -- Stars in your eyes / Graham Russell --
My heart's with you / Diane Warren -- I'd die for you / Graham
Russell -- You're only in love / Graham Russell -- Time for
love / Randy Stern and Anthony LaPeau -- Heart and soul /
Graham Russell -- Hope springs eternal / Graham Russell.
    Publisher's no.: P0746SMX.

## RECORDED MUSIC

Special rules that balance the contributions of composers and performers are provided for the entry of sound recordings. A special provision applies to recordings of improvised performances, which may be entered under the heading for a corporate body when the responsibility of the group goes beyond simply performing a written work. This provision should be applied only in cases where the group has been chiefly responsible for the intellectual content of the recording.[6] For all other sound recordings the choice of main entry is dependent on the number of works, and, when more than one, the presence of a collective title and/or the type of music. Recordings that contain only one work are entered under the heading for that work (usually the composer-uniform title) with added entries for performers:

————▶ Brahms, Johannes, 1833-1897.
    [Symphonies, no. 4, op. 98, E minor]
    Symphonie no. 4 e-moll op. 98 [sound recording] / Johannes
Brahms. -- Hamburg : Teldec, 1987.
      1 sound disc : digital, stereo. ; 4¾ in.
      Teldec: 8.43678 ZK.
      Cleveland Orchestra ; Christoph von Dohnanyi, conductor.
      Compact disc.

      I. Cleveland Orchestra. II. Dohnanyi, Christoph von.

Likewise recordings that contain more than one work by the same person are entered under the heading for that person, again with added entries for performers:

————▶ Carter, Elliott, 1908-
    Night fantasies : (1980) ; Piano sonata (1946) [sound record-
ing] / Elliott Carter. -- Amsterdam : Etcetera, p1983.
      1 sound disc (44 min.) : analog, 33⅓ rpm, stereo. ; 12 in.
      Etcetera: ETC 1008.
      Charles Rosen, piano.
      Durations: 20:58; 22:33.

————▶     I. Rosen, Charles, 1927-      II. Carter, Elliott, 1908-
Sonatas, piano. III. Title.

Note that an added entry has also been made for the second work. This function is closely related to the construction of uniform titles (see below).

    Other recordings, then must, by process of elimination, be collections. Those with collective titles are treated as performances and entered under the heading for the principal performer. A principal performer is a person or corporate body whose name is given prominence by the wording or layout of the chief source of information. If all the performers on a recording are given equal prominence, all are considered to be principal performers. The rule of three applies. That is, when there are two or three principal performers, main entry is under the heading for the first-named with added entries under the others:

————▶ Tear, Robert.
    The dicky bird and the owl [sound recording] : Victorian songs
and ballads. -- Tinton Falls, N.J. : Musical Heritage Society,
[1983], c1973.
      1 sound disc : analog, 33⅓ rpm, stereo. ; 12 in.
      Musical Heritage Society: MHS 4660.
      Songs and duets.
      Robert Tear, tenor ; Benjamin Luxon, baritone ; Andre Previn,
piano.

————▶     I. Luxon, Benjamin. II. Previn, Andre, 1929-      III. Title.
IV. Title: Victorian songs and ballads.

When there are four or more principal performers, or no principal performers (i.e., when no performers are named in the chief source of information), main entry is under the collective title.

    When such a recording has no collective title the choice of main entry is dependent on the musical character. If the works are in a popular idiom main entry is under the heading for the principal performer, the first of two or three principal performers, or the heading appropriate to the first work if there are four or more or no principal performers. Added entries are made for additional principal performers. Recordings like this are unusual in general library collections. Most contemporary commercial recordings of music in popular idioms have collective titles.

Analysis, or an added entry for each musical work recorded, is used to create access to the musical works when main entry has been made under the heading for a performer. LC makes analytical added entries for up to twenty-five musical works if they require no more than fifteen analytical added entries and if the music is Western art music.[7]

For all other recordings (that is, musics not in popular idioms), main entry is under the heading appropriate to the first work. These recordings are fairly commonly encountered in general music collections. Added entries are made for all performers and for each work, according to the provisions outlined above:

        →    Copland, Aaron, 1900-
           The red pony / Copland. Sinfonia da requiem, op. 20 /
        Britten [sound recording]. -- U.S.A. : Columbia, [1964?]
           1 sound disc : analog, 33⅓ rpm, mono. ; 12 in. -- (Columbia
        Masterworks)
           Columbia: MS 6583.
           St. Louis Symphony Orchestra ; André Previn, conductor.

        →       I. Previn, André, 1929-     II. Britten, Benjamin, 1913-1976.
        Sinfonia da requiem. III. St. Louis Symphony Orchestra.
        IV. Title.

Title added entries are always made for all distinctive titles on musical works. Traditionally, however, added entries have not been made for generic titles, the assumption being that subject analysis provides more organized access through terms denoting form of composition or medium of performance.

## Forms of Entry

There are no special provisions for forms of names associated with musical works. The general provision for regularizing names are applied. Headings are formulated to represent the name in a form that will be commonly recognized (and therefore sought) by the library users. References are created from variant forms of the name. Composers are treated as authors and headings are formulated according to the form of name that appears on title pages (or their substitutes) in published music. Language determinations rest on the language of the country of the composer's residence or activity, since textual considerations are irrelevant. This means that headings are based on title pages issued in the composer's language, or in the language of the country where the composer resided while publishing music. Performers' headings are constructed similarly, except that the chief sources of recordings are considered. For persons who are both composers and performers the determination should be based on the person's primary activity.

Because many performing ensembles have distinctive names it is often necessary to add the expression "Musical group" in parentheses after the name to avoid confusion in dictionary catalogs.

    Philadelphia Orchestra.
    Who (Musical group).

# Uniform Titles

Uniform titles draw together all variant manifestations of a work, and distinguish similarly titled but different works entered under the same personal name heading. Almost all musical works require uniform titles because of the great variety of titles proper under which manifestations of musical works appear.

Uniform titles must be formulated for all music bibliographic records. When the title proper of an item is identical with the uniform title that it would be assigned, no uniform title is displayed by LC, but the uniform title must have been formulated prior to this determination.[8] The musicological detective work required to gather the elements of a uniform title can be quite complex, but the process of formulating a uniform title for a musical work is straightforward. First a title is chosen from among the variants that appear on published manifestations, then the title is manipulated to derive an initial element to which identifying details are added. The discussion that follows outlines the steps that are applicable in all cases.

A uniform title is based on "the composer's original title in the language in which it was formulated, [unless] a later title in the same language is better known," in which case it is preferred.[9] Except for recent compositions that can be ascertained to have appeared in only one manifestation, the original title and any later, better known versions in the same language must be determined from reference sources. For the purposes of formulating uniform titles, reference sources in the language used by the composer must be consulted.

Once the basis for the uniform title is chosen, excess terms such as *medium of performance, key, opus number*, etc., are stripped away (this is the same process applied in title transcription). For example, "Piano Sonata no. 3 in F major, opus 9" is rendered *Sonata*. The words remaining are referred to as the initial title element.

If the initial title element is distinctive it is used as is, minus any initial articles. If the initial title element is generic, that is, if it is the name of a type of composition, it is manipulated further to form a uniform title. If the generic initial title element is a term that is cognate in English, French, German, and Italian, the English form is preferred. If the composer has written more than one work of this type of composition, the English plural form is used. At this stage, the title of the aforementioned piano sonata is rendered *Sonatas*.

Terms are added to indicate the medium of performance, numbering, and key, as appropriate. The purpose of these additions is first to make the uniform title unique, and second to provide a sytematic file under a composer's heading. Medium of performance is added unless it is implied by the initial title element (as is the case for "Symphony," which implies orchestra, or "Chorale prelude," which implies organ). Medium of performance is also excluded if no medium was designated by the composer, if the work is one of a set of works for differing media, or if the complexities of stating the medium make some other arrangement more useful. An example of the latter situation is the list of Mozart works titled "Divertimento." There are many of these works, and alphabetical subarrangement by medium of performance would make the file difficult to access, so the medium of performance is not given and the thematic index number is used for subarrangement.

Additions for medium of performance are made using English language terms whenever possible. Except for chamber music, no more than three terms may be used. The number of instruments is given parenthetically following the name of the instrument, unless the number is implied by other elements of the uniform title. Instruments are listed in the following order: voices, keyboard if more than one non-keyboard instrument, the order of other instruments in score order. Standard terminology is used for standard Western art music chamber combinations. For works titled "Trio," "Quartet," or "Quintet" for non-standard chamber ensembles all instruments are listed, even if the limit of three elements is exceeded.

Other additions are made to provide identifying elements. These include as many as are applicable of the following: serial number, opus number or thematic index number (if a thematic index number is used the serial number is deleted), and key or tonal center. If these elements are not available or fail to create a unique uniform title, other elements such as date of composition may be added. The uniform title for the aforementioned piano sonata has now become:

Sonatas, piano, no. 3, op. 9, F major

If the title of the work is distinctive and it conflicts with the title of another work by the same composer, either a statement of medium of performance or a descriptive word or phrase is added to create a unique uniform title. If this fails to resolve the conflict one of the identifying elements specified for use with generic titles may be added.

Excerpts are always entered using the uniform title for the *whole* work followed by a designation for the part of the work. The designation of the part may be a number, a title, or both depending on the larger work:

Schumann, Robert, 1810-1856.
    [Waldscenen. Vogel als Prophet]
    Vogel als Prophet = The prophet bird : op. 82, no. 7 / edited
and fingered by Max Vogrich. -- New York : G. Schirmer, 1895.
    5 p. of music ; 32 cm.
    Caption title.

    I. Vogrich, Max, 1852-1916. II. Title. III. Title: The prophet
bird.

If the work is not the composer's original, but rather an arrangement or a version of the original work, additions are made to indicate the manifestation in hand. These include the symbol "arr." to indicate *arrangement*, the phrases "vocal score," "chorus score," or "libretto" where applicable, a term indicating some other alteration of a musico dramatic work, or the language of liturgical works or translations of other vocal works:

Beethoven, Ludwig van, 1770-1827.
    [Symphonies, no. 3, op. 55, Eb major. Marcia funèbre;
arr.]
    Marche funèbre da la symphonie heroique / de L. van
Beethoven ; partition de piano par F. Liszt. -- Leipzig : P.
Mechetti, [1850?]
    15 p. of music ; 31 cm.
    Pl. no.: P.M.No. 3593.

    I. Liszt, Franz, 1811-1886. II. Title.

Collective uniform titles are used for collections of works by one composer. If the item contains all the works of a composer, the uniform title "Works" is used:

Handel, George Frideric, 1685-1759.
⟶   [Works]
The works of George Frederic Handel. -- Leipzig : Printed for
the German Handel Society ; [Ridgewood, N.J. : Gregg Press,
1965-1966]
1 score (97 v. in 84) : facsims. ; 28 cm.
Facsims. of original title pages.
Imprints in some volumes covered with label: Gregg Press Ltd.,
Farnborough, Hampshire, England.
Reprint of the 1858-1902 ed.; Friedrich Chrysander, editor.
Contents: v. [1-38] Operas. -- v. [39-58] Oratorios. -- v. [59-67]
Sacred vocal music. -- v. [68-77] Secular vocal music. -- v. [78-79]
Keyboard music. -- v. [80-84] Other instrumental music.

I. Chrysander, Friedrich, 1826-1901. II. Title.

If it contains three or more works of various types for various media the uniform title is
"Selections." Analytical added entries are often made for the individual works found in
collections entered under the uniform title "Selections":

Schumann, Robert, 1810-1856.
⟶   [Selections]
Konzert für Klavier und Orchester a moll op. 54 ; Introduction
und Allegro appassionato G-dur op. 92 ; Novellette F-dur op. 21
Nr. 1 ; Toccata C-dur op. 7 [sound recording] / Robert
Schumann. -- [West Germany] : Deutsche Grammophon, [1966]
1 sound disc : analog, 33⅓ rpm, stereo. ; 12 in.
Deutsche Grammophon: 138 077.
Svjatoslav Richter, piano ; Sinfonie-Orchester der Nationalen
Philharmonie Warschau ; Witold Rowicki, conductor (1st work) ;
Stanislaw Wislocki, conductor (2nd work).

I. Schumann, Robert, 1810-1856. Concertos, piano, op. 54, A
minor. 1966. II. Schumann, Robert, 1810-1856. Introduction und
Allegro appassionato. 1966. III. Schumann, Robert, 1810-1856.
Noveletten, piano, op. 21. No. 1. 1966. IV. Schumann, Robert,
1810-1856. Toccata, piano, op. 7, C major. 1966. V. Rowicki,
Witold, 1914-      VI. Richter, Sviatoslav, 1915-      VII. Wislocki,
Stanislav, 1921-      VIII. Filharmonia Narodowa (Warsaw,
Poland) IX. Title: Introduction and Allegro appassionato.

If the collection consists of works of various types in one medium of performance, the
medium of performance is used as the uniform title:

→ Kuula, Toivo, 1883-1918.
    [Choral music]
    Sekakuorolauluja [sound recording] / Toivo Kuula. --
[Helsinki?] : Finlandia, p1979.
        1 sound disc : analog, 33⅓ rpm, stereo. ; 12 in.
        Finlandia: FA 306.
        Klemetti Institute Chamber Choir ; Harald Andersén, conductor.
        Contents: Auringon noustessa -- Venelaulu -- Rukous --
Kevatlaulu -- Virta venhetta vie -- Keinutan kaikua -- Savel --
Hautalaulu -- Karavaanikuoro -- Siellón kauan jo kukkineet
omenapuut -- Meren virsi.

        I. Andersén, Harald.  II. Kuula, Toivo, 1883-1918. Auringon
noustessa.  III. Kuula, Toivo, 1883-1918. Venelaulu.  IV. Kuula,
Toivo, 1883-1913. Rukous.  V. Kuula, Toivo, 1883-1918. Kevatlaulu.
VI. Kuula, Toivo, 1883-1913. Virta venhetta vie.  VII. Kuula, Toivo,
1883-1918. Keinutan kaikua.  VIII. Kuula, Toivo, 1883-1918. Savel.
IX. Kuula, Toivo, 1883-1918. Hautalaulu.  X. Kuula, Toivo,
1883-1918. Karavaanikuoro.  XI. Kuula, Toivo, 1883-1918. Siellón
kauan jo kukkineet omenapuut.  XII. Kuula, Toivo, 1883-1918.
Meren virsi.  XIII. Klemetti-Opiston. Kamarikuoro.  XIV. Title.

If the works are all of one type of composition, the name of the type of composition is used as the uniform title.

    Schubert, Franz Peter, 1797-1828.
    [Symphonies]
    Eight symphonies / Franz Schubert ; forewords by Hermann
Grabner. -- London : E. Eulenburg ; New York : Edition
Eulenburg, [1967?].
        1 score (2 v.) ; 18 cm.
        Contents: v. 1. Nos. 1-5 -- v. 2. Nos. 6-8.

        I. Grabner, Hermann.

Finally, if the collection is incomplete, "Selections" is added unless the selections form a consecutively numbered group, in which case the numerical designation is preferred.

# Examples

    The following examples contain complete descriptive cataloging (i.e., complete descriptions and access points including uniform titles) to illustrate choice and form of access for the musical works. Readers should note especially the fact that access points are not used to amplify the description. Rather, any access point used must be explained in the descriptive portion of the record to prevent confusion when the record is retrieved.

    Mozart, Wolfgang Amadeus, 1756-1791.
    [Symphonies, K.550, G minor]
    Symphony no. 40, G minor, K.550 / Wolfgang Amadeus
Mozart. -- Score. -- New York, Broude Bros., [194-]
        1 score (49 p.) ; 28 cm.
        Pl. no.: 390.

**Main entry:** The work in this item is Mozart's 40th symphony. Mozart is the personal author and therefore the main entry. Mozart's full name, Johann Chrysostom Wolfgang Amadeus Mozart, was used as the heading under earlier rules, but the form of name used here, Wolfgang Amadeus Mozart, is the form found on title pages of his music published in German-speaking countries.

There are no added entries.

**Uniform title:** The initial title element is "Symphony," which is generic and because it is cognate in English, French, German, and Italian, it is used in English. Because it is clear that Mozart wrote more than one symphony, the plural form is used. Medium of performance is not stated because it is implied by the initial title element. The serial number is not used because a thematic index number is preferred. The key is added as the final identifying element.

> Handel, George Frideric, 1685-1759.
>    [Suites, harpsichord, HWV 432, G minor. Passacaille;
> arr.]
>    Passacaille / G.F. Haendel. -- [S.l.] : Composers Facsimile
> Edition, c1966.
>    1 score ([3] p.) ; 34 cm.
>    Arr. for 2 guitars by Herbert Haufrecht; originally for
> harpsichord.
>    Caption title.
>    Reproduced from arranger's holograph.
>
>    I. Haufrecht, Herbert, 1909-

**Main entry:** The work represented here is Haufrecht's arrangement for guitars of a movement from Handel's suite for harpsichord. Main entry is under the composer of the original work (i.e., Handel). Handel was a German born composer whose productive career was spent in England, so his name appears predominantly on English language title pages and is used in its English form, George Frideric Handel.

Haufrecht, the arranger responsible for this manifestation of the work, receives an added entry. No title added entry is made because the title is generic.

**Uniform title:** The arrangement is of a movement from a suite, that is, an excerpt. Uniform titles for excerpts consist of the uniform title of the whole work, followed by a designation for the excerpt. The fact of arrangement (the present physical manifestation) is indicated as the last element to facilitate collocation.

The uniform title for the whole work is based on the initial element "Suites," which like "Symphony" in the preceding example, is generic, cognate in the four languages, and used more than once by Handel, thus used in the English plural form. Medium of performance "harpsichord" is added as the first identifying element. Note that the original medium is used because it is the uniform title for the entire original work that is being constructed. The thematic index number and key are also added as identifying elements. Note that the item described by this bibliographic record gives no verbal clue to these identifying elements. The cataloger has had to search the thematic index looking for movements titled *Passacaille* and an incipit that matches. This is not an uncommon situation.

To the uniform title for the whole work is added the designation of the part represented in the item, *Passacaille*. The term *passacaille* is a French cognate for *passacaglia*, a type of composition. Note that as the designation for an excerpt it is used as it appeared in the thematic index and not in a regularized form.

The designation "arr." is added to the end to show this work has been arranged, or in other words, is not in its original form.

Webber, Andrew Lloyd.
   [Cats. Vocal score. Selections]
   Cats : the songs from the musical / by Andrew Lloyd Webber ;
based on 'Old Possum's book of practical cats' by T.S. Eliot. --
London : Faber Music ; Winona, MN : Distributed by
H. Leonard Pub. Corp., c1981.
   1 vocal score (111 p.) ; 31 cm.
   Title on cover: Music from Cats : vocal arrangements with
piano accompaniment.
   For voice and piano with chord symbols.
   "In Trevor Nunn I found a collaborator ..."--Composer's
prefatory note (p. [4]).
   The text of "Jellicle songs for Jellicle cats" is by Trevor Nunn
and Richard Stilgoe after T.S. Eliot; the text of "Memory" is by
Trevor Nunn after T.S. Eliot.
   Contents: Overture -- Jellicle songs for Jellicle cats -- The naming
of cats -- The invitation to the Jellicle Ball (text only) -- The old
gumbie cat -- The rum tum tugger -- Bustopher Jones : the cat
about town -- Mungojerrie and Rumpelteazer -- Old Deuteronomy
-- The aweful battle of the Pekes and the Pollicles (text only) -- The
song of the Jellicles -- Grizabella : the glamour cat -- The moments
of happiness (text only) -- Gus : the theatre cat -- Growltiger's
last stand -- The ballad of Billy M'Caw -- Skimbleshanks : the
railway cat -- Macavity : the mystery cat -- Mr. Mistoffelees --
Memory -- The journey to the Heavyside Layer -- The addressing
of cats.
   Publisher's no.: HL00359465.
   $14.95.

   I. Nunn, Trevor.  II. Eliot, T. S. (Thomas Stearns), 1888-1965.
Old Possum's book of practical cats.  III. Title.

**Main entry:** This work is a musical show, with music by Andrew Lloyd Webber, and texts based on work by T. S. Eliot. Main entry is under the heading for the composer, Webber. An added entry is made for Trevor Nunn, who adapted the Eliot work for use in this musical. The Eliot *work* receives an added entry (name-uniform title) as a related work. A routine title added entry is made.

**Uniform title:** The initial title element is "Cats," which is distinctive, and therefore used without alteration or additions. The physical manifestation is indicated with the phrase "Vocal score." This will help subarrange *versions* of this work. To indicate that not all of the music from the show is present, "Selections" is used.

Abd al-Latif, Shah, ca. 1689-ca. 1752.
  Mystic music of Shah Lateef [sound recording] / Manzoor Ali
Khan. -- Islamabad : Institute of Folk Heritage, [1981?]
  1 sound cassette (60 min.) : 3¾ ips.
  Institute of Folk Heritage: Folk 007.
  Sung in Sindhi.
  Contents: Aanku jana pand Kaich jo dinun Ra'aiy Diach -- Boond
birhay ji bahar lagi -- Sikka marunji sumhan -- Khotha Kinjhar
kinarey.

  I. Manzoor ali Khan.  II. Title.

  **Main entry:** This sound recording is a collection containing vocal music by Abd al-Latif.
Because all of the selections are composed by one person, main entry is under the heading for
him. An added entry is made for Manzoor ali Khan, the performing musician. A routine title
added entry is also made.
  No uniform title has been formulated for this recording. It is likely that the difficulty of
locating reliable bibliographic information about Shah Latif outweighs the potential
usefulness of the device.


Rabot, Francois.
  Genevan organ music [sound recording]. -- Tinton Falls, N.J. :
Musical Heritage Society, [1978]
  1 sound disc (51 min.) : 33⅓ rpm, stereo. ; 12 in.
  Musical Heritage Society: MHS 3873 511.
  Francois Rabot, playing the great organ of St. Peter's Cathedral,
Geneva.
  Durations and program notes, translated into English by S. Celt,
on container.
  Contents: Passacaille, op. 6 / Otto Barblan (11:08) -- Pour un
jour de contrition ; Pour la fête de Pâques / Alexandre Mottu
(2:25 ; 2:25) -- Prelude grave ; Prelude in E minor / Bernard
Reichel (4:35 ; 2:42) -- Psalm 150 ; Dialogue et pas[s]acaille ;
Psalm XXIII / Henri Gagnebin (3:33 ; 9:53 ; 1:34) -- First
toccata / Eric Schmidt -- Flûtes de joie / Roger Vuataz (3:42) --
Psalm 92 / Pierre Segond (3:21).

  I. Title.

  **Main entry:** This recording is also a collection. In this instance the works are composed
by various people. Because a collective title is present, main entry is under the heading for
the principal performer, Francois Rabot. A routine title added entry is made. Many music
libraries would also make analytical added entries for each of the works on this recording, to
provide direct access to the music. The Library of Congress does not analyze recital
recordings.

Feldman, Morton, 1926-
    [Spring of chosroes]
    Spring of chosroes / Morton Feldman. Sonata for violin and
piano / Artur Schnabel [sound recording]. -- Port Jefferson,
N.Y. : CP2 Recordings, p1981.
      1 sound disc : analog, 33⅓ rpm, stereo. ; 12 in.
      CP/2 Recordings: CP2/8.
      Paul Zukofsky, violin ; Ursula Oppens, piano.
      Editions recorded: Universal Edition; Boosey and Hawkes.
      Program notes by Bunita Marcus and the violonist on container.

      I. Zukofsky, Paul. II. Oppens, Ursula. III. Schnabel,
Artur, 1882-1951. Sonatas, violin, piano. 1981. IV. Title.

**Main entry:** Once again the recording is a collection, and this time there is no collective title. Because the music is art music, main entry is under the heading for the first work, Feldman's *Spring of Chosroes*. Added entries are made for the performers and for the Schnabel work. A title added entry is made for the Feldman work, which has a distinctive title, but not for the Schnabel work, which does not.

Turandot [videorecording] / ORF Productions. -- New York :
    MGM/UA Home Video, c1984.
      1 videocassette (138 min.) : sd., col. (stereo.) ; ½ in.
      Opera.
      Italian with English subtitles.
      Cast: Eva Marton, Waldemar Kmentt, John-Paul Bogart, Jose
Carreras, Katia Ricciarelli, Robert Kerns, Helmut Wildhaber,
Heinz Zednik, Kurt Rydl, Bela Perenoz, The Vienna State Opera
Orchestra and Chorus.
      Credits: Staged by Harold Price ; director, Rodney Greenberg.
      Videocassette release of the 1983 production by ORF Productions.
      VHS format.
      Summary: Set in Peking, the opera opens with the proclamation that
Princess Turandot will become the bride of the royal suitor who can
successfully answer three riddles. Unsuccessful suitors lose not only
the hand of the princess, but their heads as well. Calaf, a handsome
prince who has been travelling the countryside incognito, is so struck
by Turandot's beauty that he tries to win her hand.
      "MV800312"

      I. Marton, Eva. II. Ricciarelli, Katia. III. Carreras, Jose.
IV. Puccini, Giacomo, 1858-1924. Turandot. V. ORF Productions.
VI. MGM/UA Home Video.

**Main entry:** Note that because this is a videorecording of an opera it has become a work of multiple authorship, thus main entry is under title proper. Added entries are made for the principal performers, for the production companies, and for the *work* by Puccini.

# Notes

[1]Krummel has described the process of musical publication in similar terms. Cf. D. W. Krummel, "Musical Functions and Bibliographical Forms," *The Library* (5th ser.) 31 (December 1976): 345.

[2]21.28A ftnt 7, *Music Cataloging Bulletin* 14, no. 12 (December 1983): 4.

[3]Rule 21.39, *AACR2*, 343-45.

[4]This is *AACR2*'s definition of arrangement; many would consider any substantial alteration to constitute an arrangement.

[5]21.23C-D, *Cataloging Service Bulletin* 38 (Fall 1987): 39.

[6]Rule 21.1B2e, *AACR2*, 285.

[7]21.7B, 21.7C, *Cataloging Service Bulletin* 28 (Spring 1985): 13-16.

[8]25.25, *Music Cataloging Bulletin* 14, no. 6 (June 1983): 2.

[9]Rule 25.27A, *AACR2*, 474.

# Suggested Reading

*Music Cataloging Bulletin*. Canton, Mass.: Music Library Association, 1969- . Monthly.

Smiraglia, Richard P. *Cataloging Music: A Manual for Use with AACR 2*. 2nd ed. "Chapter 2: Choice and Form of Entry"; "Chapter 3: Uniform Titles"; and "Chapter 4: Added Entries. References." Lake Crystal, Minn.: Soldier Creek Press, 1986.

# 5
# *SUBJECT ANALYSIS*

## Introduction

Subject analysis is the process in which a bibliographic entity is examined to identify elements such as discipline, topical content, the intellectual form of a work, its intended audience and/or its physical form. These elements are then systematized for use in retrieval. The purpose of subject analysis is to provide interesting categorizations of the material in ways that will prove useful as access points beyond the traditional composer and title index entries. The outcome of this process may be verbal indexing (controlled vocabulary subject headings, for example) when the system is primarily alphabetical or it may be classification when the system involves the assignment of symbols (notation) to represent the subject. Either way, in bibliographic control the process is dependent on a structured analysis sometimes referred to as the process of "determining aboutness."

In the process of determining aboutness, the work is examined to ascertain the discipline it is treating, the specific topic treated (sometimes this aspect is subdivided into facets, which can be further subdivided into phenomena and isolates), the intellectual form of the work (such as history or criticism), the physical form of its presentation (such as periodical or dictionary), and the audience for whom the work is intended. The terms gathered in this process (sometimes referred to as a summarization) can be taken together to describe the aboutness of a work.[1]

It has often been said that the concept of aboutness is not useful or even relevant to the subject analysis of music materials because music is not about anything in the same way that textual materials are. This is only partially true. Some musical works have directly topical character (such as an emigrant ballad about the homeland). Some musical works have indirectly topical character (such as Beethoven's Pastoral symphony). Still other musical works have a sort of environmental character (such as a sonata da chiesa, or a barn dance), though this could be said to be an element of intellectual form or genre. Some musical works display more than one of these characteristics.

More to the point then, is the realization that topicality, or aboutness, is only one of several aspects that are important in the subject analysis of music materials. Other aspects that are important are form of composition, medium of performance, intended audience, chronology, culture, and physical format.

The use of these various elements and their subsequent arrangement in verbal subject analysis and classification varies from one system to another. In the remainder of this chapter the elements of subject analysis will be examined. Subsequent chapters address specific systems for subject headings and classification.

# Characteristics for
# Arranging Music Materials

## CONCEPTUAL ANALYSES

It has always been recognized by music librarians and scholars that topicality was only one of many aspects of the intellectual content of music materials, and not the most important aspect for their arrangement and retrieval. Wide-scale dissatisfaction with existing schemes has occasioned experimentation and analysis to determine which music-specific facets are critical for successful subject arrangement and retrieval. Four significant studies have clearly identified the important facets.

An early scholarly analysis by Karl-Heinz Kohler of the salient characteristics for the subject arrangement of printed music developed a classification based on four major facets: 1) species (or form of composition), 2) setting (or medium of performance), 3) content (topic, style, or character), and 4) topography (country and chronology).[2]

In a 1975 review of existing schemes for classification of scores and sound recordings, Olga Buth identified eleven characteristics that recurred in most schemes. These characteristics were:

> 1) size; 2) format; 3) alphabetical arrangement [by composer];
> 4) medium [of performance]; 5) form [of composition]; 6) subject
> content; 7) character or content; 8) language of text; 9) geographical
> [orientation]; 10) style relating to a historical period; [and] 11) opus
> and thematic numbers.[3]

It is useful to note that Buth identified two *physical* characteristics (size and format of score), two *bibliographic* characteristics (composer and opus number), and seven truly music-specific *intellectual* and *topical* characteristics.

Brian Redfern's more detailed examination of the organization of music libraries begins by considering the types of users of music collections and their varying needs. These include:

> 1) musicologists or research workers [whose] approach may well
> be simply by composer [since] they probably know what is wanted; ...
> 2) instrumentalists [who] generally [prefer] material to be arranged by
> instrument [though] form may also prove useful; ... 3) music teachers
> [for whom] arrangement according to degree of difficulty might prove
> most serviceable ... though once again instrument could be an
> important factor; 4) groups of players, singers, etc. [for whom] an
> approach might depend on the number of people involved; ...
> 5) general readers and students [requiring] many different approaches;
> ... 6) Readers who borrow discs and cassettes [for whom] a new factor
> ... is the performing artist.[4]

The importance of these observations must not be missed. No matter how many salient intellectual and physical facets may be formulated for music materials it is clear that different users will seek the materials in differing ways, consulting varying combinations of the facets depending on their purposes. Minnie Elmer, in a 1960 article about reference capabilities of the music catalog, summarized a variety of user-specific approaches:

> The question of subject coverage is a perplexing one, capable of
> various solutions in libraries of various types. The scholar, thoroughly
> familiar with the bibliographical tools of his field, has little need of

the kind of help given by subject headings: he is more concerned with an exhaustive list of all available material than with the subject content of the individual library. In the educational institution, particularly if it is historically oriented, the same kind of approach is better taught if the student is forced to use a variety of books and bibliographies, rather than permitted to depend primarily on the library's subject catalog for his material. If an open shelf library is adequately classified, the casual reader may prefer to browse. ... And for information on specific topics, an article in [a dictionary or encyclopedia] is often adequate. In many respects—aside from coverage of the most recent materials—the bibliographical references in the better dictionaries and encyclopedias are preferable to subject entries, for here, a known authority has assembled what he considers to be the most indispensable references.[5]

Redfern's secondary emphasis is on the characteristics of the materials, beginning with a discussion of the differences in treatment between the literature about music and the music itself. This consideration begins with recognition of the physical characteristics of printed music materials, most notably the format and size of scores and parts. Four music-specific intellectual facets are recognized as being critical to the arrangement of music materials. These are "composers, instruments, forms, [and] size of ensemble." Three additional facets which are of secondary importance to the arrangement of materials are "[musical] character, space, [and] time."[6]

In a 1981 conceptual analysis of the use of musical form and musical setting in the construction of thesauri, Kurt Dorfmuller noted that instrumentation continues as the basis of most shelf arrangements with musical form, time, space, and musical character serving for subarrangement.[7]

## THE CHARACTERISTICS

In the subject analysis of textual materials five areas of analysis are commonly considered: 1) discipline; 2) topic, or what the work is *about*; 3) the work's intellectual form (such as a history or a dictionary); 4) the work's physical form (such as an anthology or a serial); and 5) the intended audience. Facets, or groups of characteristics having a common feature, exist as subdivisions within each element.

With minor modification a similar approach can be taken to the subject analysis of musical materials. The discipline element, taken always to be music, can be disregarded for the purposes of this discussion. The remaining elements, taken necessarily in a slightly different order, are 1) intellectual form, 2) topicality (which may often be inapplicable), 3) the intended audience, and 4) physical form. The placement of intellectual form before all other aspects recognizes the pervasiveness of structural elements in music. The other elements and their facets can be said to always act as qualifiers for the primary elements of intellectual form.

Facets within intellectual form are medium of performance and form of composition. All musical works have a medium of performance, that is, the instruments and or voices involved in creating the musical performance. Many musical works are composed in (or can be assigned to) recognized forms (such as sonatas or concertos). There are two important problems to consider in assigning terms within these facets. First, many forms imply a specific medium of performance (such as chorale preludes or symphonies). Second, terminological confusion exists in assigning musical works to given forms because the use of terms varies from period to period.

Facets within the topicality element are 1) topic or character, 2) historical style period, and 3) cultural influences. Some musical works, including most vocal works, have topical content. Usually this is determined from the sung or spoken text. For example, the song *Frankie and Johnnie* tells the story of two people. Unfortunately, since most texts set to music exhibit the characteristics of poetry, specific topical content is difficult to determine. Some musical works imply topicality by their titles (such as Sousa's *Washington Post*). Some musical works, especially nineteenth century works, exhibit a specific character (such as the many pastoral symphonies). Many musical works are classified according to terms that denote their intended use (such as sacred or secular works, or national or political songs).

However, even these topical references can be elusive. Artists work with impressions and attempt to evoke emotions. These qualities are innately human and therefore difficult if not impossible to categorize, because their perception is not a matter of common understanding. For these reasons, among others, classifiers have always avoided attempting to categorize the topical content of most literary and other artistic works. The major exception has been fictional works (and by extension, musical works) that are considered to be illustrative.[8]

Musical works are commonly identified by terms indicating the style period in which they were composed (rococo, classical, romantic, etc.). Of course, these terms are inexact, reflecting a certain perception of music history that is not necessarily universally understood. For instance, the terms do not necessarily coincide with the similarly named periods in the visual arts. Further, the term *classical* is widely used in general speech to mean *art* music. For these reasons, specific chronological designations are preferred in many systems.

Cultural identification may have two characteristics, which are region of origin and language of text. Here again problems are paramount. While language is rather easily diagnosed, region of origin may not be clear. Is Beethoven's music better described as German, Austrian, or Western European? All three may be correct depending on the particular perception. In a cultural sense, Western European is probably the better descriptor. In a historical sense it is true that Beethoven's music comes from a distinctly rich period in Austrian (actually Viennese) artistic prominence. Even ethnic music, often described in terms of its cultural origins, is hard to pin down because as the music travels it is affected and changed by the cultural influences with which it comes in contact.

Audience, in several ways, is also a critical factor for bibliographic control. First, the intended audience may have played an important role in determining the physical characteristics of the object. For example, a study score is printed in a miniature format so that it can be easily carried about in a pocket, to be studied discreetly during a performance. Music intended for children may be in larger than standard type, and may be illustrated. Second, the intended audience may have had an effect on the creation of the intellectual entity itself. In this regard the intended use may be as important as the intended audience. For example, a mass setting intended for use in a service will be different from a setting intended for concert performance.

The final element is physical form. This element incorporates two facets, printed music and recorded music. The printed music facet may be subdivided by format of score and the presence or absence of parts. This facet also greatly affects policies for subject analysis. For instance, most sound recordings are anthologies. Should the recording be analyzed as a performance (which is to say, as a unified collection) or should the individual elements be separately analyzed?

# Examples

A few examples will serve to demonstrate the utility of this method of subject analysis as well as the pitfalls of subject analysis of music materials. For each bibliographic entity the four elements will be considered: 1) intellectual form, represented with terms denoting the facets medium of performance and form of composition; 2) topicality, represented with terms denoting the facets topic or character where explicit, historical period, region of origin, and language; 3) audience; and 4) physical form, with terms denoting the facets physical format and number of works. Each element is considered separately. Within elements, facets are separated with slashes. Within facets, semicolons are used to separate phenomena; commas are used to separate isolates.

In these examples, the standard result of subject analysis can be seen in the Library of Congress subject headings, which appear as added entries in the final paragraph of the record numbered with Arabic numerals, and the Library of Congress classification numbers, which appear in the lower left corner of the record.

> Mozart, Wolfgang Amadeus, 1756-1791.
>   [Symphonies, K. 385, D major]
>   Sinfonie D-Dur : "Haffner-Sinfonie" K.V. 385 / W.A. Mozart ; herausgegeben von Darvas Gabor. -- Budapest : Editio Musica, c1985.
>   1 miniature score (115 p.) ; 18 cm.
>   Includes preface in German, English, and Hungarian.
>   Pl. no.: Z. 40 063.
>
>   1. Symphonies--Scores. I. Darvas, Gabor.
> M1001

**Orchestra/symphony:** This summarizes the intellectual form by indicating the medium of performance and the form of composition. Some would consider the statement redundant, however, because the form symphony is by definition a composition for orchestra.[9]

**Haffner/classical(1782)/Salzburg:** Here, Haffner is included as a topical element. Because Mozart used the name in the subtitle a tenuous intellectual relationship may be said to exist. However, the work is commonly described as having been written for the occasion of Haffner's ennoblement.[10] It is unclear whether there was any attempt by Mozart to create a musical depiction of any sort (it is unlikely, probably). For this reason, subtitles and dedications are widely disregarded in the subject analysis of art music.

The cultural elements are more easily ascertained, and are more effective at revealing something about the music. We know that the work is from the classical period, and that it was written in Salzburg. This tells us something useful about the circumstances in which the music was written and the intellectual influences that would have affected its creation. Further, these elements might be useful gathering devices in an index or catalog.

**Miniature score:** No audience is explicitly identified, but the physical form indicates that a student (in the broadest sense of the term) may have been intended.

> Bizet, Georges, 1838-1875.
>   [Les pêcheurs de perles. Vocal score. French & English]
>   The pearl fishers : an opera in three acts, with French and English text / Georges Bizet ; English translation by Geoffrey Dunn. -- Melville, N.Y. : Belwin Mills, [198-?]
>   1 score (202 p.) ; 27 cm. -- (Kalmus vocal scores ; 6071)
>
>   1. Operas--Vocal scores with piano. I. Title.
> M1503

**Solo voices, chorus, piano/opera:** Once again the medium of performance is clear. To some degree the statement is redundant. Like the symphony in the preceding example, we know that an opera is usually a work for solo voices, chorus, and orchestra. In this particular instance, the orchestral parts have been rewritten for the piano. This is done to facilitate rehearsal, as well as informal performance.

**Pearl fishers;romance/Romance(1863)/France;French,English:** This first major opera by Bizet has as its libretto the tragic romantic tale of the South Pacific. Because this is essentially a dramatic work, created for the purpose of entertainment rather than education, its topical content alone is not of major significance. It derives whatever import it has from its position within Bizet's works; this by extension is important because of its occurrence historically.

The era is of more consequence. The appearance of this work in 1863 in a form that had been heretofore reserved for comic works was remarkable. This factor might mean that a chronological subarrangement of the form would be meaningful for some users. Likewise the cultural aspect—that is, the work's French origin—is meaningful. This element too, might provide useful subarrangement of the form. The language elements do not provide cultural identification here. Rather they function more like elements of physical form, or manifestation, of the work.

**Vocal score.** No particular audience is indicated. The physical format, vocal score, implies a certain use for the item. This element could be of importance in a variety of ways. For instance, a music history teacher wishing to illustrate certain operatic styles might wish to search for nineteenth century French opera in vocal score, so that a lecture could be illustrated by playing excerpts on the piano. A voice teacher (or student) might wish to search for opera in vocal score, so as to find material suitable to use in the studio. A student of orchestration, on the other hand, would not want to find this score as an early example of Bizet's orchestration.

> Blacher, Boris, 1903-1975.
>   [Hamlet (Symphonic poem)]
>   Hamlet : symphonische Dichtung, 1940 / Boris Blacher. --
> Partitur. -- Berlin : Bote & Bock, c1981.
>     1 score (57 p.) ; 32 cm.
>     For orchestra.
>     Inspired by Shakespeare's play.
>     Duration: ca. 14:00.
>     Publisher's no.: B & B 20586 (1404).
>
>     1. Symphonic poems--Scores.  I. Shakespeare, William,
> 1564-1616. Hamlet.  II. Title.
> M1002

**Orchestra/Symphonic poem:** Once again the medium of performance is suggested by the form of composition. At this point in the discussion it might be useful to note that although there has been a one-to-one correspondence between the forms and media, the same is not true of the reverse. While many forms are medium-specific, no media are form specific. The importance of this observation is that the medium facet is generally considered to be a broader class (i.e., more inclusive) than the form facet.

**Shakespeare's** *Hamlet*/**Contemporary(1940)/Western European(German):** This work specifically indicates the Shakespeare play as a source of thematic inspiration. It is perhaps the precursor of the ballet by the same title that appeared in 1949. In a sense then it is a programmatic work. However, program music is a distinctly nineteenth century phenomenon. This situation perfectly illustrates the terminological difficulties that abound in musicology. Blacher, a twentieth century composer, is categorized chronologically by the relatively meaningless term "contemporary." Although his career took place almost entirely in Berlin his work is not distinctly German in a nationalistic sense and is best described as Western European.

**Score:** Again no audience is indicated. The object is a full score, suitable for use by a conductor in performance.

> Schuman, William, 1910-
>   [Symphonies, no. 7]
>   Symphony no. 7 / William Schuman. Steel symphony /
> Leonardo Balada [sound recording]. -- New York, N.Y. : New
> World Records, p1987.
>   1 sound disc (50 min.) : digital, stereo. ; 4¾ in.
>   New World Records: NW 348-2.
>   Pittsburgh Symphony Orchestra ; Lorin Maazel, conductor.
>   Recorded Aug. 11, 1985 (1st work) and Mar. 18, 1986 (2nd
> work), in Heinz Hall, Pittsburgh.
>   Editions performed: Merion Music (1st work); Belwin-Mills
> (2nd work).
>   Compact disc.
>   Durations: 29:45; 19:48.
>   Biographical and program notes by Leonard Burkat (Schuman)
> and David Wright (Balada), including selected bibliography and
> discography (11 p.) inserted in container.
>   "Recorded Anthology of American Music, Inc."
>   Issued also as analog disc and cassette.
>     1. Symphonies. I. Maazel, Lorin, 1930-      II. Balada,
> Leonardo, 1933-      Steel symphony. 1987. III. Pittsburgh
> Symphony Orchestra. IV. Recorded Anthology of American
> Music, Inc. V. Steel symphony.
>   [M1001]

**Orchestra/Symphony:** This recording, like those that will follow, is a performance, which will eventually add a new dimension to subject analysis. At the first level, intellectual form, there is no difference from the printed music already examined in this chapter because both works are in the same form and for the same medium.

**Contemporary (1960)/U.S.**
**Steel industry/1972/U.S.:** In the examination of the second element complexities begin to appear. The first work has no topical orientation or indirect character. The second work is titled *Steel Symphony*, indicating at least an indirectly topical orientation to the steel industry.

**Recording (compact disc):** No particular audience is indicated.

> Takahashi, Aki, 1944-
>     A valentine out of season [sound recording]. -- [S.l.] : Eastworld,
> p1985.
>         1 sound disc (53 min.) : digital, stereo. ; 4¾ in.
>         Eastworld: CC33-3322.
>         Aki Takahashi, piano.
>         Analog recording; recorded Sept. 6-8, 1976, Ishibashi Memorial
> Hall (Veno Gakuen).
>         Previously released as Eastworld TA-72034.
>         Compact disc.
>         Contents: Evryali / Ianis Xenakis (8:58) -- For away / Toru
> Takemitsu (5:19) -- A valentine out of season (3:27) ; A room
> (1:40) ; Music for Marcel Duchamp (5:22) / John Cage --
> Gnossiennes (Complete) / Erik Satie (17:03) -- Brouillards (2:56) ;
> General Lavine-eccentric (2:29) ; La terrasse des audiences du clair
> de lune (4:20) (from "Preludes", Book II) / Claude Debussy.
>
>         1. Piano music. I. Xenakis, Ianis, 1922-      Evryali. 1985.
> II. Takemitsu, Toru. For away. 1985. III. Cage, John. A valentine
> out of season. 1985. IV. Cage, John. She is asleep. A room. 1985.
> V. Cage, John. Music for Marcel Duchamp. 1985. VI. Satie,
> Erik, 1866-1925. Gnossiennes. 1985. VII. Debussy, Claude,
> 1862-1918. Preludes, piano, book 2. Selections. 1985. VIII. Title.
> [M22]

**Piano/......preludes:** All of these works are for the piano. Only the final work is composed in a named form of composition.

**;Marcel Duchamp,Gnostics/Contemporary,Romantic/Greece,Japan,U.S.,France:** These terms characterize various works. None of the works have direct topicality. Two have identifiable indirect topicality. The works are from various eras in the late nineteenth and mid-twentieth centuries. The works are by various composers, all writing in Western European idioms, from various countries.

**Recording (compact disc):** No particular audience is indicated.

> All in the April evening [sound recording]. -- London : Hyperion,
>     p1983.
>         1 sound disc : 33⅓ rpm, stereo. ; 12 in.
>         Hyperion: A66064.
>         In part Scottish folk-song arrangements.
>         Philharmonic Chamber Choir; David Temple, conductor.
>         Recorded July 24-25, 1982.
>         Contents: All in the April evening / Sir Hugh Roberton ; words,
> Katherine Tynan (3:39) -- The isle of Mull / traditional, arr. Sir
> Hugh Roberton ; words, Malcolm MacFarlane (2:37) -- Steal away
> to Jesus / traditional, arr. Sir Hugh Roberton (2:48) -- The dashing
> white sergeant / traditional, arr. Sir Hugh Roberton (1:55) -- Were
> you there? / traditional, arr. Sir Hugh Roberton (2:13) --

(Example continues on p. 71)

The banks o'Doon / traditional, arr. Sir Hugh Roberton ; words, Robert Burns (2:54) -- Peat fire smooring prayer / traditional, arr. Sir Hugh Roberton ; words, Kenneth Macleod (2:42) -- Loch Lomond / traditional, arr. Ralph Vaughan Williams (Peter Jones, tenor) (3:46) -- King Arthur / traditional, arr. Sir Hugh Roberton (3:06) -- Belmont / traditional, arr. Sir Hugh Roberton ; words, Bishop Heber (2:50) -- Iona boat song / traditional, arr. Sir Hugh Roberton (2:00) -- The herdmaiden's song / traditional, arr. Sir Hugh Roberton (Vivien Smith, contralto) (2:16) -- The bluebird / Sir Charles Stanford ; words, Mary E. Coleridge (Judith Dunworth) (3:46) -- Swing low, sweet chariot / traditional, arr. Sir Hugh Roberton (2:58) -- Faery chorus : from The immortal hour / Rutland Boughton ; words, Fiona Macleod (1:03) -- Nightfall in Skye / Sir Hugh Roberton (2:34) -- An Eriskay love lilt / traditional, arr. Marjorie Kennedy-Fraser, Sir Hugh Roberton ; words, Kenneth Macleod (3:04) -- Crimond / arr. Sir Hugh Roberton ; words, Jessye Irvine (3:58).

1. Choruses, Secular (Mixed voices), Unaccompanied. 2. Folk music--Scotland. 3. Folk songs, English--Scotland. I. Temple, David. II. Philharmonic Chamber Choir (London, England).
M1579                                            84-757251/R

**Chamber choir/folk songs:** This recording contains traditional English language folk songs arranged for performance by a chamber choir. It is debatable whether the formal arrangement of the music has changed its character sufficiently so that it no longer qualifies as folk music in the traditional sense.

**Folk music/Scotland/English:** The original songs might have been sung for entertainment and/or morale building by Scots. There is no unifying theme, except perhaps the concept of "all in the April evening," which might be a time when such music would have been played or sung in the home. Topics are diverse, as is common in folk music, but underlying many of these works is the notion of the commoner's struggle with life.

**Recording (LP):** No audience is specified. It is possible that the intended audience for this recording is analogous to the group from whom the traditional songs originated.

# Issues in Subject Analysis

As the examples above make clear, the analysis of musical works, printed or recorded, is a complicated task. Several problems prevent most existing systems from adequately reflecting the true character, topic, and form of musical works simultaneously. The facets, while clearly articulated and discussed in the literature cited, are nevertheless difficult to pin down in practice. Judgment about the terminology and its meaning must be exercised by the analyst. Further, each existing system, for one reason or another, relies on its own selection of some of the important elements.

Jesse Shera and Margaret Egan summarized principles for subject analysis against which all systems, verbal or classified, should be measured:

1.  Provide access by subject to all relevant material.

2.  Provide subject access to materials through all suitable principles of subject organization, e.g., matter, process, applications, etc.

3.  Bring together references to materials which treat of substantially the same subject regardless of disparities in terminology. ...

4.  Show affiliations among subject fields. ...

5.  Provide entry to any subject field at any level of analysis, from the most general to the most specific.

6.  Provide entry through any vocabulary common to any considerable group of users, specialized or lay.

7.  Provide a formal description of the subject content of any bibliographic unit in the most precise, or specific, terms possible. ...

8.  Provide means for the user to make selection from among all items in any particular category.[11]

Shera and Egan's seventh principle, that a system should provide a formal subject description of the bibliographic entity, is the most frequently disregarded aspect of subject analysis of musical objects. As the examples above indicated, the "subject" of a musical work is complex, formed of elements of intellectual form, topic, and physical form. These elements subtly intertwine in a given work to create a true work of art. Most existing classifications and verbal subject analysis systems concentrate on medium of performance and form of composition, disregarding other aspects unless the bibliographic entity (the published work) features some other aspect. This emphasis is perhaps the result of two specific problems.

First, the medium of performance and the form of composition are easily recognized by analysts. Because terms denoting these elements frequently appear in the publications it is possible for analysts to abrogate judgment, preferring instead to simply copy terminology from the publications. On the other hand, topicality, especially in its less direct manifestations, and cultural influences are not easily ascertained and are even less easily categorized. It is rare in any field of bibliographic control for these elements to receive attention when they occur in works of art. The result is a failure of existing systems to adequately provide access to materials, Shera and Egan's first principle.

Second, it is probable that existing systems, which grew up to expedite education of Western European musicologists and art music performers in universities and conservatories, address medium of performance and form with little regard for other facets because music education consists largely of the study of these two aspects.

The second of Shera and Egan's principles, that of suitable organization, is also violated, because an entire element is disregarded. This results in the failure of existing systems to meet the objectives of the third and fourth principles, which embrace appropriate collocation of materials and the illustrations of the relationships that exist not only among the materials, but also among the terminology used to index them.

Most of the existing systems discussed in the next two chapters choose either medium of performance or form of composition as their principle access point. In some cases both elements are accommodated. In these cases, when there are no easily identifiable topical, cultural, or physical features, the access points are coextensive with (that is, they adequately describe in one phrase) the musical work. Promises of truly faceted systems, those that allow the regular use of all relevant elements, are the hope of the future for subject retrieval of musical works. Such systems, deployed in online catalogs, could resolve the dilemma of coextensivity in access points *and* facilitate the functioning of Shera and Egan's fifth and sixth principles, providing entry to a collection at any appropriate level of analysis. This would in turn help us provide truly effective service to music library users, satisfying the final objective, allowing the user to evaluate and select appropriate works. This must be the primary goal for music bibliographic control in the era of the Online Public Access Catalog (OPAC).

# Notes

[1]For a more fully developed explanation of this method of analysis, see A. G. Brown, *An Introduction to Subject Indexing: A Programmed Text* (London: C. Bingley, 1976).

[2]Karl-Heinz Kohler, "Grundzüge eines analytischen Systems der Sachkatalogisierung der "Musica Practica," *Zentralblatt für Bibliothekswissenschaft* 71 (1957): 267-80.

[3]Olga Buth, "Scores and Recordings," *Library Trends* 23 (1975): 428-29.

[4]Brian Redfern, *Organising Music in Libraries. Volume 1: Arrangement and Classification*, rev. and rewritten ed. (London: C. Bingley, 1978), 17.

[5]Minnie, Elmer, "The Music Catalog as a Reference Tool," *Library Trends* 8 (1960): 534.

[6]Redfern, *Organising Music*, 21.

[7]Kurt Dorfmuller, "Form- und Gattungsnamen im Sachkatalog der Musical practica zum Entwurf eines Thesaurus," *Fontes artis Musicae* 28 (1981): 115-29.

[8]Charles Ammi Cutter, *Rules for a Dictionary Catalog* (Washington, D.C.: Government Printing Office, 1876), 186.

[9]See, however, the definition in the *New Harvard Dictionary of Music*, ed. Don Michael Randel (Cambridge, Mass.: Belknap Press, 1986), 822-27.

[10]*New Harvard Dictionary*, [361].

[11]Jesse H. Shera and Margaret E. Egan, *The Classified Catalog* (Chicago: American Library Association, 1956), 10.

# Suggested Reading

Buth, Olga. "Scores and Recordings." *Library Trends* 23 (1975): 428-29.

*Theory of Subject Analysis: A Sourcebook.* Edited by Lois Mai Chan, Phyllis A. Richmond, and Elaine Svenonius. Littleton, Co.: Libraries Unlimited, 1985.

# 6
# *VERBAL SUBJECT ANALYSIS*

## Introduction

Verbal subject analysis, involving the use of controlled vocabulary subject headings in an alphabetical catalog, has always been the predominant method of subject indexing of music collections in the United States. This trend, which parallels developments in subject cataloging in general, may be a result of the tradition of public access to library collections, and therefore an example of Cutter's principle of user convenience at work.

Classified music catalogs, predominant in European libraries, have never been popular in the United States. The most famous classified music catalog was the now closed catalog in the Music Division at the Library of Congress. The use of the public shelflist as a classified catalog enjoyed a minor vogue in the 1960s and early 1970s.[1] Because of the complexity of subject analysis of music materials (see chapter 7), music lends itself well to classified approaches. In particular, faceted classifications have the potential for coextensivity and retrieval flexibility that many verbal subject headings systems lack.

Nevertheless, for several reasons, verbal subject headings have been the norm in music libraries in the United States. Until very recently most music libraries collected traditional Western art music, the music for which subject heading lists were developed. Further, most music libraries are part of larger library units, which, because of the ability of the catalog user to approach subject material directly under specific headings, have a tradition of verbal subject analysis.

## Historical Background

Like developments in descriptive cataloging of music materials in the United States, verbal subject analysis has historically been the province of just a few unified systems. This is a result of the cooperative efforts of organized music librarians working together through the Music Library Association (MLA) to achieve standardized access to their predominantly research-oriented music collections. These efforts date back at least to 1935 when the fledgling MLA (founded only in 1931) produced the first of two provisional lists of subject headings based on practice at the Library of Congress.[2] From this point, three separate trains of thought took off in different directions. Their paths would not converge for the next fifty years.

In 1943 the Music Division at the Library of Congress changed the subject portion of its divided catalog into a classified catalog.[3] From this time until the closing of the card catalogs in 1981, the music headings in the *Library of Congress Subject Headings* (*LCSH*) represented terms authorized for use on LC printed cards, but *not* terms used by the people who were devising them. This may be a principle reason why so many long-unresolved problems with the use of these headings for music materials exist.

The next milestones in subject analysis were the publication in 1952 and 1959 of the Library of Congress music headings and the New York Public Library music headings, respectively.[4] The Library of Congress list was developed in response to the expressed need of the MLA for a list that was more appropriate for use in a dictionary catalog than its own provisional lists of the 1930s. These two lists, LC and NYPL, were produced for use by the nation's two largest and most complex research music collections and thus were similar in many ways. Both lists were based on the principle of specific and direct entry. A major difference between the two lists was that the Library of Congress list chose form of composition modified by medium of performance as its primary access point. The New York Public list chose medium of performance as its primary access point. A more subtle difference was that of audience. The LC list was intended for use in a general dictionary catalog while the NYPL list was intended for use in the Music Division's catalog. Thus, many headings beginning with the words *Music* and *Musical* that appear in the LC list are entered directly under the secondary term in the NYPL list.[5] The NYPL list, more appropriate for research collections in many ways, was dropped in 1978 when NYPL automated its cataloging operations, at which time it adopted LC standards for all aspects of its cataloging.

The third direction was that of simplicity, based on audience. The music headings that were published in the *Sears List of Subject Headings* (similar to those in the earlier ALA *List of Subject Headings*) were intended for use in the dictionary catalogs of small and medium-sized public libraries. These headings, based on the principle of specific and direct entry, broad in scope and limited in number, were appropriate for the small collections of books about music that could be found in most medium-sized libraries, but were not intended for use in music collections. Another innovation of the 1950s was caused by the widespread introduction of sound recordings into music libraries. The Library of Congress commissioned a study of the applicability of its subject headings on cataloging for sound recordings. Apparently by 1953 this study had indicated that existing headings would be appropriate with a few minor modifications.[6] The major decision was whether or not to develop a form subdivision for "Phonorecords."[7] Without this subdivision it would mean that many headings would be used for the first time without form subdivision. It was ultimately decided *not* to develop such a form subdivision. Though the unsubdivided headings for recordings could easily have coexisted in front of the subdivided headings for printed music, this result was considered undesirable and was one factor in the creation of separate sound recording catalogs in many libraries, which were designed to prevent the intermingling of subject cards for scores and recordings. Further developments in verbal subject analysis in the United States are predominantly instances of tinkering with existing LC headings or with the rules for their application. For example, in 1981 changes that had been recommended by the MLA in 1980 were made in the application of subject headings to the musics of ethnic and national groups.[8]

It is important to realize that *LCSH*, like its cousin the NYPL list, was developed by and for musicologists and musicians working in a tradition of Western art music as it was practiced and understood at the turn of the twentieth century.[9] As musical practice expanded in the latter half of the twentieth century demand for more flexible indexing methods and less xenophobic terminology increased. In recent times more sweeping changes have been proposed. Many of these changes, long demanded by music librarians but rejected by LC in earlier times, are now made possible because LC began using its own headings in its online catalog in 1981. Beginning in 1984, the MLA has investigated the potential of conducting a music thesaurus project, the probable goal of which would be to develop an indexing protocol. To date no result of this investigation has been seen.

Meanwhile, the most significant advance in the verbal analysis of music took place in the mid-1970s with the application of PRECIS to the *British Catalogue of Music*. Derived from earlier chain-indexing procedures modified for computer application, PRECIS offers greater potential for coextensive analysis of musical materials than *LCSH*. The remainder of this chapter presents an overview of the specific application of *LCSH* and PRECIS to music materials.

# Library of Congress
# Subject Headings

The *Library of Congress Subject Headings* is an official list of authorized terms with references. Music headings are only a small part of that list. Further, many music headings fall into the category of headings that are "not printed," which means they are to be constructed as needed by the cataloger according to specific instructions.

## SINGULAR VERSUS PLURAL

Several principles, enumerated by Helen Bush and David Haykin at the time of the compilation of the first LC list, still govern the development and application of LC subject headings for music.[10] The first, and most important for use in the dictionary catalog, is the distinction between *subject* headings, used for books about music, and *form* headings, used for the music itself. This difference is expressed by the use of terms in singular form for subject headings and plural form for musical form headings. Thus, "Symphony" is a heading for a book about the symphony as a musical form, while "Symphonies" is the heading for the score of a symphony.

## SPECIFIC AND DIRECT VERSUS COEXTENSIVE

A second principle, derived from Cutter and applied throughout *LCSH*, is that of specific and direct entry. That is, a work should be entered directly under the term that best expresses its specific topic, not a broader class that includes that topic. In music, this principle finds expression through the use of headings based on the form of composition modified by the medium of performance. Thus a piano sonata is entered under "Sonatas (Piano)." Another reason for this approach is that it allows collocation of form headings for musical works and subject headings for books about them under the name of the type of composition. Thus scores and recordings of suites immediately follow books about the suite. Forms of composition that imply a medium of performance, such as symphonies, are modified only when the work entered utilizes a medium of performance other than the one that would have been expected, such as "Symphonies (Band)." Works that are not composed in any particular named form, or that are composed in a form that is not included on the LC list, are entered under a heading for the medium of performance. Thus a work titled *Impromptu* for piano would be entered under the heading "Piano music." Some headings for musical form are not qualified, presumably to avoid scattering a small file into several alphabetical sequences. Often these headings require the addition of a second heading for medium of performance.

One obvious result of the preference for form over medium is the scattering of works for a particular medium of performance. This makes the use of the LC headings less appropriate for conservatory or other performance-based collections. However, most such libraries are classified by systems that arrange material on the shelves by medium of performance, making it possible to retrieve by instrument through browsing, either at the shelf or in the shelf list. Further, this approach minimizes the number of entries found under the general medium headings such as "Orchestral music." Another problem with the principle of specific and direct entry in music is that it often is not compatible with the concept of coextensivity. Specificity requires the most specific heading available be applied to the work. Thus an anthology of Christmas carols for mixed chorus is entered under the headings "Choruses (Mixed voices) with piano," "Carols, English," and "Christmas music," because there is no specific heading that is coextensive with these concepts.

## USAGE

A broad principle of American English usage is applied to the development of terms included in the list. Thus, *Songs* is preferred to *Lieder*. This principle is problematic in a music subject heading system because of the international use of terms from a variety of Western European languages. When a foreign language term is commonly used in American English it is preferred; for example, *Continuo* is preferred to *Thorough-bass*. Likewise, some musical terms are also used in other fields, so are qualified to prevent conflicts in a general dictionary catalog. Thus *Psalms (Music)* identifies a musical setting of a *Psalm*.

Timeliness in adopting new terms as they enter common usage is as much a problem for music headings as it is for terms in other fields. It is true that the retrospective nature of musicology would seem to stabilize terminological change in music. However, some archaic forms persist long after they have been dropped from standard everyday usage. The most often cited example of this is the continued use of the term *Violoncello* for cello. Because of the domain of literary warrant in the LC collection, new terminology in common usage in the popular music industry or in ethnomusicology is also very slow to enter the list, because LC does not extensively collect or catalog this material.

## NUMBER OF HEADINGS

Traditionally the number of headings applied to a single bibliographic record has been determined by a "rule of three." This means that up to three specific terms can be used before a broader term must be preferred. For instance, a sound recording of a sonata, a suite, and a set of variations for clarinet and piano would receive three headings.

> Sonatas (Clarinet and piano)
> Suites (Clarinet and piano)
> Variations (Clarinet and piano).

However, a sound recording of a sonata, a suite, and a tango for clarinet and piano would receive a single heading, "Clarinet and piano music." (The heading "Tangos" may not be modified by, but requires the use of a second heading for, medium.) There is, however, no upper limit on the number of headings that may be used together to express unrelated concepts. It is not uncommon to find five or six headings used on bibliographic records for sound recordings.

## PHRASE HEADINGS

Phrase headings are uncommon in music. They tend to obscure the terms that are not used for the filing element. Nevertheless some exist in the list, particularly for early forms of composition.

Canons, fugues, etc.
Glees, catches, rounds, etc.

## INVERTED HEADINGS

Inverted headings are not very common in music, though a few exist. These are easily categorized. First, headings for works with words, which are used for anthologies or for ethnic vocal works, are inverted so as to allow collocation by form of composition.

Ballads, French
Songs, Japanese.

Music in the dramatic vocal forms that is either sacred or secular is represented by inverted headings.

Cantatas, Sacred
Choruses, Secular.

Those headings unqualified (i.e., "Cantatas" and "Choruses") are used for collections that include both.

Arrangements, or music that is intended to be performed with a different medium of performance than that for which it was originally written, are indicated with inverted headings.

Violin and piano music, Arranged
Operas—Excerpts, Arranged.

Music intended for children, either as performers or as audience, is indicated with inverted headings.

Piano music, Juvenile.

Headings for juvenile music, unlike other inverted headings, may be used only when they are published in the list. Languages, and the terms *Sacred, Secular,* and *Arranged* may be added as necessary.

## MEDIUM HEADINGS AND QUALIFIERS

Medium headings and form headings with medium qualifiers are not specified in the printed list except to indicate specific references. Instructions for constructing these headings appear in the "Introduction" to the eighth edition of the printed list.[11]

### Instrumental Music—Chamber Music

Music for one instrument alone is indicated by the name of that instrument (as specified in the list) and the word *music*. The same construction is used for music for two like instruments, with the addition of a parenthetical qualifier consisting of the instrument name and the number in parentheses.

Clarinet music
Flute music
Snare drum music
Harp music (Harps (2))
Violoncello music (Violoncellos (2)).

Music for two unlike instruments is indicated with a conjunctive phrase. If one of the instruments is a chordal accompanying instrument it is named in the second position.

Horn and piano music
Bass clarinet and organ music.

Otherwise, instruments are named in the following order of preference:

1. Keyboard instruments

2. Wind instruments (i.e., woodwind *and* brass instruments)

3. Plucked instruments

4. Percussion, and other instruments

5. Bowed stringed instruments

6. Unspecified instruments

7. Continuo.[17]

Within each category instruments are named in alphabetical order, except bowed stringed instruments, which are named in score order (violin, viola, violoncello, double bass).

Oboe and viola music
Harp and continuo music.

For three to nine instruments in combination a heading indicating the size of the ensemble is used (i.e., trios, quartets, quintets, sextets, septets, octets, or nonets). For standard chamber combinations, the name of the ensemble is used without qualification.

Piano trios
Piano quartets
Piano quintets
String trios
String quartets.

If the combination is not standard, however, qualification is added. Thus,

String quartets (Violin, violas (2), double bass).

If the ensemble is not one of the standard chamber combinations, it is possible to use a medium ensemble heading if all the instruments are in the same group.

Brass trios
Wind sextets.

Otherwise, the ensemble name is used unmodified.

Septets (Piano, clarinets (2), flute, horn, violin, viola, violoncello).

### Instrumental Music—Large Ensembles

For ensembles of ten or more players, one player to a part, the term *ensembles* is used without further specification of instruments.

Brass ensembles
String ensembles
Woodwind ensembles.

If the instruments are not all of one type, *Instrumental ensembles* is used.

For large ensembles, which utilize more than one player to a part, the heading consists of the name of the ensemble and the word *music.*

Orchestral music
Dance orchestra music.

### Instrumental Music—Soloist with Ensemble

Headings for soloists with ensembles are constructed as prepositional phrases using the name of the soloist and the name of the ensemble joined by the word *with.*

Flute with string orchestra.

If the work is in the form of a concerto, the accompanying medium is assumed to be orchestra unless otherwise specified.

Concertos (Piano)
but
Concertos (Violin with string orchestra).

### Vocal Music

Headings for vocal music are constructed similarly. Music for solo voice is entered under a heading consisting of the form (usually "Songs") qualified by the type of voice (high, medium, or low) and, if appropriate, a prepositional phrase to indicate the accompaniment.

Songs (High voice)
Songs (Medium voice) with piano
Songs (High voice) with orchestra.

Vocal music for two or more solo voices is entered under a phrase heading "Vocal duets [trios, etc.]," again, where appropriate, with a prepositional phrase to indicate the accompaniment.

Vocal trios with orchestra.

Choral music is entered under an inverted heading beginning with the word "Choruses," modified by the term "Sacred" or "Secular" as appropriate, qualified by a statement indicating the type ("men's," "women's," "mixed," "equal") of voices, and with a prepositional phrase to indicate the accompaniment.

Choruses, Sacred (Mixed voices) with orchestra.

(If the accompaniment is chordal or if there is no accompaniment, the number of voice parts is also specified).

Choruses, Secular (Men's voices, 5 parts) with piano.

## SUBDIVISION

### Chronological Subdivision

Historical periods can be indicated by the use of chronological subdivisions. In *LCSH* music chronological subdivisions are used only for collections of Western art music by two or more composers when the collection emphasizes a period. The subdivisions are

- —To 500
- —500-1400
- —15th century
- —16th century
- —17th century
- —18th century
   19th century
- —20th century[13]

Note that the old subdivision "—To 1800," which had been used with musical compositions, was cancelled in 1980. Other chronological subdivisions, for example those used with headings for popular music forms, are specified in the list.

### Geographic

Like other terms treated in *LCSH*, geographic subdivision may be applied whenever the list indicates by use of the phrase "[May Subd Geog]" (formerly *(Indirect)*). Extended application of geographic subdivision is made for ethnic musics (see discussion below).

### Free-floating

Free-floating subdivisions are those that may be applied whenever they are applicable. In *LCSH*, free-floating subdivisions used with music are predominantly physical form subdivisions. No free-floating subdivisions are authorized for use with sound recordings in *LCSH*.

There are three categories of free-floating subdivisions that may appear under headings for music materials.

### Musical Format Subdivisions

—Parts
—Parts (solo)
—Piano scores
—Piano scores (4 hands)
—Scores
—Scores and parts
—Scores and parts (solo)
—Vocal scores
—Vocal scores with accordion
—Vocal scores with continuo
—Vocal scores with guitar
—Vocal scores with harpsichord
—Vocal scores with organ
—Vocal scores with piano
—Vocal scores with piano (4 hands)
—Vocal scores with piano and organ
—Vocal scores with piano and organ.[14]

Musical format subdivisions may be applied to works where the medium of performance is generally stated or implicit, but not to headings for special seasons (e.g., Christmas music) or for works that are generally published in only one format (e.g., hymns, songs, unaccompanied choruses, etc.). Other musical format subdivisions that are not free-floating are "Solo with piano" and "Solos with piano" for use with music originally written for soloist(s) and accompanying ensemble.

### Form Subdivisions

—Excerpts*
—Excerpts, Arranged*
—Instructive editions
—Simplified editions
—Teaching pieces.[15]

These are only the form subdivisions. Those marked with an asterisk may be further subdivided by musical format. Topical subdivisions also exist, but are not applied to music.

### Subdivisions Controlled by the Pattern Heading for Musical Instruments

—Instruction and study (Indirect)
—Instruction and study—Fingering
—Instruction and study—Juvenile
—Instruction and study—Pedaling
—Methods
—Methods—Group instruction
—Methods—Juvenile
—Methods—Self-instruction
—Methods (Jazz [Rock, etc.])*
—Orchestra studies

—Studies and exercises
—Studies and exercises—Fingering
—Studies and exercises—Juvenile
—Studies and exercises—Pedaling
—Studies and exercises (Jazz [Rock, etc.])*[16]

These again are only those subdivisions listed under the pattern heading for musical instrument ("Piano") that would be applicable to music. Those marked with an asterisk should be accompanied by a second heading for style of music subdivided by "—Instruction and study."

Harp—Methods (Jazz)
Jazz music—Instruction and study.

Other subdivisions are listed under the pattern heading for musical compositions ("Operas").

## MUSICS OTHER THAN WESTERN ART

Special provisions, instituted as a result of much investigation and lobbying by the MLA under the leadership of Judy Kaufman, are applied to the formulation of headings for musics other than Western art (an awkward phrase used to cover non-art music from any culture, and art music from non-Western cultures). Three categories of headings are applied to examples of these musics. An attempt is made always to apply the first two categories, with the third added as appropriate.

The first category is a heading consisting of the name of the ethnic or national group with local subdivision, and the subdivision "—Music." These headings are not assigned to music of individual nationalities within their own countries.

Germans—Hungary—Music
Afro-Americans—Louisiana—Music.

The second category is a heading for broad musical genre or style or for ballads and songs with national emphasis, with local subdivision as appropriate.

Music—Japan
Folk dance music—Denmark.

The third category is a heading for language of sung or spoken material. These are always inverted headings. Local subdivision is used as appropriate.

Folk-songs, Swedish
Songs, French—Haiti.

Other headings may be applied, as appropriate.

Koto music
Sarod and tabla music.

## ANOMALIES

There are several inexplicable anomalies in the *LCSH* music headings. For instance, sacred choruses are entered under "Choruses, Sacred" as are "Cantatas, Sacred," but sacred works for solo voices are entered under "Sacred songs," "Sacred vocal duets," etc. As mentioned above, some names of types of composition, principally dance forms, are used without medium qualification, preferring instead a second heading to express the medium. A third important anomaly is the treatment of electronic media. A work for any traditional instrument and an electronic medium (such as a tape, synthesizer, etc.) is entered under a heading representing the traditional aspects with a second heading, "Electronic music." For example, a suite for violin, tape, and orchestra receives the headings:

Suites (Violin with orchestra)
Electronic music.

The latter two examples are instances when coextensivity is sacrificed without the concommitant benefit for specificity.

## PHYSICAL FORM OF THE LIST

The list is available in printed form (the eleventh edition of *LCSH* was published in three volumes in 1988 and is also available in microfiche). "Subject Heading Additions and Changes" is a column that appears monthly in the *Music Cataloging Bulletin*. This column contains comprehensive information about new, changed, and cancelled subject headings and subdivisions. The printed list is analogous to an authority file, and plans to make the headings available in machine-readable form as the LC subject authority file came to fruition in December 1987 when OCLC began offering LC subject authority records as part of its online authority file.

In either format, LC classification numbers, scope notes, references, and tracings accompany the headings themselves. Scope notes explain the application of particular headings. LC classification numbers accompany some headings and may be used as aids to classification.

References are used to create the list's syndetic structure (i.e., its network of hierarchical relationships). *See* references refer the reader from a term sought to the authorized term used in the list, and take the form USE. *See from* tracings are indicated by UF, meaning Used For, and show the location of *see* references that point to the term. *See also* references, indicated by SA, indicate narrower terms that the user may wish to consult. *See also from* references indicate broader terms (BT) and related terms (RT) that the user might wish to consult. Updates, in addition to the codes already explained, also carry the relevant MARC tags and LC subject authority file numbers that would be used in machine-readable authority records (see also chapter 10 below).

```
150        Mandola music [sh85-80451]
360            SA  Concertos, Minuets, Sonatas, Suites, and similar headings with specifi-
                   cation of instruments; Trios [Quartets, etc.] followed by specifications
                   which include the Mandola; also Plectral ensembles and headings that
                   begin with the words Mandola or Mandolas

150        Clarinette d'amour [sh85-89038]
450            UF    Clarinet d'amour
450            UF    Clarinetto d'amore
550            BT    Clarinet

150        Concertos (Ti tzu) [sh85-30371]
053                 M1034.T6
550            RT    Ti tzu with orchestra
```

## CONCLUSION

*LCSH* is the most widely used system for verbal subject analysis of music materials. It should be apparent from this brief introduction that only some of the facets relevant for the subject analysis of music materials are covered by *LCSH* headings. Medium of performance and form of composition are adequately and consistently provided. Other facets, in particular the cultural, are only occasionally covered if at all. The conception of literary warrant that governs the choice of new headings in the list effectively prevents not only new terms but also terms not needed in the collection at LC from entering the list.

These persistent problems have lead many music librarians to develop internal systems to solve specific problems and played a role in the development of content designated control elements of the MARC music record to cover chronology (field 045), geography (field 043), form of composition (field 047), and medium of performance (field 048). Additional fields have been proposed to include further elements of the cultural facet, including coded indications of cultures from the George Murdock *Outline of World Cultures* or the Sachs-Hornbostel instrument classifications.[17] Others, notably the MLA Music Thesaurus Project working group, have called for development of a thesauro-facet approach to verbal subject analysis of music materials.

In recent years LC has been sensitive to criticisms of its terminology. Many changes have been made in music headings, including the revamping of headings for popular music in the summer of 1987. It remains to be seen whether *LCSH* will continue as a viable system for verbal subject analysis of music materials in online catalogs.

# PRECIS

PRECIS is the acronym for PREserved Context Indexing System. PRECIS is not a list of terms like *LCSH*, nor is it intended to be used to organize card files. Instead, PRECIS is a system of detailed procedures for indexing bibliographic files. Though it was and is intended for use in printed indexes that are produced from machine-readable records, it has been adapted for online use. Coextensive strings (sequential descriptive phrases) are produced, detailed content designation is applied, and index entries are permuted, each of which remains coextensive.

PRECIS was developed for alphabetical subject indexing of the DDC-classified *British National Bibliography* (*BNB*). Since 1970, when a system of chain indexing was discarded, PRECIS has been used to produce printed indexes to the BNB. The use of PRECIS was extended to the *British Catalogue of Music* (*BCM*) in 1984. Since then it has been used to create alphabetical subject indexes to the classified catalog, which, since 1980, has been arranged according to numbers derived from the highly synthetic *Proposed Revision of 780 Music* (a phoenix).

## PRINCIPLES

According to Derek Austin, who was instrumental in the development of PRECIS, five requirements, or principal goals governed the development of PRECIS:

1.  The computer should handle … the "clerical drudgery" aspects of indexing…. The computer … would manipulate the single input string into a full set of entries under selected terms.

2.  Each of the entries produced … should be co-extensive with the subject as seen by the indexer: that is to say, each entry should contain an equally complete summary of the subject.

3.  The terms in every entry should be printed in what might be called a meaningful order—sufficiently close to natural language to allow the user to understand the subject without the need for complex instructions. [PRECIS] would deliberately avoid, for example, unnatural inversions, such as "Bridges, concrete."

4.  The order of terms in input strings, and in the entries generated from these strings, should be determined by a single set of logical criteria which can be applied with equal effect in any subject field, and also to any kind of document.

5.  The terms selected as entry points in the index should be supported by a system of *See* and *See also* references from other related terms that might occur to a user but had been excluded from entries on the grounds that they were sufficiently implied. This would apply, for example, to broader terms and non-preferred synonyms. These references would be extracted by the computer from a machine-held thesaurus.[18]

The statement of these five requirements describes the system quite well. Strings are derived by indexers according to specific instructions. The string is constructed to fit a basic model of codes and terms known as a paradigm. The coded strings are coextensive with the subject matter of the document. The order of terms in each string is said to be context-dependent, which means that each term places the next into its most obvious context, much like natural language. Also mimicking natural language, terms in a string may form what is called a one-to-one related sequence. This means that each term is directly related to the terms displayed on either side.

Terms designated as access points, or index entries, are moved through a series of controlled permutations into lead, or entry, position. This process is called shunting. The *BCM* index will contain alphabetical lists under each entry (the lead term) that refer the user to the classified section of the catalog, where bibliographic descriptions may be found. At any point a PRECIS entry contains a permutation of the original string, so that not only is each entry coextensive with the subject matter of the document, but each entry can be meaningful to the user because it provides contextual information. For example, the following secondary entries could be found in the *BCM* under the index phrase "Ordinary of the mass":

Ordinary of the mass
   For contralto solo, tenor solos (2), bass solo and unaccompanied
      mixed voices
   For mixed voices with keyboard
   For soprano, contralto, tenor and bass solos with mixed voices and
      chamber orchestra
   For soprano, contralto, tenor and bass solos with mixed voices and
      keyboard
   For unaccompanied mixed voices

Each secondary entry leads to the point in the catalog where bibliographic records are arrayed.

Because there is no list of preapproved terms, indexers are free to utilize terminology as required; therefore terms can appear in the index as soon as they are encountered in the documents. The PRECIS thesaurus is a list, not of approved terms, but rather of relationships among the terms that have been chosen for index entries and their synonyms.

## APPLICATION TO MUSIC

For music, the paradigms used to construct the appropriate strings are chosen according to the presence or absence of information about three fundamental facets: musical form, medium of performance, and number of performers. For instance, if none of the three facets can be identified specifically, the paradigm directs the indexer to use terms that define the music (which must by definition be a collection) in terms of its purpose, its environment, its origin, etc.[19]

Two studies have attempted to compare PRECIS indexing with subject analysis supplied by *LCSH* subject headings for music. Paula Deversdorf Gabbard compared indexing for music books, and James B. Young compared indexing for music scores.[20] Although direct comparisons are difficult because the two systems are so different, both Gabbard and Young found that between two thirds and three quarters of documents received more index entries in PRECIS than *LCSH* headings. Most documents, about 70 percent, received one more PRECIS entry than *LCSH*. Young found that only one third of the documents received only index entries for medium of performance. Further, he reported that PRECIS entries for medium were more numerous than *LCSH* for half the documents. These results would be logically consistent with the nature of the documents. Most musical works can be characterized if not by their form of composition, then by their environmental character or some other element within the topicality facet. Most musical works are composed for performing media that could best be expressed with compound phrases. Because of the flexibility of PRECIS shunting procedures, entries could be made at each potential term in such a compound phrase. Further, a majority of Western art music is probably best described in terms of its medium and musical form. In *LCSH* both must usually be expressed in a single heading, in most cases entered under the musical form. With PRECIS, index entries in each position are possible.

A simple example of a work described in terms of its medium of performance and its musical form illustrates this point. Boris Blacher's *Sonate fu[e]r Violoncello und Klavier (1940/41)* would receive the PRECIS string "Sonatas for cello with keyboard." Entries would be generated under:

Sonatas
   For cello with keyboard
and
Cello
   Sonatas for cello with keyboard.

Note that at each entry the entire phrase is repeated, indicating contextual information, and that each entry is coextensive with the subject analysis of the document. The *LCSH* approach would be to use a single heading under "Sonatas (Violoncello and piano) — Scores and parts." The subject analysis is identical, with the exception of *LCSH*'s use of physical form indicators (not used in *BCM*). However, the *LCSH* phrase is entered only at one point, under "Sonatas ..." This example would be consistent with the observation that a majority of documents had one more PRECIS entry than *LCSH*.

An example from Young's paper further illustrates the facility of PRECIS. A work titled *English romantic songs & ballads of the early 19th century with guitar accompaniments of the period* is represented by the PRECIS string: "Songs for solo voice with guitar — Collections." PRECIS entries would be generated from this string as follows:

Guitar
    Solo voice with guitar. Songs — Collections

Solo voices
    Solo voice with guitar. Songs — Collections

Songs
    For solo voice with guitar — Collections[21]

Note that entries give direct access to each element of the medium and to the musical form, and that the physical form is indicated in each phrase. Note that at each index point for medium subfiles will be arranged first by complete medium, then by form. So, for example, the guitar player who wanted some music to use with a singer (not an implausible request) would be able to find music for guitar and solo voice in the musical form "song" in a collection by beginning at "guitar." On the other hand, the *LCSH* heading that would be assigned is: "Songs (High voice) with guitar." The only access point in the *LCSH* file would be under the musical form "Songs." Our hapless user would begin at "guitar" only to find that it was necessary to look under each name of type of composition until the appropriate conditions were satisfied.

## CONCLUSION

Subject analysis in the *BCM*, regardless of PRECIS, is not significantly different from common North American use of *LCSH*. Cultural, chronological, and physical form facets, for example, are not included in PRECIS strings as applied to this collection of music. No application of PRECIS has yet been made in a significant collection of sound recordings. The application of PRECIS in the *BCM* represents a great leap forward in the subject analysis of musical documents. Its virtues are its context-dependence and coextensivity, and its multiple entry system that provides access under all significant elements of the subject analysis. PRECIS certainly has the capacity to adequately index all relevant facets of the subject analysis of music materials. Yet it remains to be seen whether PRECIS, or some other yet to be devised system, can resolve the problems of verbal subject analysis of music.

# Notes

[1]See, for example, Music Library Association. Cataloging and Classification Committee, *S L A C C: The Partial Use of the Shelf List as Classed Catalog*. MLA Technical Reports, No. 1 (Ypsilanti, Mich.: Music Library Association, 1973).

[2]Barbara Duncan, "Review of *Music Subject Headings Used on Printed Catalog Cards of the Library of Congress*," *Notes* 9 (1952): 607.

[3]Virginia Cunningham, "The Library of Congress Classed Catalog for Music," *Library Resources & Technical Services* 8 (1964): 285.

[4]Library of Congress. Subject Cataloging Division, *Music Subject Headings Used on Printed Catalog Cards of the Library of Congress* (Washington, D.C.: [U.S. Government Printing Office]), 1952; and New York. Public Library. Reference Department, *Music Subject Headings Authorized for Use in the Catalogs of the Music Division* (Boston: G. K. Hall, 1959).

[5]For a discussion of the relative merits of the two systems see Wilma Reid Cipolla, "Music Subject Headings: A Comparison," *Library Resources & Technical Services* 18 (1974): 387-97.

[6]Richard S. Angell, "Subject Headings," *Notes* 10 (1953): 198-200.

[7]A good thing, as it turned out, since the term was to undergo much convoluted shifting until "sound recording" was finally settled on in 1973.

[8][Library of Congress. Processing Services. Special Materials Cataloging Division. Music Section], "Music of Ethnic and National Groups," *Music Cataloging Bulletin* 12, no. 5 (1981): 2-4.

[9]For a good discussion of this problem see Don Michael Randel, "Defining Music," *Notes* 43 (1987): 751-66.

[10]Helen E. Bush and David Judson Haykin, "Music Subject Headings," *Notes* 6 (1948): 39-45. The discussion that follows is heavily indebted to this article.

[11]Library of Congress. Processing Services. Subject Cataloging Division, *Library of Congress Subject Headings*, 8th ed. (Washington, D.C.: Library of Congress, 1975), viii.

[12]Library of Congress. Processing Services. Subject Cataloging Division, *Library of Congress Subject Headings*, 10th ed. (Washington, D.C.: Library of Congress, 1986).

[13]*Music Cataloging Bulletin* 15, no. 1 (January 1984): 1.

[14]Ibid., 2.

[15]Ibid.

[16]Ibid.

[17]George Peter Murdock, *Outline of World Cultures*, 6th rev. ed. (New Haven, Conn.: Human Relations Area Files, 1983).

[18]Derek Austin, "PRECIS: Theory and Practice," *International Cataloguing* 13 (1984): 9.

[19]Derek Austin, *British Catalogue of Music Code of Practice for the Application of PRECIS* ([London]: The British Library, Bibliographic Services Division, 1985). This segment has been verified in this document, which is for British Library internal distribution only.

[20]Paula Beversdorf Gabbard, "LCSH and PRECIS in Music: A Comparison," *Library Quarterly* 55 (April 1985): 192-206; and James Bradford Young, "A Comparison of PRECIS and Library of Congress Subject Headings for the Retrieval of Printed Music" (Atlanta, Ga., 1986, Computer-generated typescript).

[21]Young, "A Comparison of PRECIS," 14.

## Suggested Reading

Austin, Derek, and Jeremy A. Digger. "PRECIS: The Preserved Context Index System." *Library Resources & Technical Services* 21 (1977): 13-30.

Library of Congress. Processing Services. Subject Cataloging Division. *Subject Cataloging Manual: Subject Headings*. Rev. ed. Washington, D.C.: Library of Congress, 1985- . Looseleaf.

Richmond, Phyllis A. *Introduction to PRECIS for North American Usage*. Littleton, Colo.: Libraries Unlimited, 1981.

# 7
# *CLASSIFICATION*

*Another library reports it has "no methods to report" since "the music people have control of the scores and toss and cram them everywhere. Perhaps in another fifty years."[1]*

## Introduction

Classification, perhaps the most complex aspect of bibliographic control and that most easily treated in a scientific manner, is nevertheless the least well developed aspect of the bibliographic control of music materials. Unlike descriptive cataloging, or even verbal subject analysis, there is no singular history of classification in music libraries. In the United States, many attempts were made to devise classifications for printed music and later, for sound recordings. While it has always been recognized that music materials were somehow different from books about music, there has been little agreement about how they should be treated. The most frequently encountered argument is whether they should be arranged alphabetically by composer, thus collocating as artifacts the works of an artist, or by some musical concept. In the latter camp are two major approaches, form of composition (said to be preferred by scholars) and medium of performance (said to be preferred by musicians).

The advantages of classification for subject retrieval have often been overlooked in music libraries. Only the Library of Congress is widely known to have maintained a classified catalog. As the discussion in previous chapters notes, music materials are easily susceptible to faceted subject analysis. With online bibliographic data retrieval definitely in the future, the advantages of faceted classification may now be felt. Among these advantages are freedom from terminological disparity, and the ability to combine specified elements such as forms of composition, topical character, medium of performance, cultural traditions, or chronological considerations in user-driven searches. Given the disaffection with subject related control fields in the MARC Music Format, it may be time to dispense with the "toss and cram" approach and to reexamine music classification as an approach to retrieval in the online environment.

Of the many schemes devised, four have gained wide acceptance in the United States. The music portions of the Dewey Decimal Classification (DDC) and the Library of Congress Classification (LCC) have many adherents, perhaps because of the widespread use of the general classifications in the parent libraries. Two other schemes have gained wide acceptance in libraries throughout the United States, the Dickinson classification for printed music in academic libraries and ANSCR for sound recordings in small and public libraries. This chapter examines these four schemes.

# The Dickinson Classification

## INTRODUCTION

George Sherman Dickinson (1888-1964) was the first music librarian at Vassar College, a founder of the American Musicological Society, and an early president of the MLA. Dickinson's *Classification of Musical Compositions: A Decimal-Symbol System*, first published in 1938, was designed specifically to organize the collection of music scores at Vassar. Perhaps resulting from Dickinson's strong background in musicology, his scheme illustrates great logic in its approach to the elements of published, Western art music. Though limited in its application, the scheme was particularly popular in academic music libraries in the eastern United States in the early part of the twentieth century. Various adaptations of Dickinson's original scheme found uses in the music libraries at Columbia University and the University of Buffalo (now known as SUNY Buffalo) as well.

## PRINCIPLES

Because Dickinson's scheme was not a part of a more general classification, the principles of organization he utilized more closely reflect the principles of musical analysis than do other more commonly applied classifications. That is, like subject analysis of the music he sought to organize, Dickinson's scheme is faceted and his number-building techniques are synthetic.

The classification had an admittedly limited scope. Dickinson intended it as a scheme to organize the music scores in the library at Vassar. Thus, despite relatively detailed notation, the classification was primarily intended to be used as a shelving device. The categories were derived from those already present in the *LCC: Class: M, Music and Books on Music* (*LCC:M*) schedules, which Dickinson found too rigid for his purposes.

Three principles were enumerated in Dickinson's introduction.[2] The first was musicological integrity of the facets. Categories were to be clearly defined and subsequently combined as necessary to describe the multiple varieties of musical compositions. This led to the resulting faceted approach to the organization of the classification.

The second principle was flexibility in control of the application, or combination, of the categories. It was clear to Dickinson that various types of libraries would have different priorities for retrieval depending on the needs of their users. Thus several formulae are presented for various combinations of the available facets, though all begin with the facet for medium of performance. For instance, the performance library would utilize the specific medium indicating the actual required instrumentation before subdivision, whereas the musicological library could utilize a formula requiring primary indication of the *original* form. The simplest formula, for the small public library, utilizes only a broad indication of medium subdivided by composer. Once a formula had been selected, however, the individual library had to build its own schedules from the faceted tables presented.

Dickinson's third requirement was that the notation be "mnemonically vivid." Call numbers are constructed of numerals (some decimal), letters, and symbols (such as the equals sign used to indicate an arrangement). At its most detailed the notation makes use of many conventional musical symbols such as sharps, flats, and naturals combined with upper or lower case letters to indicate key and mode (major or minor respectively).

## THE FACETS

Each of Dickinson's facets is presented in a table. Elements from the various facets are combined in a citation order specified by the aforementioned formulae. Dickinson's facets follow.

**Location**

This was a letter used to distinguish the physical location of the items. As in other schemes, "M" was most commonly used to differentiate "Music" from books about music.

**Medium of Performance**

Following the location device in Dickinson's tables is the general heading "Classification," which consists of the tables for this facet identified as "Class and Division" to which may be added four categories of "Subdivision." "Class and Division" is a decimally arranged list of numerical designations for the various performing media. Since this element was the first required in all the formulae, it is the de facto principal element for arrangement of materials in this scheme. Numbers are used decimally in the classification to indicate hierarchical relationships.

The order of the classes is similar to that used in *LCC:M*, with collected works and monuments at the beginning in a miscellaneous class. This class also includes methods, an approach which is not found in other schemes. Miscellanea are followed by instrumental music, then vocal music. The breakdown within the two main divisions is next by number of performers, in each case progressing from smaller to larger forces. Divisions within instrumental classes are essentially in score order. Within vocal classes the division is secular or sacred.

|  | Miscellaneous |
|---|---|
| 0 | Collections, manuscripts, monuments, methods, etc. |

|  | Instrumental |
|---|---|
| 1 | Keyboard, solo and ensemble |
| 2 | String solo |
| 3 | Wind solo |
| 4 | Plectral solo and Various other |
| 5 | Chamber ensemble |
| 58 | Solo with chamber ensemble |
| 6 | Orchestral ensemble |
| 68 | Solo with orchestral ensemble |

|  | Vocal |
|---|---|
| 7 | Voice solo and solo ensemble |
| 78 | Folk and patriotic |
| 8 | Choral and solo-choral ensemble |
| 88 | Liturgic |
| 9 | Dramatic ensemble |
| 95 | Ballets |
| 98 | Incidental music to dramas |

**Species**

Subdivisions are further facets that are appended to the main classes according to specific instructions found in the tables. The first of these, *species*, is the facet for form of composition. The table contains seven separate lists of numerical designations for forms that may be combined with particular instrumental or vocal divisions, or in the case of chamber music, a group of divisions. The lists are limited to the forms indicated. Forms not on the list are to be grouped in the miscellaneous subdivision, which is ingeniously the unsubdivided class or division.

### Historical Categories

The digit 9 is reserved in every case for categories designated "obsolete," "primitive," or "other." Dickinson provides no designated schedule for historical subdivision, instead indicating that these designations constitute historical categories (much like the subdivision 09 in DDC, see below). Apparently, libraries choosing to use historical subdivisions are encouraged to develop and maintain their own schedules for historical subdivision.

### Accompaniment, Voicing, Etc.

Following species and historical subdivision, Dickinson presents a group of qualifying elements that he labels "Extension." There are three broad categories of extension: medium, form, and qualification. Not all elements may be applied at any point in number construction. Like the other subdivisions, the tables specify which classes may receive each element of extension.

Accompaniment, voice range, number (i.e., duo through nonet), and tessitura constitute the first grouping of miscellaneous categories that may be used as medium extensions. Accompaniment, when added, consists of a numerical element preceded by a zero added to the class number. Dickinson's use of mnemonics is apparent here. Zero, except when used in the initial position to indicate miscellanea, always indicates accompaniment. The numbers that follow correspond to the numbers in the main classes. Thus 88 is the class number for liturgical choral settings, and 8800 is the class number for unaccompanied liturgical choral settings. Likewise, choral music may be further subdivided with a letter *m, w,* or *y* preceded by a dash to indicate men's, women's, or young voices.

A digit indicating the number of performers (e.g., 2 for a duo, 7 for a septet), again preceded by a hyphen, may be added to class numbers 12, 14, 16, or 17 (keyboard ensembles). Thus 12 is the class number for piano ensembles, but 12-5 becomes the class number for piano quintets.

Finally, *h, i,* or *L* preceded by a hyphen may be added to class numbers for vocal music to indicate high, intermediate or low tessitura.

### Arrangement

The second grouping of extension elements (referred to by Dickinson as "form") are numerical designations added following an equals sign to indicate the medium a work was arranged *for* or *from* (depending on the library's choice of formula). The numerals correspond to those used in the original nine classes, thus making use of mnemonic principles. A numeral alone represents a work arranged in its entirety, a numeral preceded by a zero represents an arranged accompaniment. Thus =2 is added to a class number representing the original medium of performance to indicate a work arranged for stringed instruments, but =02 indicates a work for which the accompaniment is arranged for stringed instruments. Alternatively, if the main classes have been used to indicate the medium of performance present in the score, these designations are used to indicate the original medium. Thus =2 would now indicate a work that had originally been composed for stringed instruments.

### Character

The third set of extension elements begins with alphanumeric designations for nationality, language, and/or religion to be added in square brackets. Dickinson suggests that other nationality or language tables (e.g., DDC) could be used as well. Thus the class mark for a work emphasizing the United States could be subdivided with either "[U6]" or

"[78]." Chronological emphasis is expressed by adding dates in parentheses. Finally, digits representing particular occasions, may be added decimally when the species indicator 6 is present.

### Book Marks

The final element of subdivision is a work mark, labeled "Distinction" by Dickinson. This procedure utilizing Cutter or Cutter-Sanborn numbers, though similar to *LCC* procedures, is remarkable for its inclusion as *part* of the classification. This means that the choice of composer, editor, compiler, or title alphanumeric subarrangements may be intellectually divorced from the similar descriptive cataloging issues.

Composer book marks are to be taken from one of the Cutter tables. Work marks are created using lowercase letters to indicate the title of the work or its genre (species). An additional letter may be added following a slash to indicate the title of an excerpt. Numbering, either opus or thematic index numbers or numbers of movements, is added parenthetically, as are letters and signs to indicate the key and mode (e.g., (18/2) for opus 18, no. 2).

## APPLICATION

The schedules are presented in the order "Class and Division," "Subdivision," and "Extension." Each element has a corresponding alphabetical symbol, an alphabetical table of which precedes the schedules proper. Most of Dickinson's instructions appear in the 183 footnotes at the end of the text. Since many of these notes are applicable to more than one segment of the schedules or more than one operation, it is necessary for the classifier to have a complete understanding of these instructions. Further, the variety of potential options inherent in Dickinson's synthetic number-building procedure requires each library to develop its own version of the schedules. Hence the various published versions from Vassar, Columbia, and SUNY Buffalo are useful illustrations of not only the flexibility of the scheme but also varieties inherent in its practical application.

The use of mnemonic devices, in particular the eight divisions for medium of performance and their subdivisions in essentially score order, and the symbolic conventions of 0 to introduce accompaniment and = to introduce arrangement, means that the numbers are easily remembered by classifiers and easily read by users.

The flexibility of the system is further demonstrated in the following examples. For each of the musical works represented below, Dickinson's formulae for performance libraries, musicological libraries, and small general libraries will be examined.

> Brahms, Johannes, 1833-1897.
> [Symphonies, no. 4, op. 98, E minor]
> Symphony 4, E minor, opus 98 / Brahms. -- London ; New
> York : Boosey & Hawkes, [1967?]
> 1 miniature score (168 p.) ; 19 cm. -- (Hawkes pocket scores ;
> no. 143)
> Pl. no.: B.&H.8486.
>
> 1. Symphonies--Scores. II. Series.

For the performing collection, classifying by specific medium divided by form of composition then arranged by composer, the call number would be:

| | | |
|---|---|---|
| 611 | Orchestra, full, symphony | |
| B73 | Brahms | |
| sy(4)B | "Sy"mphony, no. 4, "B"oosey ed. | |

Another possible approach for a musicological collection, arranging all the works by a composer within a broad class, then subdividing by specific medium and form of composition would be:

```
6 B73      Orchestra, Brahms
11           Full orch., symphony
sy(4) B         "Sy"mphony, no. 4, "B"oosey ed.
```

For the general public library the classification would be much simpler:

```
61         Orchestra, full
B73sy(4)      Brahms, "Sy"mphony no. 4
```

> Schoenberg, Arnold, 1874-1951.
>   [Verklärte Nacht; arr.]
>   Verklärte Nacht / Arnold Schönberg ; arr. by Edward
> Steuermann for violin, cello and piano. -- Newton Centre, Mass. :
> Margun Music, c1979.
>   1 score (59 p.) + 2 parts ; 31 cm.
>   Originally for string sextet.
>   Duration: ca. 30:00.
>
>   1. Piano trios, Arranged--Scores and parts.  I. Steuermann,
> Edward.  II. Title.
>   M314.S35V4

For the performing collection, arranging by medium of performance of the score in hand, subdivided by the original medium, the call number would be:

```
12-3 = 52-6     Piano trio arranged from a string sextet
Sch6            Schoenberg
vS                 "V"erklärte ... ed. by "S"teuermann
```

For the musicological collection, arranging by original medium, subdivided by medium of the score in hand, the call number would be:

```
52 = 12     String chamber work arr. for piano ensemble
Sch6-3        Schoenberg, for a trio
v S              "V"erklärte ... ed. by "S"teuermann
```

Another approach for the musicological collection, arranging broadly by original medium subdivided by medium of arrangement, then further by composer and size of ensemble is:

```
52         String chamber work
Sch6-3        Schoenberg, for a trio
v = 12 S         "V"erklärte ..., arr. for piano ensemble, ed. by "S"teuermann
```

For the small public library the number consists of the medium of the score in hand divided by size of ensemble.

```
12-3       Piano ensemble for trio
Sch6v         Schoenberg, "V"erklärte
```

Schoenberg, Arnold, 1874-1951.
   [Verklärte Nacht; arr.]
   Verklärte Nacht : Op. 4 / Schoenberg ; Bearbeitung für
Streichorchester vom Komponisten. -- Revision 1943. -- [Wien] :
Universal Edition ; Los Angeles : for sale in the USA only through
Belmont Music Publishers, c1943.
   1 miniature score (36 p.) ; 25 cm.
   For string orchestra; originally for string sextet.
   Plate no.: UE 14 486.

   1. String-orchestra music, Arranged.  I. Title.

For the performing collection:

| | |
|---|---|
| 62 = 52-6 | String orch., arr. from string ens., 6 players |
| Sch6 | Schoenberg |
| v S | "V"erklärte ... ed. by "S"choenberg |

For the musicological collection:

| | |
|---|---|
| 52 = 62 | Chamber ens., strings, arr. for string orch. |
| Sch6 | Schoenberg |
| v S | "V"erklärte ... ed. by "S"choenberg |

For the general library:

| | |
|---|---|
| 62 | String orchestra |
| Sch6v | Schoenberg, "V"erklärte ... |

Schubert, Franz, 1797-1828.
   [Piano music. Selections]
   Piano pieces / Franz Schubert. -- Huntington Station, L.I.,
N.Y. : E. F. Kalmus, c1968.
   103 p. of music ; 18 cm. -- (Kalmus study score series ; no. 787)
   Reproduced from Breitkopf & Härtel ed.
   Contents: Fantasy in C major, op. 15 "Wanderer" -- Four
impromptus, op. 90 -- Four impromptus, op. 142 -- Moments
musicaux : op. 94.

   1. Piano music.  I. Schubert, Franz, 1797-1828. Fantasien, piano,
D. 760, C major. 1968.  II. Schubert, Franz, 1797-1828. Impromptus,
piano, op. 90. 1968.  III. Schubert, Franz, 1797-1828. Impromptus,
piano, op. 142. 1968.  IV. Schubert, Franz, 1797-1828. Moments
musicaux. 1968.  V. Series.

For performing and musicological collections:

| | |
|---|---|
| 11 | Keyboard, piano, solo, collection |
| Sch8 | Schubert |
| p K | "P"iano music, "K"almus |
| 1968 | 1968 ed. |

The call number would be essentially the same for the general library. Only the level of detail in the book mark changes.

11          Keyboard, piano, solo, collection
Sch8p          Schubert, "P"iano ...

     Britten, Benjamin, 1913-1976.
      [Spring symphony]
      Spring symphony : for soprano, alto and tenor soli, mixed chorus, boy's choir and orchestra : op. 44 / Benjamin Britten. -- London ; New York : Boosey & Hawkes, c1950.
      1 miniature score (126 p.) ; 19 cm. -- (Hawkes pocket scores ; no. 66)
       Duration: 45:00.
       Plate no.: B.&H.16904.

      1. Choruses, Secular (Mixed voices) with orchestra--Scores.
     I. Title.

For the performing collection:

81          Vocal, choral, secular, orch. acc.
B778          Britten
sB          "S"pring ..., "B"oosey

Again, the number for the other collections would be essentially the same, differing only in the level of detail in the book mark. For the general library:

81          Vocal, choral, secular, orch. acc.
B778s          Britten, "S"pring ...

## CONCLUSION

It is clear that Dickinson's scheme is highly developed. It utilizes many of the elements of music subject analysis, which are represented by mnemonic facet indicators, and which may be combined in a variety of useful patterns. The chief advantage of the scheme would be its ability to provide shelf arrangement by a classification considered most advantageous for item browsing and retrieval, while still allowing full access to all of the other facets through a classified catalog. The use of symbols in the synthesis makes the mnemonics of the classes even clearer than in the popular DDC. Chief drawbacks for modern use of Dickinson are the absence of a facet to indicate physical form, the lack of classes for non-Western instruments and cultures, and the absence of formulae that would allow primary arrangement by some element other than medium of performance, all elements that could be devised and added to the existing scheme.

# *Library of Congress Classification:M*

## *INTRODUCTION*

The first edition of *LCC:M* was published in 1904. It was developed by Oscar G. Sonneck, who was at that time Chief of the Music Division at LC. Unlike classifications of recorded knowledge applied to library collections, the LC classification was developed with a particular set of materials in mind. Part of the library-wide effort to create a classification that would be suitable for a research library, the *M* schedule also had to incorporate thousands of pieces of music received through copyright deposit programs. At the time the scheme was developed, the Music Division possessed approximately 375,000 pieces of music and approximately 6,000 pieces of musical theory and instruction.[3] This enormous collection was described by Sonneck as organically developed, for it consisted largely of U.S. and Western European compositions published or deposited for copyright after 1891.[4] Walter Whittlesey, Sonneck's predecessor as chief, had arranged the music by instrument, and divided vocal music by sacred and secular, then by number of performers.[5]

Derived from an educated turn of the century view of music and musicology and based on the literary warrant of the Music Division, the *LCC:M* still embodies Whittlesey's original divisions by medium of performance, though in much greater detail. The scheme clearly is designed to give wide latitude to the materials of Western art music as it was understood at the beginning of the twentieth century. This view is apparent in the few classes (e.g., piano, violin) that are subdivided by traditional forms of composition (e.g., suite, sonata). Few changes have been made in the scheme since the beginning. A third edition published in 1978 incorporated modern terminology, expanded lists of subdivisions, and included an updated index, but made no changes in the basis of the classification itself.

## *SCOPE*

*LCC:M* was designed as a shelf classification for scores, books on music, and materials for teaching music theory and performance (e.g., methods, tutors, studies, etc.). These three groups of materials are classified in three broad divisions, M, ML, and MT, respectively. The discussion that follows is about the provisions of division M, for music itself.

Despite its origin as a shelf classification, *LCC:M* was used for over forty years as the principal means of subject access to the collections of the Music Division. From 1943 until the close of the card catalogs in 1981, the Music Division maintained a classified catalog that was unique in the United States. For the classified catalog additional entries were made under supplementary numbers to indicate elements of character, form of composition, or number of parts when these were not provided in the main schedule. These numbers are still printed in the schedule and may be used by other libraries as they judge it appropriate for their collections.

Beginning in 1972, class numbers only were provided on cataloging for sound recordings.[6] These suggested numbers appeared in square brackets because LC did not use them for shelving, preferring instead a system utilizing manufacturer's label name and number. However, it is fair to say that *LCC:M* is as suitable for sound recordings as many other classifications. Since the introduction of unit description of sound recordings in 1981, it has been possible to assign classification numbers to collective main entries with more sensible results than was the case when class numbers were assigned to correspond only to the first work on a recording. The result is very often arrangement of many recordings within broad general classes with subarrangement by performer.

Because of the continuing policy of literary warrant applied at LC it is important to note that *LCC:M* is not particularly well suited to detailed classification of the burgeoning field of musics other than Western art. Musics in popular idioms are classified ultimately by nationality of performing group. Classes for national musics are subdivided by idiom (art, popular) and within idiom subdivided by physical form (collection, separate). These portions of the schedules remain underdeveloped, as do provisions for non-traditional instruments, because LC does not collect this material in sufficient quantity to require more detailed classification.

Similarly, *LCC:M* makes few provisions for music of periods earlier than the mid-eighteenth century (sometimes referred to as the "classical" period), or later than the late nineteenth century (sometimes referred to as the "romantic" period). "Music printed in the United States before 1860," "music before 1700," and "chamber music for obsolete instruments" are the only classes that are available for this music. In many libraries that use *LCC:M* music for instruments of earlier times is classified with the music of modern instrumental successors. Likewise, chance composition, electronic music, and jazz are three classes available for post-nineteenth century music.

## PRINCIPLES

### Martel's Seven Points

Charles Martel was responsible for many of the principles that guided construction of *LCC*. A set of basic features called "Martel's Seven Points" recurred throughout *LCC* whenever it was deemed appropriate by the subject specialists who developed the individual schedules. The points were:

1. General form divisions.

2. Theory. Philosophy.

3. History. Biography.

4. Treatises. General works.

5. Law. Regulation. State relations.

6. Study and teaching. Research. Textbooks.

7. Subjects and subdivisions of subjects.

The seven points are all present in *LCC:M*. Points 2 and 6, theory and study and teaching, make up the contents of division MT. Points 1, 3-5, and 7 can be seen to make up the literature of music, and are embodied in division ML. In division M, points 1 and 7 can be observed.

Class M begins with a group of generalia that includes miscellaneous anthologies, monuments, collected works, and historical editions, encompassing Martel's first point (except for manuscript facsimiles, which are classified with paleography in class ML). Detailed division is then by medium of performance, beginning at every level of the hierarchy with miscellaneous collections. The classes proceed from solo instruments through ensembles of increasing size to large ensemble works. Within each of these groupings, the subarrangement is keyboard, string, wind, plectral (or plucked), percussion, other. The notation, though enumerative, employs some mnemonic devices. For example, 300s through 900s are used to indicate ensembles for trio (300s) through nonet (900s). The divisions within these classes are also mnemonic; thus 357 is a separate, original, work for wind trio, and 457 is a separate, original work for wind quartet.

Vocal music is arranged similarly, in the two main divisions secular and sacred, progressing by number of performers from solo to ensemble, and ending in each case with dramatic works and vocal music of topical character.

Works are classed according to the medium of performance of the score in hand. Two subarrangements are common throughout: 1) physical form, collection and separate, and 2) original works and arrangements.

There is no consistent attempt to provide for any other facets of music subject analysis. Subdivisions by form of composition occur for piano, organ, violin, and orchestral compositions. Classes are available for songs, but not instrumental works, of national character, but cross-national cultural identities are not provided. Classes are provided for some songs of topical character (e.g., protest songs, or baseball songs), or for special occasions (e.g., Christmas). Subdivisions are provided for liturgies of various Christian churches, and hymns of particular churches. It is clear that these scattered provisions reflect the scope and size of the bodies of literature for individual performing media rather than any attempt to provide consistent access by elements other than medium of performance.

### Index

Like all schedules in *LCC* an individual index accompanies class M. This index is an internal locating device, which is to say it contains the terms found throughout the schedules in alphabetical sequence. Thus it is not the best approach to the classification. *LCSH* can be used as a guide to the classification, for the headings are accompanied by broad indications of appropriate class numbers. However, classifiers quickly learn the broad outlines of *LCC:M* and gain entry through the hierarchy of the classification itself. As new terms are added to the classification, mostly new alphanumeric subdivisions for instruments, they are also added to the index. Additions to the index are reported in the monthly *Music Cataloging Bulletin* and cumulated in its five-year *Supplement* volumes.

### *OUTLINE OF CLASS M*

The partial outline below is drawn from the schedules and is intended to illustrate the main provisions of the classification. Only the major segments are illustrated.

M     Music
| | |
|---|---|
| 1.A1-A15 | Music printed in U. S. before 1860 |
| 2-2.3 | Collections of musical sources |
| 3-3.1 | Collected works, indiv. composers |
| 3.3 | First editions |

Instrumental Music
| | |
|---|---|
| 6-175 | Solo instruments |
| 177-990 | Music for two or more solo instruments |
| 180-298.5 | Duets |
| 300-386 | Trios |
| 400-486 | Quartets |
| 500-586 | Quintets |
| 600-686 | Sextets |
| 700-786 | Septets |
| 800-886 | Octets |
| 900-986 | Nonets, larger chamber ensembles |
| 990 | Chamber music 18th cent. or earlier |
| 1000-1075 | Orchestra |
| 1100-1160 | String orchestra |

(Outline continues on page 102.)

| | |
|---|---|
| 1200-1269 | Band |
| 1356-1356.2 | Dance orchestra |
| 1366 | Jazz ensembles |
| 1375-1420 | Instrumental music for children |
| 1450 | Dance music |
| 1470 | Chance music |
| 1473 | Electronic music |
| 1490 | Music before 1700 |

| | | |
|---|---|---|
| | Vocal Music | |
| 1497-1998 | Secular vocal music | |
| 1500-1527.8 | | Dramatic music |
| 1528-1529.5 | | Duets, trios, etc. |
| 1530-1610 | | Choruses |
| 1611-1624.8 | | Songs for one voice |
| 1627-1853 | | National music |
| 1900-1980 | | Songs of special character |
| 1990-1998 | | Secular music for children |
| 1999-2199 | Sacred vocal music | |
| 1999 | | Collections |
| 2000-2007 | | Oratorios |
| 2010-2017.7 | | Services |
| 2018-2019.5 | | Duets, trios, etc. |
| 2020-2101.5 | | Choruses |
| 2101-2114.8 | | Songs for one voice |
| 2115-2146 | | Hymnals |
| 2147-2188 | | Liturgy and ritual |
| 2190-2196 | | Sacred vocal music for children |
| 2198-2199 | | Songs of special character |
| 5000 | | Unidentified compositions |

| | | |
|---|---|---|
| MT | | Musical Instruction and Study |
| | 2-5 | History and criticism |
| | 6-7 | Music theory |
| | 20-32 | Special methods |
| | 40-73 | Composition. Instrumentation. |
| | 90-145 | Analytical guides |
| | 170-810 | Instrumental techniques |
| | 820-949 | Singing and voice culture |

## *APPLICATION*

### Notation

Call numbers produced from *LCC:M* are constructed quite simply. The class number is represented by an initial letter indicating the division (M, ML, or MT) and a one- to four-digit integer, occasionally with decimal subdivision, indicating the class. Some subdivisions utilize alphanumeric work marks ("cutter" numbers), constructed according to the rules for book numbers (see below). These are indicated in the schedule by the instruction "A-Z." In many cases LC's own authorized alphanumeric symbols are incorporated in the schedule. These lists are updated in the *Music Cataloging Bulletin* and cumulated in its five-year *Supplement* volumes.

**Pattern Subdivisions**

There are several patterns for subdivision that are repeated throughout *LCC:M*. These are always indicated with footnotes in the schedule, and the instruction "Subarranged like ...." The first is a five-integer pattern used to subarrange music for all instruments where subdivision by musical form is not used. The pattern is:

| | |
|---|---|
| 15 | Miscellaneous collections |
| | Original compositions |
| 16 | Collections |
| 17 | Separate works |
| | Arrangements |
| 18 | Collections |
| 19 | Separate works |

Whenever the instruction "subarranged like M15-19" is encountered it means that the first integer of the five-integer range should be assigned to anthologies that include both original works and arranged works. The second integer is assigned to collections of original works (for instance, a collection of Chopin piano music) and the third to single original works (for instance, a Chopin *Nocturne*). The fourth and fifth integers are assigned to collections of works that are all arrangements, and separate arranged works, respectively. It is the third integer, for separate original works, that is used most frequently. In some instances a two-integer range is used with the instruction "subarranged like ..." to indicate use of the first integer for collections, and the second for separates.

| | |
|---|---|
| 355 | Miscellaneous collections |
| | Original compositions |
| 356 | Collections |
| 357 | Separate works |
| | General |
| .2 | Woodwinds only |
| .4 | Brasses only |
| | Arrangements |
| 358 | Collections |
| 359 | Separate works |

In this pattern the distribution of original and arranged collections and separate works is the same as in the M15-19 range. However, original separate works may be subdivided by specific group of wind instruments. Therefore a *wind* trio (e.g., a work for flute, clarinet, and horn) would be classed in M357, a *woodwind* trio (e.g., a work for flute, oboe, and clarinet) in M357.2, and a *brass* trio (e.g., a work for trumpet, trombone, and horn) in M357.4. Likewise a *wind* quintet is classed in M557, a *woodwind* quintet in M557.2, and a *brass* quintet in M557.4.

The next pattern subdivision is found with concertos. The instruction "Subarranged like M1005-1006" is used with each solo instrument to indicate the following pattern:

| | |
|---|---|
| 1005 | Scores |
| | Class here full and reduced scores |
| | Including arrangements for reduced orchestra |
| .2 | Cadenzas. By composer of concerto, A-Z |
| | Assign a second cutter for composer of cadenza |
| 1006 | Solo(s) with piano |

This pattern is used for works for one or more like solo instruments and orchestra or string orchestra accompaniment. The first integer in the sequence is used for the original composition (e.g., concertos for organ solo with accompaniment of full orchestra). The subdivision .5 is added for cadenzas, thus a separately published cadenza for an organ concerto would be classed in M1005.5. The cadenzas are subarranged by the *complete work mark* for the concerto into which the cadenza is to be interpolated. A second cutter is added for the composer of the cadenza. Thus Silverstein's cadenza for Beethoven's violin concerto would be classified M1012.5.B3 op.61 .S5, where B3 op.61 is for the Beethoven concerto and S5 is for Silverstein. The second full integer in the range is used for arrangements of the concertos where the solo part or parts are unaltered, but the accompaniment has been arranged for piano.

Another common pattern is the subarrangement for popular songs found in the classes for national secular vocal music. Identified by the instruction "Subarranged like M1678-1679.2" the pattern is:

|      |       | General |
|------|-------|---------|
| 1678 |       | Collections |
| 1679 |       | Separate works |
|      |       | Popular music |
|      | .18   | Collections |
|      | .2    | Separate works |

This pattern is intended to collocate national songs, folk songs, and popular songs by nationality. Though it is not indicated in the schedule, these vocal ranges are also used for instrumental music of national character. The important feature is the use of the second integer subdivided decimally .18 for collections in the popular idiom. Thus a collection of English folk songs would be classed at M1740, a separately published English folk song would be classed at M1741, an anthology of Beatles songs (or one of their recordings) would be classed at M1741.18, and a separately published Beatles song (such as Paul McCartney's *Michele*) would be classed at M1741.2. (This breakdown is also found at 1729.3-1729.6, and 1755.3-1755.6.)

A modification of this pattern is found at M1684-1685 and is used for ranges of numbers that apply to regions of the world that use cutters for national subdivision.

|      |       | General |
|------|-------|---------|
| 1684 |       | Collections |
|      | .A1   | General |
|      | .A5-Z | By region or country |
| 1685 |       | Separate works. By region or country, A-Z |
|      |       | Popular music |
|      | .x18  | Collections |
|      | .x2   | Separate works |

This is the same pattern found at 1678-1679 and elsewhere, but a cutter for specific region or country must be used. Thus a collection of Central American folk songs would class in M1684.A1, and a collection of Panamanian folk songs would class in M1684.P3, a separately published folk song from Central America would class in M1685, and a separately published Panamanian folk song would class in M1685.P3. Popular music from Panama would then follow, collections in M1685.P318 and separately published works in M1685.P32. This arrangement is somewhat awkward, disrupting collocation by nationality, presumably because regional collocation is more important. It is likely that this is another reflection of the small number of these materials in LC's collection.

A pattern subdivision "By language, A-Z" is used with special parts of liturgical texts set as separate compositions. The LC cutters are found at 2079, listed under their Latin titles. For example:

| | |
|---|---|
| .L1-99 | Latin texts |
| .L1 | Two or more |
| .L11 | Adeste fidelis |
| .L21 | Benedictus qui venit |
| .L5 | Kyrie |

and so forth. Settings in languages other than Latin use the same numeric portion of the cutter, substituting the initial of the language. For instance, an English setting of the Kyrie ("Lord have mercy") would class in M2079.*E5*, and a French setting would class in M2079.*F5*.

The final pattern of subarrangement that is repeated is used in the MT schedule to arrange works intended for use in learning instrumental techniques. There are two versions of this pattern. The first version is used with instruments that are given a nine integer range. It is repeated from MT360-368, the range for oboe:

| | |
|---|---|
| 360 | General |
| 362 | Systems and methods |
| | Studies and exercises |
| 365 | General |
| 366 | Orchestral studies |
| 368 | Self-instructors |

The other iteration of this pattern is slightly different and is used for instruments that employ decimal divisions of a single integer. This is repeated from MT192-192.8, for electronic keyboards:

| | |
|---|---|
| 192 | General |
| .2 | Systems and methods |
| .3 | Studies and exercises |
| .4 | Orchestral studies |
| .5 | Teaching pieces |
| .6 | Instructive editions |
| .7 | Two instruments |
| .8 | Self-instructors |

### Shelf Arrangement

Shelf arrangement employs work marks that consist of alphanumeric symbols or cutter numbers that are constructed according to LC's own tables. These cutters are also used whenever the schedules instruct arrangement by alphanumeric symbols or cutters A-Z. The simple LC cutter tables (reproduced in several sources) rely on the use of the first letter of the relevant word, name, title, etc., and numbers assigned to represent the second and third letters of the word as appropriate.[7]

An initial cutter number is always used to represent the main entry, either a title or a composer. Works entered under title usually require no further notation. Works entered under composer will require a second work mark if the work has a distinctive title, in which case a cutter for the title is used. Extra digits may be added to title cutters for vocal works to subarrange by language of text or translation. If the work is a collection, a cutter for the editor or publisher is used.

Works with non-distinctive titles, particularly those whose titles are the same as the name of their class (e.g., "Piano sonata = M23") employ a musical identifying element if possible. Such elements are serial, opus or thematic index number, key or tonal center, or date of composition. A cutter may be added following the identifying element to represent the editor, arranger, or publisher, as appropriate. Some libraries (but not LC) always prefer to arrange music by identifying element whether works have distinctive titles or not, because of the widespread recognition of opus numbers or thematic index numbers among the users of music collections.

Dates of publication may be added as the final element of any call number to arrange subsequent editions of a work. Conflicts may be resolved by the addition of extra digits to cutters, or lowercase letters to dates when necessary.[8]

LC call numbers are written in a variety of ways by various libraries. The separate elements may be written on different lines or the class number may appear on the top line, the cutter(s) on the second line, identifying elements and dates on subsequent lines. Class numbers are always filed numerically, and cutter numbers are always filed decimally. The examples that follow illustrate these provisions.

> Powell, Robert J.
>   Cathedral pieces / by Robert J. Powell. -- Chapel Hill, N.C. :
> Hinshaw Music, c1978.
>     16 p. of music ; 31 cm.
>     For organ.
>     Contents: Cathedral windows -- Trumpets -- Plainsong --
> Bells -- The church.
>     Publisher's no.: HMO-128.
>
>     1. Organ music.  I. Title.

M
11          Other separate works,
                  Original compositions,
                        Organ
                              Solo instruments
                                    Instrumental music
.P69        Powell
C3          *Cathedral ...*

> School of classical organ trios from 1512 to 1916 : for the
>   organ / by Schlick ... [et al.]; -- Melville, NY : Belwin
>   Mills, [19--].
>     37 p. of music ; 23 x 31 cm. -- (Kalmus organ series ; 4481)
>     Contents: 1. Maria zart / Arnold Schlick -- 2. Vom Himmel
> hoch, da komm ich her / Johann Pachelbel -- 3. Vater unser im
> Himmelreich / Dietrich Buxtehude -- 4. Christe, der du bist Tag
> und licht / Georg Bohm -- 5. In dulci jubilo / Johann Gottfried
> Walther -- 6. Ein feste Burg ist unser Gott / Joh. Gottfr.
> Walther -- 7. Aria / Johann Sebastian Bach -- 8. Andante /
> Johann Ludwig Krebs -- 9. Largo / Johann Ludwig Krebs --
> 10. Ach Gott vom Himmel sieh darein / Johann Ludwig Krebs --
> 11. Moderato / Johann Ludwig Krebs -- Gottfried August
> Homilius -- 14. Schmücke dich, o liebe Seele / Johannes Brahms --
> 15. Canon in der Quarte / Max Reger.
>
>     1. Organ music.  I. Schlick, Arnolt, fl. 1512.

M
7          General collections,
                Original compositions,
                    Organ
                        Solo instruments
                            Instrumental music
.S36       *School ...*


           Cavalcade of rock through the years. -- New York, N.Y. : Warner
               Bros. Publications, c1984.
               1 vocal score (351 p.) ; 31 cm.
               Songs arr. for voice and piano, with guitar chord diagrams.
               Includes index.
               Publisher's no.: VF1124.
               $16.95.

               1. Rock music.  2. Popular music.


M
1630.18    Collections
                Popular music
                    United States
                        National music
                            Secular vocal music
.C3        *Cavalcade ...*


           MacDowell, Edward, 1860 1908.
               [Sonatas, piano, no. 4, op. 59]
               Sonata for piano solo, no. 4, op. 59 / MacDowell. -- Melville,
           N.Y. : Belwin Mills, [198-?]
               31 p. of music ; 31 cm. -- (Kalmus piano series ; 3653)

               1. Sonatas (Piano)


M
23         Sonatas
                Special collections and separate works
                    Original compositions
                        Piano
                            Solo instruments
                                Instrumental music
.M32       MacDowell
op.59      Opus 59
B4         Belwin Mills

# Dewey Decimal Classification: 780

## INTRODUCTION

Melvil Dewey's *A Classification and Subject Index for Cataloguing and Arranging the Books and Pamphlets of a Library* was published (anonymously) in 1876. Dewey's notion, to produce a logical classification of knowledge that could serve as a retrieval and browsing mechanism for the records of knowledge, revolutionized library service and continues to be the most widely used library classification more than a century later.

Music materials, however, were never a strong point of the Decimal Classification (DDC), a classification that was designed to include records of knowledge rather than its artifacts. The best that could be accomplished was to prefix DDC numbers with a letter M to represent music itself, as distinct from the books about music. The original schema was sparse:

| | |
|---|---|
| 780 | Music. |
| 781 | Theory. |
| 782 | Dramatic. |
| 783 | Church. |
| 784 | Vocal. |
| 785 | Instrumental. |
| 786 | Piano and Organ. |
| 787 | Stringed instruments. |
| 788 | Wind instruments. |
| 789 | Associations and institutions.[9] |

Intervening decades, punctuated by frequent criticism and repeated adaptations based on the practice of thousands of libraries, have seen increased detail in the schema with no real improvement in the results. Now in its nineteenth edition, DDC perpetuates its original fault of making no separate provision for the materials of music, intertwining them with the books about music. A phoenix schedule has been prepared for inclusion in the twentieth edition. The phoenix makes extensive use of synthetic principles and may serve to bridge the gap between the traditional enumerative properties of DDC and its potential for use as a faceted classification.

A summary from the nineteenth edition shows how little DDC has changed:

| | |
|---|---|
| 780 | Music |
| 781 | General principles |
| 782 | Dramatic music |
| 783 | Sacred music |
| 784 | Voice & vocal music |
| 785 | Instrumental ensembles & their music |
| 786 | Keyboard instruments & their music |
| 787 | String instruments & their music |
| 788 | Wind instruments & their music |
| 789 | Percussion, mechanical, electrical[10] |

The logical inference is that dramatic music (782), sacred (meaning liturgical) music (783), and (apparently) secular music (784-789) constitute three major divisions of music. Further, dramatic and liturgical musics are arranged by form; secular musics are arranged by medium of performance.

Within the divisions, the typical DDC principle of hierarchical arrangement, proceeding from the general to the specific, is preserved. Within a range, the first portion covers general works while the last portions include specific treatments of the topic. Close examination of the 780 schedules will reveal the classification of musical concepts, including provision for score at the bottom of each hierarchical sequence. While this approach preserves a certain logic within DDC allowing the artifacts of a given topic to collocate with the books about it, it disregards the fundamental elements of music materials as described earlier. Printed scores are presented in each case as a representation of a given physical form of a specific topic. Thus 787.1 is a book about violin and 787.151-787.154 are the scores and parts for violin. Likewise, 786.81 is the number for books about organ sonatas, 786.8152-786.8154 are the numbers for publications that *are* organ sonatas. Thus the number expresses the medium of performance and the physical form as an element of topic, rather than the two elements as facets of musicality. Like other schemes, cultural, chronological, topical, and intellectual form characteristics cannot be expressed in most instances. Like *LCC:M*, subdivisions for forms of composition occur only under some performing media such as keyboard and orchestral, but not bowed strings.

Nevertheless, a certain logic can be observed in the use of the subdivisions. Miscellaneous collections are allowed to gather in the generalia division of each class, introduced with the subdivision 08, and specific scores follow, by form or medium, introduced with the subdivision 5. A library choosing this approach may thus intershelve the scores and books. Or the library may choose to use unsubdivided numbers prefaced with the letter M for scores and shelve them all in a separate section.

## APPLICATION OF DDC 19

The following are the classes in the nineteenth edition of DDC that admit provisions for music materials. In most instances scores and parts are indicated by "adding" subdivisions. In DDC the instruction to add a number means to "append" it to a given base number. Thus, given 782.87 as the base number for television music and 54 as the subdivision to be added for scores, the number for scores of television music is 782.8754.

### 780.8   Collected Works

Provision is made within the generalia division for collected sets of all kinds. Subdivisions are provided for collections of works by individual composer (.81), and more than one composer (.82). Iterations of this pattern are repeated wherever subdivision for music is allowed. Additionally, all miniature study scores may be classified at 780.84, following collected sets (which would usually be reference items), and preceding all other scores. This pragmatic approach to shelving is uncharacteristically practical for DDC.

### 781.7   Music of Ethnic Groups

Within division 781, "General principles," which otherwise is the class for music theory and compositional techniques, is the subdivision 781.7 for music of ethnic or geographic character. Numbers are derived by adding notation from auxiliary table 5 (for racial, ethnic, or national groups) or table 2 (areas) to base numbers 781.71 (for non-literate peoples, by area), 781.72 (for literate peoples by group), or 781.73-781.79 (for literate peoples by specific locality). Books and music will intershelve unless the M device is used to separate them.

### 782 Dramatic Music

Division 782 is for dramatic music, and the 81 and 82 mnemonic device (introduced at 780.81, etc.) is used here for arrangements, abridgments, excerpts, and scores that include librettos. Opera is treated at 782.1, other secular dramatic forms at 782.81-782.87, and ballet at 782.9. Beginning at this point scores are introduced in the following pattern of subdivision:

5       Scores and parts
52          Collections by more than one composer
54          Separate works and collections by one composer

Librettos and plot synopses are collocated with the scores by use of subdivisions 2 and 3, respectively. Scores of dramatic music may be classed by medium in 784-789 if preferred.

### 783 Sacred Music

The next division of 780 is 783 for "Sacred Music." Like 782, the library is given the option of preferring to class sacred music by medium of performance, in 784-789, if desired. Libraries choosing to use this class must then decide whether to class music by form (liturgy, oratorio, hymn, etc.) or by denomination. These options are mutually exclusive.

If the choice is to arrange music by denomination, synthesis is used to append numbers representing religions to base numbers representing music. This is accomplished using the numbers in the religion schedules following 28 for Christian sects or 29 for non-Christian sects. The resulting numbers representing religions are then added to base numbers 783.026 or 783.029, respectively.

The alternative is to use the by now common form subdivisions 5, 52, and 54 as directed under the sections for types of music. Sections are present for liturgy and ritual, oratorio, and hymns among miscellaneous non-liturgical sacred songs (including Christmas carols and Negro spirituals) and choral music. Thus 783.21 is the number for a mass and 783.2154 is a score of a mass by an individual composer.

### 784-789 Instrumental Music

The numbers derived from this part of the schedule are highly synthetic. Works for solo instruments or voices are classified in the base numbers enumerated in the schedule. A table of precedence (voice, string, wind, percussion, keyboard) is applied in synthesizing numbers for chamber ensembles that combine media. Thus a work for piano is classed in 786.41-786.49 (subdivided by form of composition) and a work for trombone in 788.2(541). Chamber music classes in 785.71 (for miscellanea) and 785.72-785.79 (for duets through nonets). Thus a duo for trombone and piano is classed in 785.72/82.

### *SHELF ARRANGEMENT*

Most libraries use Cutter or Cutter-Sanborn author numbers assigned to represent the main entry, and a lowercase letter assigned to represent the title of the work. Because of the use of titles that are names of types of composition it is usually necessary to follow the title symbol with a serial number or some other designation for subarrangement. It is not uncommon to find opus numbers, etc., used, as in the *LCC:M* scheme for shelf arrangement.

## ADAPTATIONS

Because DDC's approach to integrating scores and books on music was so universally rejected for collections of music materials, several attempts have been made to devise better schemes for the classification of music materials. An adaptation by Lionel McColvin and Harold Reeves, published in 1937, places all music in 780-782, reserving 783-789 for the books about music.[11] Vocal music is placed in 780, divided into secular (subdivided by number of voices) and sacred (subdivided by form). Instrumental music, divided by medium, is placed in 781-782. No provision is made for any other elements such as form of composition, character, etc. This scheme was widely adopted in British music libraries.

A Music Library Association committee published an adaptation of its own in 1951.[12] Based on the fifteenth edition of DDC and the Columbia adaptation of Dickinson, the scheme retains some of the original DDC notation. Miniature scores are to be kept together at M780, subarranged by composer. Collections are to be classed in the M780.8 (as in the current DDC). M781 is reserved for instructive editions for no particular medium (editions for specific media are to be indicated using the form subdivision 07). Otherwise the major DDC divisions are retained. M784.4 is reserved for national musics, to be subarranged by adding country notations from DDC 15 930-999. No provision is made for forms of composition; thus all orchestral scores are classed in M785 arranged by composer and parts are classed in M785.1. M789.91-789.95, reserved in DDC for discography and criticism, is here adapted for sound recordings. Recordings are to be classified by type (781.921 = 78 rpm, 781.923 = 33 rpm, 781.924 = 45 rpm, etc.) and subarranged by composer and title.

None of the adaptations gained wide acceptance, as most libraries preferred not straying from the published schedules. In the United States, most academic music libraries have chosen *LCC:M* for the arrangement of music materials; thus interest in improving DDC has come mostly from public libraries or other general collections.

## PHOENIX

In 1979 a *Proposed Revision of 780 Music* was published as a separate volume by the Forest Press and distributed widely for comment.[13] After extensive review, including application in the *British Catalogue of Music*, this phoenix schedule is expected to be incorporated in the forthcoming twentieth edition of DDC. Highly synthetic, utilizing advanced concepts of classification theory and of the classification of music, the phoenix 780 promises to be the first truly useful, faceted classification of music materials suitable for use as an online retrieval device.

While the general arrangement of classes is not radically different from that of DDC 19, the phoenix recognizes the essential distinction between music (which should be arranged by medium, or "executant" in the terms of the schedule) and books about music (most successfully arranged by composer). Therefore, the summary outline of the phoenix is as follows:

| | |
|---|---|
| 780.0001-.0999 | Relation of music to other subjects |
| 780.1-.9 | Standard subdivisions, modified |
| 781 | General principles |
| 781.1 | Basic principles |
| 781.2 | Elements |
| 781.3-.4 | Techniques |
| 781.5-.6 | Character and traditions |
| 781.7-.9 | Forms |
| 782-788 | Executants |
| 782-783 | Voices and vocal music |
| 782 | Opera and choral |
| 783 | Single voices |
| 784-788 | Instruments and their music |
| 784 | Orchestras and bands |
| 785 | Chamber ensembles |
| 786-788 | Specific instruments and their music |
| 786 | Keyboard, mechanical, electrophonic, percussion |
| 787 | Stringed |
| 788 | Wind |
| 789 | Individual composers[14] |

It can be observed at once that the books about music will occur in the three general classes, 780 for generalia, 781 for theory and composition, and 789 for biography. The music itself is to be classed by medium of performance in 782-788, each medium further subdivided by size of ensemble. The revision of these classes reflects an attempt to reconcile the schedules with the recognized international classification of musical instruments by C. Sachs and E. M. von Hornbostel, thereby making it possible to classify in an integrated manner music from all traditions.[15] Scores may be further distinguished by the addition of a standard subdivision 027. The digits 0 and 1 have been reserved for use as facet indicators, thus increasing dramatically the potential for synthetic classification.

### Citation Order

The citation order, or order of facets in the classification number, for music is to be executant, form, character, technique, standard subdivisions. Like Dickinson's *formulae* the citation order is comprehensive. That is, not all elements will be applicable or needed in every case. The phoenix recommends that no classification number contain more than three elements. The following examples illustrate the synthetic properties of the phoenix 780.

> Beethoven, Ludwig van, 1770-1827.
>    [Rondos, violin, piano, K. 41, G major]
>    Rondo for violin and piano / Ludwig van Beethoven ; edited by
> Rok Klopcic. -- New York : G. Schirmer, c1974.
>    1 score (13 p.) + 1 part ; 31 cm. -- (Schirmer's library of musical
> classics ; v. 1912)
>
>    1. Rondos (Violin and piano)--Scores and parts.

| | | |
|---|---|---|
| 787.2174 | | |
| | 787.2 | Violin |
| | 1 74 | Forms Rondo forms |

This number illustrates the simplest form of synthesis, adding a number to represent a form of composition (from 781.1-781.9) to the base number representing the medium of the solo instrument. The digit 1 is used to introduce the form of composition facet. It also illustrates one potential drawback of the scheme, which is its placement of music for keyboard and one other instrument in the class with music for solo instrument alone. Thus, in 787.2 will be found music for violin alone, and music for violin and keyboard, interfiled by composer.

> Mozart, Wolfgang Amadeus, 1756-1791.
> [Concertos, piano, orchestra. Selections]
> Piano concertos nos. 11-16 : in full score : from the Breitkopf & Härtel complete works edition / Wolfgang Amadeus Mozart ; with Mozart's cadenzas for nos. 12-16. -- New York : Dover, 1987.
> 1 score (252 p.) ; 31 cm.
> Reprint. Previously published: Leipzig : Breitkopf & Härtel, 1878. Originally published in series: Wolfgang Amadeus Mozart's Werke. Kritisch durchgesehene. Serie 16, 22.
> Contents: No. 11 in F major, K. 413 (1782-83) -- No. 12 in A major, K. 414 (1782) -- No. 13 in C major, K. 415 (1782-83) -- No. 14 in E-flat major, K. 449 (1784) -- No. 15 in B-flat major, K. 450 (1784) -- No. 16 in D major, K. 451 (1784).
> ISBN 0-4862-5468-2.
>
> 1. Concertos (Piano)--Scores.

784.262186

| | |
|---|---|
| 784 | Full orchestra |
| .26 | Specific solo instruments |
| 2 | Piano |
| 1 86 | Forms  Concerto forms |

In this instance the medium and form of composition are expressed quite clearly through use of synthesis. The number 62 for piano is taken from the base number for piano 786.2. The form of composition is added as before. Collections are not distinguished from separate works in the phoenix.

> Faure, Gabriel, 1845-1924.
> [Cantique de Racine; arr.]
> Cantique de Jean Racine : op. 11 : A song of praise / Gabriel Faure ; SATB with piano acc. ; English text adapted by Howard D. McKinney. -- Glen Rock, N.J. : J. Fischer, [1970]
> 1 vocal score (20 p.) ; 27 cm.
> Acc. originally for orchestra.
> English and French words.
>
> 1. Choruses, Sacred (Mixed voices, 4 parts) with orchestra--Vocal scores with piano. 2. Racine, Jean, 1639-1699--Musical settings.

782.5265

| | |
|---|---|
| 782 | Vocal music |
| .5 | Choral music, Mixed voices |
| 5 | Accompanied |
| 265 | Anthems |

This number reflects the complex synthesis allowed for vocal music. Vocal music is divided by number of voices and type of voices, then numbers may be added to indicate the presence or absence of accompaniment, and vocal forms of composition (specified at 782) may be indicated.

## CONCLUSION

The phoenix holds great promise for advancing the scientific classification of music, particularly for online retrieval of bibliographic records. Of the prevailing classifications it is the most detailed and based on the most sound principles of music analysis.

# ANSCR

## INTRODUCTION

*The Alpha-Numeric System for Classification of Sound Recordings* was introduced to the small and public library community in 1969.[16] Commonly designated by its acronym ANSCR (pronounced "answer"), the scheme gained wide acceptance in public libraries, where it was well suited to bin arrangement of small circulating collections of twelve-inch, long-playing disc sound recordings. ANSCR was not designed as a classification of knowledge, so it satisfies few of the principles of classification that are adhered to by major schemes such as DDC and *LCC*. ANSCR is quite utilitarian, however, based on experience gained through trials in small library collections. Main classes were derived from observations of the sound recordings collected in such libraries and reflect not so much musical knowledge as commercial categories of recordings. ANSCR can be used appropriately for browsing collections of disc or tape recordings. In some ways ANSCR can be seen as a realization of the formula for the small library presented in the Dickinson scheme (see above).

The ANSCR approach (described by the authors as a system) proceeds from three concepts: 1) a broad classification of "subject" categories (primarily forms of composition), 2) a "basic rule" that stipulates class location according to the length of the musical works, and 3) creation of unique class numbers for each recording.

## THE BASIC RULE

ANSCR's simple approach begins with an examination of the recording and an application of its basic rule. If the first work on the first side of a recording occupies one-third or more of the side (measured in space on a disc or time on a tape), then the class is chosen to correspond to that work. Otherwise, the class will be chosen to correspond to the collective nature of the recording.

The logic in this approach is clear and is similar to the logic employed in rules for choice of main entry for sound recordings in *AACR2*. Recordings are divided into two broad groupings, those that feature a particular musical work and those that feature a type of music. Recordings falling into the first category will be collocated by the form of that work, subdivided by composer. Recordings falling into the second category will be collocated by the style or character of the recording, and will be subdivided by performer or title. Popular music is not measured in this way, but is placed directly in a class by itself and subdivided by performer.

*OUTLINE*

Mnemonic devices are employed in the outline of ANSCR's main classes. Although the alphabetical class and name symbols are enumerative and utilitarian, the letter symbols for the divisions correspond to the headings for those divisions, and the use of the letter A is always to represent a miscellaneous division. There are thirty-six main classes. The progression is from vocal, through instrumental, commercial, cultural, and holiday music, followed by several classes for spoken-word recordings. Within the musical categories progression is by size of performance force from largest to smallest.

A    Music Appreciation--History and Commentary
B    Operas: Complete and Highlights
C    Choral Music
D    Vocal Music
E    Orchestral Music:
      EA    General Orchestral
      EB    Ballet Music
      EC    Concertos
      ES    Symphonies
F    Chamber Music
G    Solo Instrumental Music:
      GG    Guitar
      GO    Organ
      GP    Piano
      GS    Stringed Instruments
      GV    Violin
      GW    Wind Instruments
      GX    Percussion Instruments
H    Band Music
J    Electronic, Mechanical Music
K    Musical Shows and Operettas: Complete and Excerpts
L    Soundtrack Music: Motion Pictures and Television
M    Popular Music:
      MA    Pop Music
      MC    Country and Western Music
      MJ    Jazz Music
P    Folk and Ethnic Music: National
Q    International Folk and Ethnic Music
R    Holiday Music
S    Varieties and Humor
T    Plays
U    Poetry
V    Prose
W    Documentary: History and Commentary
X    Instructional
Y    Sounds and Special Effects
Z    Children's Recordings:
      ZI    Instructional
      ZM    Music
      ZS    Spoken[17]

The order of classes is, again, strictly utilitarian and is designed to facilitate browsing. Four large groups of what are perceived to be different user classes are apparent: art music, commercial music, spoken word, and children's material. Band music and stage music (musicals and operettas) are perceived to be commercial or "popular" forms and thus fall out of place in relation to orchestral and opera music. Jazz is perceived to be a form of "popular" music and is thus separated from instrumental and vocal music. These observations indicate why ANSCR would not be an appropriate scheme for a research or teaching collection of recordings. By the same token, the utilitarian separation of materials by class of user is a valid approach to shelf classification that has been very successful in public library browsing and circulating collections.

## CALL NUMBER CONSTRUCTION

ANSCR call numbers consist of four elements (called "terms"): a class number, an alphabetic work mark, a symbol representing the number or title of a work, and an alphanumeric symbol representing a portion of the manufacturer's serial number.

The work marks can represent composers, performers, titles, or broad subject subdivisions such as geographic location, depending on the class in question. Usually the first four consecutive letters of a name or word are used, all written as capitals. Lists of composer and language abbreviations, as well as certain types of terms (e.g., instructional skills for class X) are included in the instructions.

The third element of the call number is a serial number or a three-letter alphabetical abbreviation of a collective title or other term. The fourth element is a letter associated with the performance, such as the conductor or other featured performer, followed by the final two digits of the manufacturer's serial number. This means that within each class, the recordings will be subarranged by performer, thus allowing a user to contrast performances. The addition of the digits from the manufacturer's serial number guarantees a unique identifier that will be easily associated with the item itself.

> Mississippi folk voices [sound recording]. -- [U.S.] : Southern
> Folklore Records, [1973]
> 1 sound disc : analog, 33⅓ rpm ; 12 in.
> Southern Folklore Records: SF 101.
> "Mississippi Folk Voices is part of Folklore project sponsored by the Mississippi Department of Archives and History in the state capitol of Jackson."
> Notes on the artists and music by Ferris, with texts, bibliographies, discographies, and films (55 p. ill.) in slipcase.
> Contents: Somebody knocking on my door ; Baby please don't go. Glory glory hallelujah (Napoleon Strickland, vocal, fife, harmonica) -- Pico Polka ; High level ; Tom & Jerry (Bill Mitchell, fiddle) -- The blues : conversation between Bruce Payne and James Thomas -- Cool water ; Momma talk to your daughter (James Thomas, vocal,
> guitar) -- Hobo's meditation (John Arnold, vocal, guitar) -- We so glad to be here ; God spoke ; He's my rock, my sword, my shield (Chapman Family) -- Light at the river ; As I go along my way (J. L. Jones and the Good Buys) -- When I can read my titles clear ; Love divine (Mississippi Sacred Harp Singers) -- Oh Rosie : chopping wood ; Lazarus : hoes (Inmates, Parchman State Penitentiary, Camp B, Lambert).
>
> 1. Folk music--Mississippi. 2. Sacred songs. 3. Afro-American songs--Mississippi. 4. Folk music--Mississippi--Bibliography. 5. Folk music, American--Mississippi--Discography.
> I. Mississippi. Dept. of Archives and History.

The ANSCR call number for this recording would be:

P           Folk music
COLL             Collective
MIS              Title "Mississippi"
S 01                   "Southern" ... 01

The recording would collocate with all U.S. folk music. Special categories for use in the work mark exist for Cajun, Eskimo, Indian (Native American), and Hawaiian music. Everything else is to be designated as collective and subarranged by title proper.

> Handel, George Frideric, 1685-1759.
>     [Music for the royal fireworks]
>     Music for the royal fireworks / George Frideric Handel.
> Suites / [Lully ... et al.][sound recording]. -- Tinton Falls,
> N.J. : Musical Heritage Society, [1982], p1976.
>     1 sound cassette : analog.
>     Musical Heritage Society: MHC 6505.
>     Title from container.
>     Bande des hautbois Michel Piguet ; Edward Tarr Brass
> Ensemble ; Michel Piguet, artistic director.
>     Program notes by M. Piguet on container.
>     Contents: Suites: Les airs de trompettes, timbales et hautbois /
> Jean-Baptiste Lully -- Suite for oboes, horns and bassoons / Georg
> Philipp Telemann -- Partie for oboes / Johann Philipp
> Krieger -- March for trumpet, oboes and bassoons / George
> Frideric Handel.
>
>     1. Suites (Orchestra) 2. Suites. I. Piguet, Michel. II. Lully, Jean
> Baptiste, 1632-1687. Airs de trompettes, timbales et hautbois.
> III. Telemann, Georg Philipp, 1681-1767. Suites, winds. IV. Krieger,
> Johann Phillip, 1649-1725. Partie, oboes. V. Handel, George
> Frideric, 1685-1759. Marches, winds. VI. Bande des hautbois
> Michel Piguet. VII. Edward Tarr Brass Ensemble. VIII. Title: Music
> for the royal fireworks.

The ANSCR call number for this recording would be:

EA          Orchestral music: General
HAND             Handel
ROY              Royal Fireworks
P 05                   Piguet ... MHS 505

Special classes of orchestral music are provided for ballet suites and symphonies. This recording will collocate with the general class that includes everything else. Subdivision is by composer and title. Recordings of this popular work will then be subdivided further by conductor, and each conductor's performances will be arranged by manufacturer's serial number.

Dvořák, Antonín, 1841-1904.
[Quartets, strings, B. 92, Eb major]
Streichquartett Nr. 10 Es-dur op. 51 ; Streichquartett Nr. 8 E-dur
op. 80 [sound recording] / Anton Dvorák. -- [Hamburg] :
Deutsche Grammophon, p1976.
1 sound disc (59 min.) : analog, 33⅓ rpm, stereo. ; 12 in.
Deutsche Grammophon: 2530 719.
Prager Streichquartett.
Durations: 31:38; 27:08.

1. String quartets. I. Dvořák, Antonín, 1841-1904. Quartets,
strings, B. 57, E major. 1976. II. Prazske kvarteto.

The ANSCR call number for this Dvorak recording would be

| | | |
|---|---|---|
| F | Chamber music | |
| DVOR | By Dvořák | |
| QS-10 | | Quartet, strings, no. 10 |
| P 19 | | Prager Streichquartett, DGG ... 19 |

Chamber music for ensembles of three to nine performers, each playing one to a part, is grouped by composer in class F. Subdivision within composer division is by musical form. A list of approved forms is included in the scheme. Serial number is preferred to opus number or thematic catalog number. The name of the featured performing group is used to organize the performances. The scheme directs the use of the name used by the performer on his works for this division, which may differ from the *AACR2* authorized official name for a corporate body.

MacDermot, Galt.
[Hair. Selections]
Hair [sound recording] / [book and lyrics by] Ragni, Rado ;
[music by] MacDermot. -- New York : RCA Victor, c1968.
1 sound disc (63 min.) : analog, 33⅓ rpm, stereo. ; 12 in.
RCA Victor: LSO-1150.
"The American tribal love-rock musical."
"Original cast from the Broadway musical."
Orchestra directed by Galt MacDermot.
Contents: Aquarius -- Donna ; Hashish -- Sodomy -- Colored
space -- Manchester England -- I'm black ; Ain't got no -- Air --
Initials ; I got life -- Hair -- My confiction -- Don't put it
down -- Frank Mills -- Be in -- Where do I go? -- Black boys ;
White boys -- Easy to be hard -- Walking in space -- Abie Baby --
Three-five-zero-zero ; What a piece of work is man -- Good
morning starshine -- The flesh failures (Let the sunshine in).

1. Musical revues, comedies, etc.--Excerpts. 2. Rock music--United
States. I. Ragni, Gerome. II. Rado, James. III. MacDermot,
Galt.

The ANSCR call number for this Broadway rock musical would be

| | |
|---|---|
| K | Musical shows |
| HAIR | Hair (show title) |
| HAI | Hair (album title) |
| R 50 | RCA ... 50 |

The class K is for musical shows, and is collocated with L for movies and television and M for popular music, but not with B for opera. The main division of class K is to be by show title, each show then subdivided by album title. The scheme indicates the vocalist with the highest voice range should be used for form in the performance division; however, it is impossible to determine ranges for this recording (voice range is irrelevant in rock music), so the record company name is preferred.

*CONCLUSION*

The ANSCR scheme is simple to use and provides a convenient basis for browsing a collection of circulating records. It is the only classification in use with music materials that uses form as the initial class element. The choice of those forms is based on the audience element and classification is accomplished by a heavy reliance on the commercial nature and physical presentation of sound recordings. For these reasons ANSCR is unique among the major classifications used with music materials.

It is debatable whether the scheme could be adapted for use with printed music, although the categories of musical anthologies often collected by small public libraries have much in common with the categories of sound recordings that form the basic classes in ANSCR. Because of ANSCR's utilitarian structure (i.e., it is not a classification of knowledge) it would be an unlikely choice for online retrieval. It is likely, however, that the principles used to formulate ANSCR could be easily applied to the condensation of major schemes in use in general libraries, thus preserving a unified approach to bibliographic control of the entire collection through classification.

# Notes

[1] W. C. Look, "The Classification and Cataloging of Music Scores in Libraries" (M.A. diss., University of Chicago, 1951), 33-34.

[2] George Sherman Dickinson, *Classification of Musical Compositions: A Decimal-Symbol System* (Poughkeepsie, N.Y.: Vassar College, 1938), 7-8.

[3] O. G. Sonneck, "Prefatory Note (First Edition)," in Library of Congress. Processing Department. Subject Cataloging Division, *Classification. Class M: Music and Books on Music*, 2nd ed. with supplementary pages (Washington, D.C.: The Library, 1917, reissued 1968), 3.

[4] Ibid., 5.

[5] Carol June Bradley, "Notes of Some Pioneers: America's First Music Librarians," *Notes* 43 (1986): 272-73.

[6] "Class Numbers for Records." *Library of Congress Information Bulletin* (17 February 1972): 70.

[7] The LC work number tables are found in *Cataloging Service Bulletin* 3, no. 20, along with several examples. Extensive detailed instructions for the construction of workmarks are found in Richard P. Smiraglia, *Shelflisting Music: Guidelines for Use with the Library of Congress Classification: M*, MLA Technical Reports, No. 9 (Philadelphia, Pa.: Music Library Association, 1981).

[8]See the instructions in Smiraglia, *Shelflisting*, 17-18; and LC's amplification in "Shelflisting: Adding Dates to Monographic Call Numbers," *Cataloging Service Bulletin* 19 (Winter 1982): 25-26.

[9][Melville Dewey], *A Classification and Subject Index for Cataloguing and Arranging the Books and Pamphlets of a Library* (Amherst, Mass., 1876), 20.

[10]Melvil Dewey, *Dewey Decimal Classification and Relative Index, Volume 1*, 19th ed., under the direction of Benjamin A. Custer (Albany, N.Y.: Forest Press, 1979), 480.

[11]Lionel McColvin and Harold Reeves, "Special Scheme," in *Music Libraries* (London: Grafton, 1937).

[12]Music Library Association. Classification Committee, "Proposed Alternate Scheme for Dewey M780," *Notes: Supplement for Members* 17 (1951): 5-15.

[13]*Proposed Revision of 780 Music: Based on Dewey Decimal Classification and Relative Index* (Albany, N.Y.: Forest Press, 1980).

[14]Ibid., xiii.

[15]E. M. von Hornbostel and C. Sachs, "Systematik der Musikinstrumente; ein Versuch," *Zeitschrift für Ethnologie* 4-5 (1914). Non-Western music may optionally be arranged at 781.9 "Traditions" subarranged by ethnic group or nationality.

[16]Caroline Saheb-Ettaba and Roger B. McFarland, *ANSCR: The Alpha-Numeric System for Classification of Recordings* (Williamsport, Pa.: Bro-Dart, 1969).

[17]Ibid., 7.

# Suggested Reading

Bradley, Carol June. *The Dickinson Classification: A Cataloguing & Classification Manual for Music. Including a Reprint of the George Sherman Dickinson Classification of Musical Compositions.* Carlisle, Pa.: Carlisle Books, c1968.

Music Library Association. Cataloging and Classification Committee. *S L A C C: The Partial Use of the Shelflist as Classed Catalog.* Donald Seibert, Chairman. MLA Technical Reports, No. 1. Ann Arbor, Mich.: Music Library Association, 1973.

*Proceedings of the Institute on Library of Congress Music Cataloging Policies and Procedures.* Transcribed and compiled with editorial comments by David Sommerfield. MLA Technical reports, No. 3. Ann Arbor, Mich.: Music Library Association, 1975.

*Proposed Revision of 780 Music: Based on Dewey Decimal Classification and Relative Index.* Prepared under the direction of Russell Sweeney and John Clews, with assistance from Winton E. Matthews. Albany, N.Y.: Forest Press, 1980.

Saheb-Ettaba, Caroline, and Roger B. McFarland. *ANSCR: The Alpha-Numeric System for Classification of Recordings.* Williamsport, Pa.: Bro-Dart, 1969.

Smiraglia, Richard P. *Shelflisting Music: Guidelines for Use with Library of Congress Classification: M.* MLA Technical Reports, No. 9. Philadelphia, Pa.: Music Library Association, 1981.

# 8
# MACHINE-READABLE CATALOGING (MARC)

*There exists a dichotomy about the MARC format which, I think, is caused by an unclear concept ... of what the format should do. As I understand it, the format was basically devised for the transmission of cataloging information, however, along the way, information retrieval has slipped in.*[1]

## Automated Cataloging:
### A Historical Overview

### INTRODUCTION

Machine-readable music cataloging (MARC) as we know it and conceive of it today had its beginnings in the 1950s. Much like their colleagues in other subfields of librarianship, music librarians were drawn to the tremendous potential benefits of computers for information storage and retrieval. Not surprisingly, the earliest efforts were aimed at automating card production, with the secondary benefit of shared cataloging also providing a strong incentive. Music librarians have always been enthusiastic supporters of shared cataloging initiatives, and it was only with the implementation of computer techniques that their dream of a shared cataloging database met its realization.

Among the earliest efforts involving music catalogs was the use of punched cards in the record library at Radio Marocco in 1957. The principal advantages of this system were its use of encoding to systematize discographical data and the concomitant increased ability of the librarian to sort the entries according to new combinations of bibliographic elements.[2] Through the next decade sporadic reports of similar attempts at computerization appeared in the literature. The most significant, and probably the largest, project was that at the State University of New York at Buffalo. This project also utilized punched cards, but an intermediate product was a magnetic tape that could be used to share data as well as to produce cards for the catalog. Library system developers at Buffalo were attempting to create a system that was compatible with the MARC-II format, then in use for books. An interesting sidelight of this project was the fact that the content designation, or tag, for a uniform title was 15t, a subdivision of the field for composer main entry (10t).[3]

Through the early 1970s machine-readable music cataloging took two tracks. In the United States efforts were underway to design and implement a MARC-compatible music format. In Europe experiments with non-MARC based systems continued.

## THE MARC MUSIC FORMAT

The original developments that led to the construction of what is known as the MARC Music Format are attributed to Mary Lou Little, Music Librarian at Harvard in the 1960s. Little, like many of her colleagues elsewhere, was dismayed at the prospect of manually updating a seriously flawed sound recordings card catalog. Taking the approved MARC-II format for books, Little and her staff added subfield content designation for the music-specific elements of the uniform title, for the language of printed accompanying matter for recordings, and for plate numbers and label-names and numbers. They also added extra fields for performer notes and added entries, and developed a complex intrarecord linking technique designed to produce genuine analytics (as opposed to the usual analytical added entries) for specific musical works on a recording.

By mid-1970 Little had communicated with the Library of Congress, where she had found a willing cooperative partner in format development. Though the Library of Congress announced that it had no plans to automate its own music cataloging, it took the draft format under its wing and in January 1971 issued the first published draft format for sound recordings. Abandoning printed music for the time being, this draft incorporated most of Little's additions but dropped the intrarecord linking technique. The LC draft incorporated the 007 fixed field for physical description and the 008 fixed field accompanying material codes, which were borrowed from the now completed film format.

Anxious to encourage such promising developments, the Music Library Association appointed a liaison, and a year later a joint committee, to advise the Library of Congress on the development of the format. It was on the advice of the music librarians that the draft was altered to again include provisions for printed music. It was also during this period that open discussions of the format led many to begin to view it not so much as a device for printing cards, but as a tool for communicating bibliographic and musical data. That is, the information retrieval potential of such a tool, which Bowles noted in the letter quoted at the top of this chapter, was at last comprehended.

It was this realization that radically changed the shape of the music format. Forward thinking music specialists requested that format developers add the capability of retrieving music chronologically, and by form of composition, medium of performance, and nationality. These were all aspects of "subject" analysis that had eluded satisfactory solution in manual catalogs, but which promised to be easily accomplished given the anticipated power of automated searching.

A second draft was issued by the Library of Congress in 1972. Following four years of often heated discussion in the joint committee, the current version was published in 1976.[4] The new format was implemented on a large scale by the Online Computer Library Center (OCLC), then the Ohio College Library Center, in late 1978. Research Libraries Information Network (RLIN) implementation followed in 1980. Unique among the special formats, the Library of Congress abrogated its role as purveyor of the format, not implementing the music format internally or for record distribution until 1985. In the intervening years music librarians working through network user groups built the body of practice reflected in the remaining sections of this chapter. The large national database of shared bibliographic records for music materials was built by the cooperative efforts of music librarians around the country.[5]

Though slightly altered over the years in attempts by MARC development personnel to better integrate the various material-specific formats, the music format remains a highly detailed and flexible device for communication of bibliographic data about music materials.

## CONCEPTS OF THE MUSIC FORMAT

> Essential to the concept of machine-readable cataloging is the existence of a machine format for bibliographic records. A format in this context refers to a method of organizing data so that the record and parts of the record can be identified ... explicitly for machine manipulation.... This is in contrast with traditional catalog cards where identification of cataloging information is implicit.[6]

The MARC Music Format, which is designed to carry bibliographic records for printed music and sound recordings, is really very much like the other material-specific formats. Because it was developed relatively early in the history of automated cataloging, it has undergone a fair amount of refinement since its inception, and attempts to simplify its internal structure continue.

Nevertheless, the format is intended to serve more than one master. That is, its purpose is threefold: 1) to contain catalog records and produce catalog products for musical materials, 2) to support automated library activities that are dependent on bibliographic data (such as circulation, acquisitions, serials control, etc.), and 3) to generate indexes that can be used for sophisticated information retrieval activities. To this end, the format contains a few music-specific areas (such as a field for music publisher's numbers), quite a few more music-specific code lists and applications practices for general bibliographic areas (such as relator codes to identify performers in fields that store access points), and several archival features that are intended to support specialized searching in archives of printed music or sound recordings (such as 007 subfields for physical characteristics of master recordings). These encoded fields carry bibliographic data beyond those that have traditionally been found in card catalog records. These data represent a powerful information retrieval potential in future online systems.

In the sections that follow, the music-specific aspects of the format will be enumerated and their applications explained, and a variety of fully formatted bibliographic records is presented.

# Formatting Machine-Readable Records

## INTRODUCTION

Formatting, or content-designation, is the process by which eye-readable bibliographic records are encoded for machine manipulation and retrieval. Each element of the bibliographic record is preceded by a code derived from the *MARC Formats for Bibliographic Data* (*MFBD*).[7] Some fields are extraneous to the traditional card catalog record. These fields carry encoded data that are potentially useful for retrieval but have not been specified in the cataloging rules, subject heading lists, or classification schedules. It cannot be overemphasized that the MARC record is designed to contain and communicate bibliographic data that have already been generated in the cataloging process. That is, the cataloger's first priority is to create the bibliographic data, and only subsequently enter them into a MARC formatted record. Consequently, many potential areas of the MARC format are unused in any given bibliographic record, depending on the content of the bibliographic data.

*MARC FIELDS FOR PRINTED MUSIC*

Following is a discussion of each element of the MARC record that is encoded differently for music or not found in the MARC record for books. Isolated examples are used here to illustrate the content designation of specific fields. Complete examples of formatted bibliographic records are illustrated with explanations of their features at the end of the chapter.[8]

Leader, Byte 6 (Record type)
   c = printed music
   d = manuscript music

This byte ("Type" in OCLC, "BLT" in RLIN) identifies the type of music bibliographic record.

008, Byte 35-37 (Language of Sung or Spoken Text)

A three-character alphabetic code (from the MARC Code List found in *MFBD*) is entered here ("Lang" in OCLC, "L" in RLIN) to represent the language of sung or spoken words in a musical work:

Title: Jesu, der du meine Seele ...
008 35-37: ger

When the musical work has words in more than one language, the first language is encoded here, and subsequent languages are encoded in field 041 (see below). When the musical work has no sung or spoken text, this byte is coded "N/A" (not applicable) in OCLC or "ƀ" (blank) in RLIN.

008, Bytes 18-19 (Form of composition)

A code from the approved list found in *MFBD* is entered here ("Comp" in OCLC, "FCP" in RLIN) when there is only one musical work in the item being cataloged. When no appropriate code appears on the list "zz" is entered. When more than one work is present in the item, "mu" is entered here and the individual codes are entered in field 047 (see below).

008, Byte 20 (Format of Music Manuscript or Printed Music)

   a = Full score
   b = Miniature score
   c = Accompaniment reduced for keyboard
   d = Voice score
   e = Condensed score
   g = Close score
   m = Multiple formats
   n = Not printed music (i.e., sound recording)
   u = Unknown
   z = Not score format (i.e., music for solo instrument or voice)

A code is entered here ("Format" in OCLC, "SCO" in RLIN) to reflect the specific material designation that appears in field 300.

1 score (23 p.)
008 20: a

1 miniature score (59 p.)
008 20: b

17 p. of music
008 20: z

008, Byte 21 (Existence of Parts)
ƀ = No parts exist
a = Parts exist
n = Not applicable
u = Unknown

A code is entered ("Prts" in OCLC, "PTS" in RLIN), again to reflect the specific material designation that appears in field 300. In some network applications, when LC copy indicates that parts exist, even though they are not held in the contributing library, code "a" is entered.

1 score (12 p.) + 3 parts
008 21: a

008, Bytes 24-29 (Accompanying matter)
ƀ = No accompanying matter
a = Discography
b – Bibliography
c = Thematic index
d = Libretto or text
e = Biography of composer
f = Biography of performer/history of ensemble
g = Technical/historical information on instruments
h = Technical information on music
i = Historical information
k = Ethnological information
r = Instructional materials
s = score
z = Other

Codes from *MFBD* are entered ("Accomp mat" in OCLC, "ATC" in RLIN) only when the information contained in the accompanying textual matter is substantial or unique and could not be found in a standard reference work. When the accompanying matter has been described in a note in the bibliographic record, the appropriate codes should be entered here.

500 ƀƀ Words printed also as text.
008, 24-29: d

When codes are entered in this field, the language of the accompanying matter must be entered in field 041 $g (see below).

008, Byte 32 (Main Entry in Body of Entry)
    1 = Name used as main entry named in 245
    0 = Title main entry, or name used as main entry not named in 245

This byte ("MEBE" in OCLC, "MEI" in RLIN) contains a code indicating whether the name found in a 1xx field also appears in subfield "c" (statement of responsibility) of field 245. This is analogous to the "M" portion of the "M/F/B" byte in the books format.

008, Bytes 35-37 (Language Code)

The appropriate three-character alphabetic language code from *MFBD* is entered here ("Lang" in OCLC, "L" in RLIN) when the musical work has sung or spoken text.

    Title: Jesu, der du meine Seele ...
    008 35-37: ger

When the musical work has words in more than one language, the first language is encoded here, and subsequent languages are encoded in field 041 (see below). When the musical work has no sung or spoken text, this byte is coded "N/A" (not applicable) in OCLC or "ƀ" (blank) in RLIN.

028 (Publisher's Number for Music)
First Indicator for Music
    2 = Plate number
    3 = Publisher's number
Second Indicator
    0 = No note; no added entry
    1 = Note; added entry
    2 = Note; no added entry
    3 = No note; added entry
Subfields
    a = Numerical portion
    b = Designation of source

The content of this field should reflect the notes required by *AACR2* cataloging. This field is indexed by most networks. The indicators for this field can be used not only to store the numbers among the control fields, but also to generate notes required by *AACR2* and added entries for catalogs with plate number files (or indexes).

For plate numbers, the numerical portion (the plate number itself) is entered in $a, the name of the publisher in $b.

    028 22 $a B. & H. 8813 $b Breitkopf & Hártel

In some applications this will generate a note on printed output or in screen displays:

    Pl.no.: B. & H. 8813.

For publisher's numbers that contain an epithet, the numerical portion is entered in $a, and the name of the publisher in $b, disregarding the epithet. The note generation process will not work for this type of publisher's number, so the number is also entered in field 500.

On the first page of the score:
>  Edition Peters No. 1234

Entered in field 028 as:
>  028 30  1234 $b C. F. Peters

Entered in field 500:
>  500 ƀƀ  Publisher's no.: Edition Peters No. 1234.

In OCLC applications, the *epithet* is entered in $b, disregarding the name of the publisher.

041 (Languages)
First Indicator
>  0 = Item is not a translation and does not include a translation
>  1 = Item is a translation or includes a translation

Second Indicator
>  ƀ

Subfields
>  a = Language of sung or spoken text
>  h = Language of original or intermediate translation
>  b = Language of summaries or abstracts
>  d = Language of libretto
>  g = Language of accompanying matter

This field carries language codes from *MFBD* that either supplement the code found in field 008 byte 35-37 (see above), or that indicate the language of accompanying textual matter (see field 008 bytes 24-29 above).

A Mozart symphony with substantive critical notes:
35-37: ƀ          ["N/A" in OCLC]
24-29: i
041 0ƀ  $g ger

Handel's *Messiah* with German text, libretto printed separately in German, French, and English, performance instructions in German.

35-37: ger
24-29: dh
041 1ƀ  ger $h eng $d gerfreeng $g ger

045 (Chronological Code or Date/Time)
First Indicator
>  ƀ = No specific date recorded
>  0 = Single date
>  1 = Multiple single dates
>  2 = Range of dates

Second Indicator
>  ƀ

Subfields
>  a = Chronological code
>  b = Date

When the specific date of composition is known, $b is used.

    Composed 1817:
    045 0ƀ  $b d1817

    Composed 1893-1895:
    045 2ƀ  $b d1893 $b d1895

When the specific date of composition is not known, the period is estimated based on information in the item. This estimate is used to construct a chronological coverage code.

    Composed after 1810; composer died 1827:
    045 ƀƀ  w1w2


        047 (Form of Composition)
Indicators
        ƀ
Subfields
        a = Form of composition code

Multiple codes from *MFBD* are entered in field 047 when fixed field Comp has been coded "mu."

    A string quartet:

        008, 18-19: zz

    Anthology with sonatas, fantasias and variations:

        008, 18-19: mu
        047 ƀƀ  sn $a ft $a vr


        048 (Number of Instruments or Voices)
Indicators
        ƀ
Subfields
        a = performer or ensemble
        b = soloist with accompaniment

This field is not usually used for collections for miscellaneous instrumentation, operas, or other large vocal works, folk songs or folk music, school songbooks without specified instrumentation, or hymns and liturgical chants.

Codes are entered in separate subfields and are followed with a two-digit number indicating the number of performers. If the number of parts is unknown only the code is supplied.

    A string quartet:

        048 ƀƀ  sa02 $a sb01 $a sc01

    Song for soprano and piano:

        048 ƀƀ  $b va01 $a ka01

Chorus with orchestra:

    048 ƀƀ $b ca04 $a oa

Duet for flute (or violin) and piano:

    048 ƀƀ wa01 $a ka01
    048 ƀƀ sa01 $a ka01


    240 (Uniform Title)
First Indicator
    1 = Printed on cards
Second Indicator
    0 = Nonfiling characters
Subfields
    a = Uniform title
    k = Form subheading
    l = Language
    n = Number
    p = Name of part or section of work
    s = Version
    m = Medium of performance
    o = Arrangement
    r = Key

The uniform title formulated according to *AACR2* is entered in this field. The various elements of the uniform title are separately subfielded. In some online systems, separately subfielded elements can be accessed. All uniform title subfields are coded in the same way regardless of the field in which they appear (6xx, 7xx, 8xx).

The indicator values for this field are essentially obsolete. The first indicator values were designed to be used for books in the period before the implementation of *AACR2* when the Library of Congress rarely displayed uniform titles on cards for books. In most networks, the indicator values are disregarded even for card printing. Consequently, the first indicator is usually set to 1 for music, because a uniform title, if present, should always be displayed. The second indicator records the number of non-filing characters (letters and spaces in initial articles) in uniform titles. The Library of Congress routinely drops initial articles from all headings. *AACR 2* will incorporate this policy in its 1988 revision.

    [Quartets, strings, no. 3, op. 25, D major]
    240 10 Quartets, $m strings, $n no. 3, op. 25, $r D major

    [Aïda. Vocal score. English]
    240 10 Aïda. $s Vocal score. $l English

    [Aïda. Celeste Aïda]
    240 10 Aïda. $p Celeste Aïda

    [Songs. Selections; arr.]
    240 10 Songs. $k Selections; $o arr.

245 (Title and Statement of Responsibility)
First Indicator
    0   = No title added entry
    1   = Title added entry
Second Indicator
    0-9 = Nonfiling characters
Subfields
    a   = Title proper
    b   = Other title information
    c   = Remainder of title transcription

This field carries the information transcribed into area 1 of the description according to *AACR2*. The first indicator is set to 1 to make an automatic added entry under the title proper, when required by *AACR2*. The second indicator records the number of non-filing characters (letters and spaces) in initial articles.

Placement of the subfield indicators follows the ISBD punctuation conventions of area 1 of the description. That is, subfield "a" contains the title proper, subfield "b" follows the colon preceding other title information (if any), and subfield "c" follows the slash preceding a statement of responsibility (if any). The placement of the subfield "b" indicator is very important, because it delimits the amount of information that will be used in the title added entry generated by first indicator 1 and therefore the amount of information that will be contained in the title index of an online system.

        Symphony, no. 40, G minor, K. 550 / Mozart.
245 00  Symphony, no. 40, G minor, K. 550 / $c Mozart.

        Chez le docteur : piano et chant / Erik Satie ; [paroles de
Vincent Hyspa].
245 10  Chez le docteur : $b piano et chant / $c Erik Satie ; [paroles de
Vincent Hyspa].

        1001 great country hits.
245 00 1001 great country hits.


254 (Musical Presentation Area)
Indicators
     ƀ
Subfields
     a

This field carries the data transcribed in area 3 of the *AACR2* description for printed music.

    Area 3: Partitur und Stimmen. --

    254 ƀƀ  Partitur und Stimmen.


300 (Physical Description)
Indicators
     ƀ
Subfields
    a = Extent of item
    b = Other physical details
    c = Dimensions

This field carries the physical description from area 5 of the *AACR2* description for printed music.

A score and 3 parts of the same size:

   300 ƀƀ 1 score (14 p.) + 3 parts ; $c 31 cm.

A score and 4 parts of different sizes:

   300 ƀƀ 1 score (74 p.) ; $c 19 cm. $a + 4 parts ; $c 31 cm.


   306 (Duration)
Indicators
   ƀ
Subfields
   a

Duration of musical works is given in the form HHMMSS. If a score contains more than one work, enter the duration for each piece in a separate $a. Durations for printed music are derived from physical description notes (500) or contents notes (505).

One hour, seventeen minutes:

   306 ƀb 006017
   500 ƀb Duration: 60:17


## MARC FIELDS FOR MUSICAL SOUND RECORDINGS

This section discusses each element of the MARC record for musical sound recordings that is not found in the MARC record for music or that is encoded differently for sound recordings.

Leader, Byte 6 (Record Type)

   j = Musical sound recording

This byte ("Type" in OCLC, "BLT" in RLIN) identifies the type of sound recording bibliographic record.

008, Byte 6 (Type of Date)

   p = Date of issue and recording differ by at least one year
   r = Reissue

As for all other materials, this field ("Dat tp" in OCLC, "PC" in RLIN) carries a code that indicates the type of dates included in area 4 of the description as formulated according to *AACR2*.

For sound recordings, the date of release is compared to the date of recording, if the date of recording has been given in a note. When there is a difference between the two dates of one year or more, code "p" is recorded here, and the date of release is recorded in Date 1 (008, Byte 7-10) and the recording date in Date 2 (008, Byte 11-14).

260 0ƀ  New York : $b Angel, $c p1985.
518 ƀƀ  Recorded Nov. 4, 1982.
008, 6: p
008, 07-14: 1985,1982


260 0ƀ  Holland : $b Phillips, p1985.
500 ƀƀ  Originally released in 1976.
008, 6: r
008, 07-14: 1985,1976


260 0ƀ  New York : $b Columbia, $c p1983.
500 ƀƀ  "All selections previously released."
008, 6: r
008, 07-14: 1983,ƀƀƀƀ


008, Bytes 30-31 (Literary Text)

This field is not used for musical sound recordings.


007 (Physical Description Fixed Field)
Indicators
    ƀ
Subfields
    a = GMD
    b = Specific Material Designation
    d = Speed
    e = Kind of sound
    f = Groove width
    g = Dimensions
    h = Tape width
    i = Tape configuration
    m = Recording and reproduction characteristics

This field carries a coded version of the information present in field 300 (see below), area 5 of the description according to *AACR2*. Subfield c, "Original vs. Reproduction Aspect," is obsolete. Subfields j-l are for archival uses only.

300 ƀƀ  1 sound disc : $b analog, 33⅓ rpm, stereo. ; $c 12 in.
007 ƀƀ  s $b d $d b $e s $f m $g e $h n $i n $m n

300 ƀƀ  1 sound disc (35 min.) : $b digital, stereo. ; 4¾ in.
007 ƀƀ  s $b d $d z $e s $f z $g z $h n $i n $m e

300 ƀƀ  1 sound cassette : $b analog, stereo., Dolby processed
007 ƀƀ  s $b s $d l $e s $f n $g j $h l $i c $m c

024 (Standard Recording Number)
First Indicator
    1 = Universal Product Code
Second Indicator
    &#7775;
Subfields
    a = Number

Input the digits that appear underneath the bar code symbol of a Universal Product Code that appears on the container. Enter only ten-digit codes. Input the number without hyphens or spaces.

028 (Publisher's Number for Music)
First Indicator
    0 = Issue number
    1 = Matrix number
Second Indicator
    0 = No note; no added entry
    1 = Note; added entry
    2 = Note; no added entry
    3 = No note; added entry
Subfields
    a = Numerical portion
    b = Designation of source

This field should reflect the note required by *AACR2*. The name of publisher, entered in $b, should match the name in field 260 $b (label name). The number is entered as it appears on the label.

028 01  6514 379 $b Philips

In OCLC applications, sequential numbers in a set are entered in one $a, separated by two hyphens.

028 01 S 36482--S 36489 $b Angel

In other applications, multiple fields are used.

Non-sequential numbers in a set are entered in separate 028 fields. The note generation will be unwieldy, so the second indicator is set to 0 (no note) and the numbers are entered in field 500.

028 00 MS 6712 $b Columbia
028 00 MS 6872 $b Columbia
028 00 MS 7124 $b Columbia
500 &#7775;&#7775;  Columbia: MS 6712, MS 6872, MS 7124.

033 (Capture Date and Place)
518 (Data on Recording Session)

These two fields must be used in conjunction with one another. Field 033 is not used unless data on the recording session is recorded in note field 518. When field 518 is present, field 033 is also used to encode the data. Codes for field 033 come from the schedules in the *Library of Congress Classification: Class: G, Maps.*

033
First Indicator
    ƀ = No date information present
    0 = Single date
    1 = Multiple single dates
    2 = Range of dates
Second Indicator
    ƀ
Subfields
    a = Capture date
    b = Geographic classification area code
    c = Geographic classification subarea code

518
Indicators
    ƀ

033 0ƀ 19780916 $b 3964 $c N2
518 ƀƀ Recorded in Nashville, Sept. 16, 1978.

041 (Languages of Sung or Spoken Text)

When the text sung in a performance is a translation, or when accompanying textual matter is present and noted in field 008 bytes 24-29 (see above), the language of sung or spoken text (already recorded in field 008 bytes 35-37) is entered in $d. All other codes are the same as for printed music.

100, 110, 111, 700, 710, 711 $4 (Headings—Relator Codes)

For sound recordings, relator codes can be used in subfield 4 to differentiate among headings for composers, arrangers, performers, conductors, etc. MARC records for sound recordings sometimes contain these codes. These codes take the place of the obsolete fields 705 and 715, which were once used for performer added entries.

Beethoven's *Symphony no. 1* performed by the Detroit Symphony Orchestra with Antal Dorati conducting:

    100 10  Beethoven, Ludwig van, $d 1770-1827. $4 cmp
    240 10  Symphonies, $n no. 1, op. 21, $r C major
    700 10  Dorati, Antal. $r cnd
    710 20  Detroit Symphony Orchestra. $r prf

The Library of Congress only uses the relator codes "prf" and "cnd" in name headings for musical sound recordings.

245 (Title and Statement of Responsibility)
First Indicator
    0  = No title added entry
    1  = Title added entry
Second Indicator
    0-9 = Nonfiling characters
Subfields
    a  = Title proper
    b  = Other title information
    c  = Remainder of title transcription
    h  = GMD

Field 245 is encoded for recordings exactly as for scores with the single exception of the use of subfield "h" to designate the GMD.

> Sheer heart attack [sound recording]
> 245 10  Sheer heart attack $h [sound recording]

When two titles proper occur side-by-side, all are part of subfield "a" and a 740 title added entry is required to achieve a distinct title added entry for the second title proper:

> Lulu suite ; Lyric suite [sound recording] / Alban Berg.
> 245 10  Lulu suite ; Lyric suite $h [sound recording] / $c
>        Alban Berg.
> 740 01  Lyric suite.

> Dedicated to the one I love / Lowman Pauling, Ralph Bass ; [performed by] The Temprees ; arr. by Lester Snell and Tom Nixon. Explain it to her Mama / Cleophus Fultz & Leon Moore ; arr. by Jo Bridges & Tom Nixon ; [performed by] the Temprees ; rhythm by We Produced Band [sound recording].
> 245 10  Dedicated to the one I love / $c Lowman Pauling, Ralph Bass ; [performed by] The Temprees ; arr. by Lester Snell and Tom Nixon. Explain it to her Mama / Cleophus Fultz & Leon Moore ; arr. by Jo Bridges & Tom Nixon ; [performed by] the Tempress ; rhythm by We Produced Band $h [sound recording].
> 740 01  Explain it to her Mama.

300 (Physical Description)
Indicators
      Ƀ
Subfields
    a = Extent of item
    b = Other physical details
    c = Dimensions
    d = Accompanying material

This field carries the physical description from area 5 of the *AACR2* description for sound recordings.

A compact disc:

> 300 ƀƀ  1 sound disc (45 min.) : $b digital, stereo. ; $c 4¾ in.

An analog LP disc:

300 ƀƀ  1 sound disc (52 min.) : $b analog, 33⅓ rpm, stereo. ; $c 12 in.

A cassette tape:

300 ƀƀ  1 sound tape (62 min.) : $b analog, Dolby processed.


511 (Participant or Performer Note)
First Indicator
    0 = General
    1 = Cast
    2 = Presenter
    3 = Narrator
Second Indicator
    ƀ
Subfields
    a

    511 0ƀ  The Ambrosian Singers, with instrumental ensemble ; Denis
        Stevens, conductor.


518 (Data on Recording Session)

(See 033-518 above)

# Examples of Formatted Records

Because the MARC formats are designed for machine manipulation and communication of bibliographic data, there is no standard display format. That is, the same bibliographic record may be displayed in different ways in different systems. Often, the fixed field (008) is represented with different mnemonic subfield tags, line numbers may or may not be present, and subfield codes may be displayed at the start of their respective portions of a field, or less frequently as a group at the start of each field.

The example below is a MARC record for a score from the Library of Congress' MUMS system. Note that the numerical symbols on the far left are line numbers, not field tags (the field tags follow the colon), that the subfield codes are displayed as a group at the start of each field, and that the fixed field (field 008) is displayed with numeric rather than mnemonic tags (these tags do not correspond to the byte numbers) at the end of the record.

```
   INP SRCE   m  LOCATION  PERSON   VK03   AP    DATE   00/00/00
-- 010 :001:a:85-753437
-- 020 :0500:ab:M2013:.M9 K. 427 1956
-- 030 :10010:ad:Mozart, Wolfgang Amadeus,:1756-1791.
-- 040 :24010:anrsl:Masses,:K. 427,:C minor.:Vocal score.:Latin
-- 050 :24500:abc:Missa c Moll KV 427 (417a) =:C minor KV 427
(417a) /:W.A. Mozart ; herausgegeben von H.C. Robbins Landon ;
Klavier-Auszug von Josef Nebois.
-- 060 :2600:abaabc:Zurich ::Edition Kunzelmann ;:Frankfurt ;:New
York ::C.F. Peters,:c1956.
-- 070 :300:ac:1 vocal score (133 p.) ;:27 cm.
-- 080 :02822:ab:E.E. 6057a:Edition Kunzelmann
-- 090 :02830:ab:4856:Edition Peters
-- 100 :500:a:For soloists (SSTB), chorus (SSAATTBB), orchestra,
and organ; acc. arr. for piano.
-- 110 :500:a:Publisher's no.: Edition Peters Nr. 4856.
-- 120 :650-0:ax:Masses:Vocal scores with piano.
-- 130   :70010:aqd:Landon, H. C. Robbins:(Howard Chandler
Robbins),:1926-
-- 140 :70010:a:Nebois, Josef.
-- 150 :0450:b:d1783
-- 155 :048:bbbaa:va02:vd01:vf01:ca08:ka01
-- 160 :0390:abcde:2:3:3:3:3
-- 170 :908
-- 180 :FFD
01.-     02.ms    03.c     04.a     05.x     06.------07.n
08.      09.      10.-     11.      12.      13.      14.
15.lat   16.      17.      18.      19.      20.s     21.1956
22.----  23.sz    24.      25.-     26.      27.m     28.-
29.-     30.y     31.4     32.-     33.7     34.      35.7
36.a     37.      38.m     39.u     40.      41.c
```

Hindemith, Paul, 1895-1963.
   Lustige Sinfonietta : für kleines Orchester / Paul
Hindemith. -- Partitur. -- [Mainz : B. Schott's Söhne], c1980.
   1 score (118 p.) ; 35 cm.
   For chamber orchestra; in D minor.
   Reproduced from holograph.

   1. Symphonies (Chamber orchestra)--Scores. 2. Music--
Manuscripts--Facsimiles. 3. Hindemith, Paul, 1895-1963--
Manuscripts--Facsimiles. I. Title.
M1001.H66 L9                    81-770441/M/r85
                                   AACR 2      MARC

This first example of a full score illustrates the routine content-designation of a bibliographic record. The 245 field's first indicator is set to 1 to generate a title added entry, which will include all the words up to the subfield "b" indicator. Field 254 has been used to designate the musical presentation statement.

Note that the OCLC record has system generated line numbers beginning immediately after field 008 (the fixed field), but that RLIN does not. Note also that the placement of subfield indicators in both OCLC and RLIN records is the same, but that the OCLC system input convention requires spaces on either side of the subfield indicator. RLIN's input convention requires no spacing around subfield indicators.

No field 240 (uniform title) appears in this record because, according to the Library of Congress implementation of *AACR2*, when the uniform title is identical to the title proper it is not included in the bibliographic record.

In the OCLC record, the subfield "w" codes in name headings indicate that the headings are represented in the online Library of Congress authority file. These codes were inserted by the system at some point during a machine conversion (see subfield "d m/c" in field 040). The RLIN system has no comparable coding. The 040 fields on the two machine-readable records also indicate that the OCLC record was entered during a MARC tape load, but the RLIN record was keyed in by hand (by Stanford University Library).

No language code is used in field 008 byte 35-37 ("Lang," in OCLC coded "N/A"; "L" in RLIN coded ƀ) because the music has no sung or spoken text. The form of composition used as a subject heading (field 650) has also been used to encode field 008 bytes 18-19 (form of composition; "Comp" in OCLC, "FCP" in RLIN), and the medium of performance is given in encoded form in field 048. The physical format from field 300 is given in encoded form (a = full score) in field 008 byte 20. Field 008 byte 21 ("Prts" in OCLC, "PTS" in RLIN) is coded "u" (unknown), which means the originating library (Library of Congress) did not know of the availability of performance parts as a component of this bibliographic unit. Note that field 045 carries the date of composition, which is not traditionally given in the card-formatted catalog record.

```
OCLC: 12916128     Rec stat: n Entrd: 850810        Used: 870420
Type: c Bib lvl: m Lang:  N/A Source:   Accomp mat:
Repr:    Enc lvl: 1 Ctry:  gw  Dat tp: s MEBE: 1
         Mod rec:   Comp:  sy  Format: a Prts:
Desc: a Int lvl:   LTxt:  n     Dates: 1980,
   1 010      81-770441/M/r85
   2 040      DLC $c DLC $d m/c
   3 045 0     $b d1916
   4 048      ob
   5 050 0    M1001.H66 $b L9
   6 090       $b
   7 049      YCLM
   8 100 10   Hindemith, Paul, $d 1895-1963. $w cn
   9 245 10   Lustige Sinfonietta : $b fur kleines Orchester / $c Paul
Hindemith.
  10 254      Partitur.
  11 260 0    [Mainz : $b B. Schott's Sohne], $c c1980.
  12 300      1 score (118 p.) ; $c 35 cm.
  13 500      For chamber orchestra; in D minor.
  14 500      Reproduced from holograph.
  15 650 0    Symphonies (Chamber orchestra) $x Scores.
  16 650 0    Music $x Manuscripts $x Facsimiles.
  17 600 10   Hindemith, Paul, $d 1895-1963 $x Manuscripts $x Facsimiles.
$w cn
```

```
ID:DCLC81770441-C   RTYP:c    ST:p    FRN:     MS:n      EL:1       AD:08-10-85
CC:9120   BLT:cm     DCF:a    CSC:    MOD:     SNR:      ATC:       UD:01-01-01
CP:gw     L:         FCP:sy   INT:    MEI:1    AMC:
PC:s      PD:1980/            SCO:a   PTS:u    REP:
MMD:      OR:    POL:     DM:      RR:       COL:       EML:      GEN:   BSE:
010       81770441/M/r85
040       $dCStRLIN
045  0    $bd1916
048       ob
050  0    M1001.H66$bL9
100  10   Hindemith, Paul,$d1895-1963.
245  10   Lustige Sinfonietta :$bf_ur kleines Orchester /$cPaul Hindemith.
254       Partitur.
260  0    [Mainz :$bB. Schott's S_ohne],$cc1980.
300       1 score (118 p.) ;$c35 cm.
500       For chamber orchestra; in D minor.
500       Reproduced from holograph.
650  0    Symphonies (Chamber orchestra)$xScores.
650  0    Music$xManuscripts$xFacsimiles.
600  10   Hindemith, Paul,$d1895-1963$xManuscripts$xFacsimiles.
```

Wilkins, Margaret Lucy.
  Study in black & white : for piano, op. 40 / Margaret Lucy
Wilkins. -- Huddersfield, West Yorkshire, Great Britain : Satanic
Mills Press, c1983.
  7 p. of music ; 42 cm.
  cover title.
  Reproduced from holograph.
  Duration: ca. 6:00.

  1. Piano music.  2. Music--Manuscripts--Facsimiles.
3. Wilkins, Margaret Lucy--Manuscripts--Facsimiles.  I. Title.
II. Title: Study in black and white.
M25.W                                    84-758876/M
                              AACR 2    MARC

In this score example the use of field 306 to give the duration of performance in encoded form is illustrated.
Field 045 records a specific date of composition. Note that the medium of performance is coded "uu" for unknown in field 008 bytes 18-19.

```
OCLC: 12056207      Rec stat: n Entrd: 840802        Used: 861115
Type: c Bib lvl: m Lang:  N/A Source:   Accomp mat:
Repr:    Enc lvl:   Ctry:  enk Dat tp: s MEBE: 1
         Mod rec:   Comp:  uu  Format: z Prts:
Desc: a Int lvl:    LTxt:  n    Dates: 1983,
     1 010       84-758876/M
     2 040       DLC $c DLC $d m/c
     3 045 0     $b d198309
     4 048       ka01
     5 050 0     M25 $b .W
     6 090        $b
     7 049       YCLM
     8 100 10    Wilkins, Margaret Lucy. $w cn
     9 245 10    Study in black & white : $b for piano, op. 40 / $c Margaret
Lucy Wilkins.
     10 260 0    Huddersfield, West Yorkshire, Great Britain : $b Satanic
Mills Press, $c c1983.
     11 300      7 p. of music ; $c 42 cm.
     12 306      000600
     13 500      Cover title.
     14 500      Reproduced from holograph.
     15 500      Duration: ca. 6:00.
     16 650  0   Piano music.
     17 650  0   Music $x Manuscripts $x Facsimiles.
     18 600 10   Wilkins, Margaret Lucy $x Manuscripts $x Facsimiles. $w cn
     19 740 01   Study in black and white.
```

```
ID:DCLC84758876-C   RTYP:c    ST:p    FRN:     MS:n      EL:        AD:08-02-84
CC:9110  BLT:cm     DCF:a   CSC:    MOD:     SNR:      ATC:       UD:01-01-01
CP:enk      L:      FCP:uu  INT:    MEI:1    AMC:
PC:s     PD:1983/           SCO:z   PTS:n    REP:
MMD:     OR:    POL:    DM:     RR:        COL:      EML:      GEN:  BSE:
010      84758876/M
040      $dCStRLIN
045 0    $bd198309
048      ka01
050 0    M25$b.W
100 10   Wilkins, Margaret Lucy.
245 10   Study in black & white :$bfor piano, op. 40 /$cMargaret Lucy Wilkins.
260 0    Huddersfield, West Yorkshire, Great Britain :$bSatanic Mills Press,$c
         c1983.
300      7 p. of music ;$c42 cm.
306      000600
500      Cover title.
500      Reproduced from holograph.
500      Duration: ca. 6:00.
650  0   Piano music.
650  0   Music$xManuscripts$xFacsimiles.
600 10   Wilkins, Margaret Lucy$xManuscripts$xFacsimiles.
740 01   Study in black and white.
```

Dedman, Malcolm.
    [Sonatas, piano, no. 2]
      Sonata no. 2, for piano, 1984 : In search / Malcolm Dedman. --
Paigles, Essex : Anglian Edition, c1984.
      28 p. of music ; 32 cm. -- (Anglian new music series ;
ANMS 139)
      Duration: 15:00.

      1. Sonatas (Piano)  I. Title: In search.
    M23.D314 no. 2 1984                   85-750559/M
                                        AACR 2   MARC

Field 240 appears in this record to contain the *AACR2* prescribed uniform title. Note the use of the subfield indicators to designate the statements of medium ("m") and serial number ("n").

In this example the first indicator in field 245 is set to 0 because no title added entry is required by *AACR2* when a title proper is generic. However, field 740 is used to obtain a title added entry under the subtitle of the work *In Search*.

Field 008 byte 20 is encoded "z" (not a score). This corresponds to the use of the phrase "p. of music" in field 300, which is required by *AACR2* to describe music for one solo instrument.

```
OCLC: 12915659      Rec stat: n Entrd: 850219      Used: 870714
Type: c Bib lvl: m Lang:  N/A Source:   Accomp mat:
Repr:     Enc lvl:   Ctry:  enk Dat tp: s MEBE: 1
          Mod rec:   Comp:  sn  Format: z Prts:
Desc: a Int lvl:    LTxt: n    Dates: 1984,
   1 010       85-750559/M
   2 040       DLC $c DLC $d m/c
   3 045 0     $b d1984
   4 048       ka01
   5 050 0     M23 $b .D314 no. 2 1984
   6 090       $b
   7 049       YCLM
   8 100 10    Dedman, Malcolm. $w cn
   9 240 10    Sonatas, $m piano, $n no. 2
  10 245 00    Sonata no. 2, for piano, 1984 : $b In search / $c Malcolm
Dedman.
  11 260 0     Paigles, Essex : $b Anglian Edition, $c c1984.
  12 300       28 p. of music ; $c 32 cm.
  13 306       001500
  14 440 0     Anglian new music series ; $v ANMS 139
  15 500       Duration: 15:00.
  16 650 0     Sonatas (Piano)
  17 740 01    In search.
```

```
ID:DCLC85750559-C    RTYP:c    ST:p    FRN:      MS:n      EL:        AD:02-19-85
CC:9110   BLT:cm     DCF:a     CSC:    MOD:      SNR:      ATC:       UD:01-01-01
CP:enk    L:         FCP:sn    INT:    MEI:1     AMC:
PC:s      PD:1984/             SCO:z   PTS:n     REP:
MMD:      OR:    POL:     DM:      RR:           COL:      EML:      GEN:    BSE:
010       85750559/M
040       $dCStRLIN
045 0     $bd1984
048       ka01
050 0     M23$b.D314 no. 2 1984
100 10    Dedman, Malcolm.
240 10    Sonatas,$mpiano,$nno. 2
245 00    Sonata no. 2, for piano, 1984 :$bIn search /$cMalcolm Dedman.
260 0     Paigles, Essex :$bAnglian Edition,$cc1984.
300       28 p. of music ;$c32 cm.
306       001500
440  0    Anglian new music series ;$vANMS 139
500       Duration: 15:00.
650  0    Sonatas (Piano)
740 01    In search.
```

> The Reader's Digest country and western songbook / editor,
> William L. Simon ; music arranged and edited by Dan
> Fox. -- Pleasantville, N.Y. : Reader's Digest Association,
> c1983.
> 1 score (252 p.) ; 32 cm.
> For voice and piano.
> Includes chord symbols and guitar chord diagrams.
> ISBN 0-8957-7147-0.
>
> 1. Country music.  I. Simon, William L.  II. Fox, Dan.
> III. Reader's Digest Association.  IV. Title: Country and western
> songbook.
> M1630.18.R332 1983                    84-755167/M/r87
>                                        AACR 2   MARC

The title proper of this item begins with an initial article, so the second indicator in field 245 is coded 4 to represent four nonfiling characters (three letters and a space). The first indicator is set to 0 because main entry is under title. Field 740 is used to create a partial title added entry under the significant words of the title proper.

Because this score contains songs, which have words that will be sung, field 008 bytes 35-37 is coded "eng" (English). Field 045 here contains a range of dates (indicated by setting the first indicator to "2").

Note that field 043 has been used to encode the geographic area "n-us---" (United States), but the Library of Congress has neglected to use the subdivision in the subject heading (field 650). Also, field 008 bytes 18-19 are coded "sg" for songs, even though the code list includes a code "cy" (country music). This OCLC record has not undergone machine-conversion, so subfield "w" codes are not present in the name headings.

```
OCLC: 9591740       Rec stat: c Entrd: 840301        Used: 881101
Type: c Bib lvl: m Lang:  eng Source:   Accomp mat:
Repr:    Enc lvl:    Ctry: nyu Dat tp: s MEBE: 0
         Mod rec:    Comp:  sg Format: a Prts:
Desc: a Int lvl:    LTxt:  n    Dates: 1983,
    1 010       84-755167/M/r87
    2 040       DLC $c DLC
    3 019       12142276
    4 020       0895771470
    5 043       n-us---
    6 045 2     $b d1900 $b d1983
    7 048       $b vn01 $a ka01
    8 050 0     M1630.18 $b .R332 1983
    9 090       $b
   10 049       YCLM
   11 245 04  The Reader's Digest country and western songbook / $c
editor, William L. Simon ; music arranged and edited by Dan Fox.
   12 260 0    Pleasantville, N.Y. : $b Reader's Digest Association, $c
c1983.
   13 300       1 score (252 p.) ; $c 32 cm.
   14 500       For voice and piano.
   15 500       Includes chord symbols and guitar chord diagrams.
   16 650  0  Country music.
   17 700 10  Simon, William L.
   18 700 10  Fox, Dan.
   19 710 20  Reader's Digest Association.
   20 740 01  Country and western songbook.


ID:DCLC84755167-C   RTYP:c   ST:p   FRN:     MS:c    EL:       AD:03-01-84
CC:9110  BLT:cm      DCF:a   CSC:    MOD:     SNR:    ATC:      UD:11-30-87
CP:nyu   L:eng       FCP:sg  INT:    MEI:0    AMC:
PC:s     PD:1983/            SCO:a   PTS:     REP:
MMD:     OR:   POL:     DM:     RR:        COL:     EML:     GEN:    BSE:
010      84755167/M/r87
020      0895771470
043      n-us---
045 2    $bd1900$bd1983
048      $bvn01$aka01
050 0    M1630.18$b.R332 1983
245 04   The Reader's Digest country and western songbook /$ceditor, William L
. Simon ; music arranged and edited by Dan Fox.
260 0    Pleasantville, N.Y. :$bReader's Digest Association,$cc1983.
300      1 score (252 p.) ;$c32 cm.
500      For voice and piano.
500      Includes chord symbols and guitar chord diagrams.
650  0   Country music.
700 10   Simon, William L.
700 10   Fox, Dan.
710 20   Reader's Digest Association.
740 01   Country and western songbook.
```

Gilbert, Pia, 1921-
    Food : soprano and baritone soloists, trumpet, percussion, and
piano / Pia Gilbert. -- New York : C.F. Peters, c1981.
    1 score ([3], 22 p.) ; 28 cm. -- (Contemporary American music)
    English words, also printed as text on 3rd prelim. p.
    The text consists of excerpts from John Cage's Where are we
eating? And what are we eating? (38 variations on a theme by
Alison Knowles).
    "Inter-American Music Awards, published by C.F. Peters
Corporation under the sponsorship of Sigma Alpha Iota"--
Cover.
    Duration: ca. 7:00.
    Publisher's no.: Edition Peters no. 66886.

    1. Vocal duets with instrumental ensemble--Scores. 2. Cage,
John--Musical settings. I. Cage, John. II. Title.
M1528.G5F6 1981               85-750822/M
                        AACR 2   MARC

    This record includes a publisher's number, which includes an epithet. Note that the
second indicator in field 028 is set to 0 (no note; no added entry) and a general note field 500
has been used to record the eye-readable text required by *AACR2*.

```
OCLC: 13437561      Rec stat: c Entrd: 850307        Used: 881108
Type: c Bib lvl: m Lang:  eng Source:    Accomp mat:
Repr:      Enc lvl:    Ctry:  nyu Dat tp: s MEBE: 1
           Mod rec:    Comp:  uu  Format: a Prts:
Desc: a Int lvl:    LTxt:  n     Dates: 1981,
  1 010       85-750822/M
  2 040       DLC $c DLC $d m/c $d OCL
  3 019       17710195
  4 028 30    66886 $b C.F. Peters
  5 048       bb01 $a va01 $a ve01 $a pn01 $a ka01
  6 050 0     M1528.G5 $b F6 1981
  7 090        $b
  8 049       YCLM
  9 100 10    Gilbert, Pia, $d 1921- $w cn
 10 245 10    Food : $b soprano and baritone soloists, trumpet,
percussion, and piano / $c Pia Gilbert.
 11 260 0     New York : $b C.F. Peters, $c c1981.
 12 300       1 score ([3], 22 p.) ; $c 28 cm.
 13 306       000700
 14 440  0    Contemporary American music
 15 500       English words, also printed as text on 3rd prelim. p.
 16 500       The text consists of excerpts from John Cage's Where are we
eating? And what are we eating? (38 variations on a theme by Alison
Knowles).
 17 500       "Inter-American Music Awards, published by C.F. Peters
Corporation under the sponsorship of Sigma Alpha Iota"--Cover.
 18 500       Duration: ca. 7:00.
 19 500       Publisher's no.: Edition Peters no. 66886.
 20 650  0    Vocal duets with instrumental ensemble $x Scores.
 21 600 10    Cage, John $x Musical settings. $w cn
 22 700 10    Cage, John. $w cn
```

```
ID:DCLC85750822-C   RTYP:c    ST:p    FRN:     MS:n     EL:       AD:03-07-85
CC:9110  BLT:cm      DCF:a   CSC:    MOD:     SNR:     ATC:      UD:01-01-01
CP:nyu   L:eng       FCP:uu  INT:    MEI:1    AMC:
PC:s     PD:1981/            SCO:a   PTS:a    REP:
MMD:     OR:    POL:     DM:    RR:         COL:     EML:    GEN:   BSE:
010       85750822/M
028 30    66886$bC.F. Peters
040       $dCStRLIN
048       bb01$ava01$ave01$apn01$aka01
050 0     M1528.G5$bF6 1981
100 10    Gilbert, Pia,$d1921-
245 10    Food :$bsoprano and baritone soloists, trumpet, percussion, and piano
          /$cPia Gilbert.
260 0     New York :$bC.F. Peters,$cc1981.
300       1 score ([3], 22 p.) ;$c28 cm.
306       000700
440 0     Contemporary American music
500       English words, also printed as text on 3rd prelim. p.
500       The text consists of excerpts from John Cage's Where are we eating? A
          nd what are we eating? (38 variations on a theme by Alison Knowles).
500       "Inter-American Music Awards, published by C.F. Peters Corporation un
          der the sponsorship of Sigma Alpha Iota"--Cover.
500       Duration: ca. 7:00.
500       Publisher's no.: Edition Peters no. 66886.
650 0     Vocal duets with instrumental ensemble$xScores.
600 10    Cage, John$xMusical settings.
700 10    Cage, John.
```

> Two sentimental pieces : for violin and piano / edited by Rok
> Klopcic. -- New York : G. Schirmer, c1987.
> 1 score (11 p.) + 1 part (3 p.) ; 31 cm. -- (Schirmer's library of
> musical classics ; v. 1958c)
> The 1st work originally for piano, the 2nd for voice and piano.
> Contents: Valse sentimentale / Peter I. Tchaikovsky --
> Vocalise / Sergei Rachmaninoff.
> Minimal level cataloging.
>
> 1. Violin and piano music, Arranged--Scores and parts.
> I. Klopcic, Rok.
> M222.T9 1987                        87-770692/M/r88
>                                     AACR 2   MARC

This record contains a plate number, and the second indicator of field 028 has been set to 2 (note; no added entry), which will cause the system to generate a note in a card-formatted screen display or during card printing.

The code 7 in leader byte 17 ("Enc lvl" in OCLC; "EL" in RLIN) reflects the fact that this record contains minimal level cataloging.

```
OCLC: 17876107      Rec stat: c Entrd: 871218        Used: 880531
Type: c Bib lvl: m Lang:  N/A Source:   Accomp mat:
Repr:     Enc lvl: 7 Ctry: nyu Dat tp: s MEBE: 0
          Mod rec:    Comp:  wz  Format: a Prts:
Desc: a Int lvl:   LTxt: n    Dates: 1987,
    1 010      87-770692/M/r88
    2 040      DLC $c DLC
    3 028 22   48720 $b G. Schirmer
    4 050 0    M222 $b .T9 1987
    5 090       $b
    6 049      YCLM
    7 245 00   Two sentimental pieces : $b for violin and piano / $c
edited by Rok Klopcic.
    8 260 0    New York : $b G. Schirmer, $c c1987.
    9 300      1 score (11 p.) + 1 part (3 p.) ; $c 31 cm.
   10 490 0    Schirmer's library of musical classics ; $v v. 1958c
   11 500      The 1st work originally for piano, the 2nd for voice and
piano.
   12 505 0    Valse sentimentale / Peter I. Tchaikovsky -- Vocalise /
Sergei Rachmaninoff.
   13 500      Minimal level cataloging.
   14 650  0   Violin and piano music, Arranged $x Scores and parts.
   15 700 10   Klopcic, Rok.
```

```
ID:DCLC87770692-C   RTYP:c    ST:p   FRN:     MS:c      EL:7       AD:12-18-87
CC:9550  BLT:cm     DCF:a  CSC:    MOD:    SNR:      ATC:       UD:05-29-88
CP:nyu    L:        FCP:wz INT:    MEI:0   AMC:
PC:s      PD:1987/         SCO:a  PTS:a   REP:
MMD:      OR:    POL:    DM:    RR:       COL:      EML:    GEN:  BSE:
010      87770692/M/r88
028 22   48720$bG. Schirmer
050 0    M222$b.T9 1987
245 00   Two sentimental pieces :$bfor violin and piano /$cedited by Rok Klop_
         ci_c.
260 0    New York :$bG. Schirmer,$cc1987.
300      1 score (11 p.) + 1 part (3 p.) ;$c31 cm.
490 0    Schirmer's library of musical classics ;$vv. 1958c
500      The 1st work originally for piano, the 2nd for voice and piano.
505 0    Valse sentimentale / Peter I. Tchaikovsky -- Vocalise / Sergei Rachma
         ninoff.
500      Minimal level cataloging.
650  0   Violin and piano music, Arranged$xScores and parts.
700 10   Klop_ci_c, Rok.
```

Beethoven, Ludwig van, 1770-1827.
    [Concertos, piano, orchestra, no. 5, op. 73, Eb major]
    Konzert für Klavier und Orchester Nr. 5 Es-Dur op. 73 [sound recording] / Ludwig van Beethoven. -- Hamburg : Deutsche Grammophon, [1984], p1962.
    1 sound disc (39 min.) : 33⅓ rpm, stereo. ; 12 in. -- (Signature)
    Deutsche Grammophon: 410 842-1.
    Wilhelm Kempff, piano ; Berliner Philharmoniker ; Ferdinand Leitner, conductor.
    "Previously released as DG 138 777"--Container.
    Issued also as cassette: 410 842-4.

    1. Concertos (Piano)  I. Kempff, Wilhelm, 1895-
II. Leitner, Ferdinand.  III. Berliner Philharmoniker.
[M1010]                     84-759233/R
                            AACR 2   MARC

Because this record is for a sound recording, field 245 contains a GMD preceded by the subfield code "h." Field 511 is used to contain the performer statement of responsibility note prescribed by *AACR2*.

Note that area 4 of the record contains both the date of release "[1984]" and the date of copyright "p1982." This is reflected in encoded form in field 008 byte 6 ("Dat tp" in OCLC; "PC" in RLIN), which is coded "r" (reprint), and field 008 bytes 7-14 ("Dates" in OCLC; "PD" in RLIN), where both dates are recorded.

Three fields 028 are used in this record. The first reflects the label-name and number of this recording. The second and third record the label-name and numbers of the previous issue and the cassette version, both of which are indicated in notes on edition and history and other formats available as required by *AACR2*. The first 028 field has a second indicator 2 set to generate a note, but the others have second indicator 0 because a cataloger-composed note is required.

The name heading fields for the performer added entries (700, 710) contain relator codes "prf" (performer) in subfield 4.

Multiple 050 fields record two different Library of Congress call numbers. The first field contains the recommended *LCC:M* classification number, which would appear in brackets at the lower left corner of a printed card. The second field contains the label-name and number, which is used by the Library of Congress for shelving sound recordings.

Field 008 bytes 20-21 are set to "n" (not a score) because this record is for a sound recording. Field 007 contains codes identifying the physical characteristics of the disc and the recording and playback characteristics as indicated in field 300, according to *AACR2*.

```
        OCLC: 12915556      Rec stat: n Entrd: 840831        Used: 880730
        Type: j Bib lvl: m Lang:  N/A Source:   Accomp mat:
        Repr:    Enc lvl:  Ctry:  gw  Dat tp: r MEBE: 1
                 Mod rec:  Comp:  co  Format: n Prts:
        Desc: a Int lvl:   LTxt:       Dates: 1984,1962
            1 010      84-759233/R
            2 040      DLC $c DLC $d m/c
            3 007      s $b d $c u $d b $e s $f m $g e $h n $i n $j m $k p $l l $m
        u
            4 028 02   410 842-1 $b Deutsche Grammophon
            5 028 00   138 777 $b Deutsche Grammophon
            6 028 00   410 842-4 $b Deutsche Grammophon
            7 045 0     $b d1809
            8 048        $b ka01 $a oa
            9 050 1    M1010
           10 050 0    Deutsche Grammophon 410 842-1
           11 090       $b
           12 049      YCLM
           13 100 10   Beethoven, Ludwig van, $d 1770-1827. $w cn
           14 240 10   Concertos, $m piano, orchestra, $n no. 5, op. 73, $r Eb
        major
           15 245 00   Konzert fur Klavier und Orchester Nr. 5 Es-Dur op. 73 $h
        [sound recording] / $c Ludwig van Beethoven.
           16 260 0    Hamburg : $b Deutsche Grammophon, $c [1984], p1962.
           17 300      1 sound disc (39 min.) : $b 33 1/3 rpm, stereo. ; $c 12 in.
           18 306      003900
           19 490 0    Signature
           20 511 0    Wilhelm Kempff, piano ; Berliner Philharmoniker ; Ferdinand
        Leitner, conductor.
           21 500      "Previously released as DG 138 777"--Container.
           22 500      Issued also as cassette: 410 842-4.
           23 650  0   Concertos (Piano)
           24 700 10   Kempff, Wilhelm, $d 1895-  $w cn
           25 700 10   Leitner, Ferdinand. $w cn
           26 710 20   Berliner Philharmoniker. $w cn
```

```
   ID:DCLC84759233-R    RTYP:c    ST:p   FRN:     MS:n      EL:        AD:08-31-84
   CC:9110  BLT:jm      DCF:a   CSC:    MOD:     SNR:      ATC:       UD:01-01-01
   CP:gw    L:          FCP:co  INT:    MEI:1    AMC:
   PC:r        PD:1984/1962     LIT:
   RMD:d  OR:u  SPD:b  SND:s  GRV:m  DIM:e  WID:n  TC:n  KD:m  KM:p  KC:l   RC:u
   010      84759233/R
   028 02   410 842-1$bDeutsche Grammophon
   028 00   138 777$bDeutsche Grammophon
   028 00   410 842-4$bDeutsche Grammophon
   040      $dCStRLIN
   045 0    $bd1809
   048      $bka01$aoa
   050 1    M1010
   050 0    Deutsche Grammophon 410 842-1
   100 10   Beethoven, Ludwig van,$d1770-1827.
   240 10   Concertos,$mpiano, orchestra,$nno. 5, op. 73,$rEb major
   245 00   Konzert f_ur Klavier und Orchester Nr. 5 Es-Dur op. 73$h[sound record
            ing] /$cLudwig van Beethoven.
   260 0    Hamburg :$bDeutsche Grammophon,$c[1984], p1962.
   300      1 sound disc (39 min.) :$b33 1/3 rpm, stereo. ;$c12 in.
   306      003900
   490 0    Signature
   511 0    Wilhelm Kempff, piano ; Berliner Philharmoniker ; Ferdinand Leitner,
            conductor.
   500      "Previously released as DG 138 777"--Container.
   500      Issued also as cassette: 410 842-4.
   650  0   Concertos (Piano)
   700 10   Kempff, Wilhelm,$d1895- $4prf
   700 10   Leitner, Ferdinand.$4prf
   710 20   Berliner Philharmoniker.$4prf
```

Sibelius, Jean, 1865-1957.
  [Voces intimae]
  String quartet in D minor, op. 56 : Voces intimae / Jean
Sibelius. String quartet no. 14 in F sharp major, op. 142 / Dmitri
Shostakovich [sound recording]. -- Finland : Finlandia, p1982.
  1 sound disc : 33⅓ rpm, stereo. ; 12 in.
  Finlandia: FA 324.
  Sibelius Academy Quartet.
  Recorded Dec. 2-3, and 7, 1980 (1st work) and Nov. 5 and 8, 1981
(2nd work) in the Sibelius Academy Concert Hall, Helsinki.
  Durations: 27:36; 26:28.

  1. String quartets.  I. Shostakovich, Dmitrii Dmitrievich,
1906-1975. Quartets, strings, no. 14, op. 142, F# major. 1982.
II. Sibelius-Akatemia (Helsinki, Finland). Kvartetti.
[M452]                                          84-760191/R/r882
                                                AACR 2   MARC

Field 306 contains the individual durations of the two works on this recording.

Field 518 contains the note about the recording sessions required by *AACR2*, and these data appear in encoded form in two fields 033. Note that the first field 033 records a range of dates (corresponding to the phrase "Dec. 2-3 and 7), coded 2 in the first indicator, but the second field 033 records multiple single dates (corresponding to the phrase "Nov. 5 and 8"), coded 1 in the first indicator.

This recording contains two distinct works, so the analytical added entry required by the Library of Congress' implementation of *AACR2* for the second work is contained in field 700 with the second indicator set to 2 (analytical added entry).

Because the date of recording differs from the date of release, both dates are recorded in field 008 bytes 7-14, which is reflected by the code "p" in field 008 byte 6.

Field 045 has its first indicator set to 1 to indicate multiple single dates, reflecting the fact that dates of composition of two works are recorded.

```
OCLC: 12903380      Rec stat: c Entrd: 841204        Used: 880701
Type: j Bib lvl: m Lang:  N/A Source:   Accomp mat:
Repr:     Enc lvl:   Ctry: fi Dat tp: p MEBE: 1
          Mod rec:   Comp:  uu Format: n Prts:
Desc: a Int lvl:   LTxt:      Dates: 1982,1980
   1 010      84-760191/R/r882
   2 040      DLC $c DLC
   3 007      s $b d $c u $d b $e s $f m $g e $h n $i n $j m $k p $l l $m
u
   4 028 02  FA 324 $b Finlandia
   5 033 2   19801202 $a 19801203 $a 19801207 $b 6964 $c H4
   6 033 1   19811105 $a 19811108 $b 6964 $c H4
   7 045 1    $b d1909 $b d1973
   8 048      sa02 $a sb01 $a sc01
   9 050 1   M452
  10 050 0   Finlandia FA 324
  11 090      $b
  12 049     YCLM
  13 100 10  Sibelius, Jean, $d 1865-1957.
  14 240 10  Voces intimae
  15 245 00  String quartet in D minor, op. 56 : $b Voces intimae / $c
Jean Sibelius. String quartet no. 14 in F sharp major, op. 142 / Dmitri
Shostakovich $h [sound recording].
  16 260 0   Finland : $b Finlandia, $c p1982.
  17 300     1 sound disc : $b 33 1/3 rpm, stereo. ; $c 12 in.
  18 306     002736 $a 002628
  19 511 0   Sibelius Academy Quartet.
  20 518     Recorded Dec. 2-3, and 7, 1980 (1st work) and Nov. 5 and 8,
1981 (2nd work) in the Sibelius Academy Concert Hall, Helsinki.
  21 500     Durations: 27:36; 26:28.
  22 650 0   String quartets.
  23 700 12  Shostakovich, Dmitrii Dmitrievich, $d 1906-1975. $t
Quartets, $m strings, $n no. 14, op. 142, $r F# major. $f 1982.
  24 710 20  Sibelius-Akatemia (Helsinki, Finland). $b Kvartetti. $4 prf
```

```
ID:DCLC84760191-R   RTYP:c    ST:p    FRN:     MS:c      EL:        AD:12-04-84
CC:9110  BLT:jm     DCF:a   CSC:    MOD:     SNR:      ATC:       UD:07-02-88
CP:fi    L:         FCP:uu  INT:    MEI:1    AMC:
PC:p        PD:1982/1980       LIT:
RMD:d  OR:u  SPD:b  SND:s  GRV:m  DIM:e  WID:n  TC:n  KD:m  KM:p  KC:l   RC:u
010      84760191/R/r882
028 02  FA 324$bFinlandia
033 2   19801202$a19801203$a19801207$b6964$cH4
033 1   19811105$a19811108$b6964$cH4
045 1   $bd1909$bd1973
048     sa02$asb01$asc01
050 1   M452
050 0   Finlandia FA 324
100 10  Sibelius, Jean,$d1865-1957.
240 10  Voces intimae
245 00  String quartet in D minor, op. 56 :$bVoces intimae /$cJean Sibelius.
        String quartet no. 14 in F sharp major, op. 142 / Dmitri Shostakovich$h
        [sound recording].
260 0   Finland :$bFinlandia,$cp1982.
300     1 sound disc :$b33 1/3 rpm, stereo. ;$c12 in.
306     002736$a002628
511 0   Sibelius Academy Quartet.
518     Recorded Dec. 2-3, and 7, 1980 (1st work) and Nov. 5 and 8, 1981 (2nd
        work) in the Sibelius Academy Concert Hall, Helsinki.
500     Durations: 27:36; 26:28.
650 0   String quartets.
700 12  Shostakovich, Dmitri_i Dmitrievich,$d1906-1975.$tQuartets,$mstrings,$
        nno. 14, op. 142,$rF# major.$f1982.
710 20  Sibelius-Akatemia (Helsinki, Finland).$bKvartetti.$4prf
```

Christ, Peter, oboist.
   Oboist Peter Christ [sound recording]. -- Sedro Woolley,
WA : Crystal Records, p1986.
    1 sound disc : digital, stereo. ; 4¾ in.
   Crystal Records: CD321.
   The 4th work is for narrator and oboe.
   Peter Christ, oboe ; Crystal Chamber Soloists.
   Recorded in Los Angeles, 1972 (3rd work) and 1978 (the
remainder).
   Previously released on S321 and S812.
   Compact disc.
   Contents: Suite for oboe, clarinet & viola / Randall Thompson
(15:39) -- Parable : for solo oboe / Vincent Persichetti (4:55) --
Duo for flute & oboe / Alberto Ginastera (8:07) -- The Sparrow
and Mr. Avaunt / William Schmidt (8:08) -- Miniatures : for flute,
oboe & piano / William Grant Still (12:14).

   1. Suites (Clarinet, oboe, viola)  2. Oboe music.  3. Flute and
oboe music.  4. Monologs with music (Oboe)  5. Trios (Piano,
flute, oboe)  I. Thompson, Randall, 1899-     Suite, oboe, clarinet,
viola. 1986. II. Persichetti, Vincent, 1915-     Parable, no. 3.
1986. III. Ginastera, Alberto, 1916-     Duet, flute, oboe, op. 13.
1986. IV. Schmidt, William, 1926-     Sparrow and the amazing
Mr. Avaunt. 1986. V. Still, William Grant, 1895-     Miniatures.
1986. VI. Crystal Chamber Soloists.  VII. Title.
[M5]                             86-754385
                                  AACR 2   MARC

   This anthology is entered under the heading for a principal performer and the name heading in field 100 contains the subfield 4 relator code "prf." Also, because this recording contains works for differing performing media, multiple fields 048 are used to reflect the specific instrumentation of each work. Although several works are recorded here, only one is in a type of composition corresponding to a code in the list for field 008 bytes 18-19, so field 047 is not required and the code "su" (suite) is entered in field 008.

```
OCLC: 16710104      Rec stat: n Entrd: 861009        Used: 880711
Type: j Bib lvl: m Lang:  eng Source:    Accomp mat:
Repr:     Enc lvl:    Ctry:  wau Dat tp: r MEBE: 1
          Mod rec:    Comp:   su  Format: n Prts:
Desc: a Int lvl:     LTxt:       Dates: 1986,
    1 010      86-754385
    2 040      DLC $c DLC
    3 007      s $b d $c u $d z $e s $f n $g z $h n $i n $j m $k l $l n $m
e
    4 028 02   CD321 $b Crystal Records
    5 028 00   S321 $b Crystal Records
    6 028 00   S812 $b Crystal Records
    7 033 0    1972 $b 4364 $c L8
    8 033 0    1978 $b 4364 $c L8
    9 045 0     $b d1971
   10 048      wb01 $a wc01 $a sb01
   11 048      wb01
   12 048      wa01 $a wb01
   13 048      vn01 $a wb01
   14 048      wa01 $a wb01 $a ka01
   15 050 1    M5
   16 050 0    Crystal Records CD321
   17 090       $b
   18 049      YCLM
   19 100 10   Christ, Peter, $c oboist. $4 prf
   20 245 10   Oboist Peter Christ $h [sound recording].
   21 260 0    Sedro Woolley, WA : $b Crystal Records, $c p1986.
   22 300      1 sound disc : $b digital, stereo. ; $c 4 3/4 in.
   23 306      001539 $a 000455 $a 000807 $a 000808 $a 001214
   24 500      The 4th work is for narrator and oboe.
   25 511 0    Peter Christ, oboe ; Crystal Chamber Soloists.
   26 518      Recorded in Los Angeles, 1972 (3rd work) and 1978 (the
remainder).
   27 500      Previously released on S321 and S812.
   28 500      Compact disc.
   29 505 0    Suite for oboe, clarinet & viola / Randall Thompson (15:39)
-- Parable : for solo oboe / Vincent Persichetti (4:55) -- Duo for flute
& oboe / Alberto Ginastera (8:07) -- The Sparrow and Mr. Avaunt /
William Schmidt (8:08) -- Miniatures : for flute, oboe & piano / William
Grant Still (12:14).
   30 650  0   Suites (Clarinet, oboe, viola)
   31 650  0   Oboe music.
   32 650  0   Flute and oboe music.
   33 650  0   Monologs with music (Oboe)
   34 650  0   Trios (Piano, flute, oboe)
   35 700 12   Thompson, Randall, $d 1899-  $t Suite, $m oboe, clarinet,
viola. $f 1986.
   36 700 12   Persichetti, Vincent, $d 1915-  $t Parable, $n no. 3. $f
1986.
   37 700 12   Ginastera, Alberto, $d 1916-  $t Duet, $m flute, oboe, $n
op. 13. $f 1986.
   38 700 12   Schmidt, William, $d 1926-  $t Sparrow and the amazing Mr.
Avaunt. $f 1986.
   39 700 12   Still, William Grant, $d 1895-  $t Miniatures. $f 1986.
   40 710 20   Crystal Chamber Soloists. $4 prf
```

```
ID:DCLC86754385-R    RTYP:c    ST:p    FRN:      MS:n      EL:       AD:10-09-86
CC:9110  BLT:jm       DCF:a    CSC:    MOD:      SNR:      ATC:      UD:01-01-01
CP:wau     L:eng      FCP:su   INT:    MEI:1     AMC:
PC:r       PD:1986/            LIT:
RMD:d  OR:u  SPD:z  SND:s  GRV:n  DIM:z  WID:n  TC:n  KD:m  KM:l  KC:n    RC:e
010       86754385
028 02    CD321$bCrystal Records
028 00    S321$bCrystal Records
028 00    S812$bCrystal Records
033 0     1972$b4364$cL8
033 0     1978$b4364$cL8
045 0     $bd1971
048       wb01$awc01$asb01
048       wb01
048       wa01$awb01
048       vn01$awb01
048      ·wa01$awb01$aka01
050 1     M5
050 0     Crystal Records CD321
100 10    Christ, Peter,$coboist.$4prf
245 10    Oboist Peter Christ$h[sound recording].
260 0     Sedro Woolley, WA :$bCrystal Records,$cp1986.
300       1 sound disc :$bdigital, stereo. ;$c4 3/4 in.
306       001539$a000455$a000807$a000808$a001214
500       The 4th work is for narrator and oboe.
511 0     Peter Christ, oboe ; Crystal Chamber Soloists.
518       Recorded in Los Angeles, 1972 (3rd work) and 1978 (the remainder).
500       Previously released on S321 and S812.
500       Compact disc.
505 0     Suite for oboe, clarinet & viola / Randall Thompson (15:39) -- Parabl
          e : for solo oboe / Vincent Persichetti (4:55) -- Duo for flute & oboe
          / Alberto Ginastera (8:07) -- The Sparrow and Mr. Avaunt / William Schm
          idt (8:08) -- Miniatures : for flute, oboe & piano / William Grant Stil
          l (12:14).
650 0     Suites (Clarinet, oboe, viola)
650 0     Oboe music.
650 0     Flute and oboe music.
650 0     Monologs with music (Oboe)
650 0     Trios (Piano, flute, oboe)
700 12    Thompson, Randall,$d1899- $tSuite,$moboe, clarinet, viola.$f1986.
700 12    Persichetti, Vincent,$d1915- $tParable,$nno. 3.$f1986.
700 12    Ginastera, Alberto,$d1916- $tDuet,$mflute, oboe,$nop. 13.$f1986.
700 12    Schmidt, William,$d1926- $tSparrow and the amazing Mr. Avaunt.$f1986.
700 12    Still, William Grant,$d1895- $tMiniatures.$f1986.
710 20    Crystal Chamber Soloists.$4prf
```

Françaix, Jean, 1912-
  [Selections]
    Quatuor à cordes ; Trois epigrammes : quatre voix mixtes et quintette a cordes ; L'heure du berger : quatuor à cordes, contrebasse et piano ; Huit danses exotiques : pour deux pianos ; Juvénalia : cantate satirique pour quatre voix mixtes et deux pianos [sound recording] / Jean Françaix. -- St.-Mandé : A. Charlin ; N[ew] Y[ork] : Distributed by Qualiton Imports, p1985.
    1 sound disc : analog, 33⅓ rpm, stereo. ; 12 in. -- (Musique française)
    A. Charlin: CCPE 1.
    The 3rd work is a suite.
    Suzanne Lafaye, soprano, Genevieve Macaux, mezzo-soprano, Paul Derenne, tenor, Andre Veissiere, bass (works 2 and 5) ; Gaston Logerot, double bass (works 2-3) ; Claude and Jean Françaix, pianos (works 4-5) ;  Quatuor Lowenguth (works 1-3).
    Distributor from label mounted on container.

    1. Instrumental music.  2. Vocal music.  I. Lafaye, Suzanne.
  II. Macaux, Genevieve.  III. Derenne, Paul.  IV. Veissiere, Andre.
  V. Logerot, Gaston.  VI. Françaix, Claude.  VII. Françaix, Jean,
  1912-        VIII. Françaix, Jean, 1912-        Quartets, strings. 1985.
  IX. Françaix, Jean, 1912-        Epigrammes. 1985.  X. Françaix,
  Jean, 1912-        Heure du berger. 1985.  XI. Françaix, Jean,
  1912-        Danses exotiques. 1985.  XII. Françaix, Jean, 1912-
  Juvénalia. 1985.  XIII. Quatuor Lowenguth.  XIV. Title: Trois
  epigrammes.  XV. Title: 3 epigrammes.  XVI. Title: Epigrammes.
  XVII. Heure du berger.  XVIII. Title: Huit danses exotiques.
  XIX. Title: 8 danses exotiques.  XX. Title: Danses exotiques.
  XXI. Title: Juvénalia.  XXII. Series.
  [M3.1]                                                      85-754322/R
                                                          AACR 2    MARC

    Notice in these records the analytical added entries, and the analytical title added entries in 740 fields.
    This anthology also contains works composed in several different forms. Three of these forms correspond to terms on the list for field 008 bytes 18-19, so the code "mu" (multiple) is entered there, and field 047 is used with repeating "a" subfields to record the three types of composition: "su" (suite), "df" (dance forms), and "ct" (cantata).

```
OCLC: 13438093     Rec stat: c Entrd: 851004        Used: 880420
Type: j Bib lvl: m Lang:  fre Source:    Accomp mat:
Repr:    Enc lvl:    Ctry:  fr Dat tp: s MEBE: 1
         Mod rec:    Comp:  mu Format: n Prts:
Desc: a Int lvl:    LTxt:        Dates: 1985,
     1 010       85-754322/R
     2 040       DLC $c DLC $d m/c
     3 007       s $b d $c u $d b $e s $f m $g e $h n $i n $j m $k p $l l $m
u
     4 028 02   CCPE 1 $b A. Charlin
     5 045 1     $b d1934 $b d1938 $b d1947 $b d1957
     6 047       su $a df $a ct
     7 048       sa02 $a sb01 $a sc01
     8 048        $b va01 $b vb01 $b vd01 $b vf01 $a sa02 $a sb01 $a sc01 $a
sd01
     9 048       sa02 $a sb01 $a sc01 $a sd01
    10 048       ka01 $a ka01
    11 048        $b va01 $b vb01 $b vd01 $b vf01 $a ka01 $a ka01
    12 050 1    M3.1
    13 050 0    A. Charlin CCPE 1
    14 090       $b
    15 049       YCLM
    16 100 10   Francaix, Jean, $d 1912- $w cn
    17 240 10   Selections
    18 245 00   Quatuor `a cordes ; Trois epigrammes : $b quatre voix
mixtes et quintette `a cordes ; L'heure du berger : quatuor `a cordes,
contrebasse et piano ; Huit danses exotiques : pour deux pianos ;
Juv'enalia : cantate satirique pour quatre voix mixtes et deux pianos $h
[sound recording] / $c Jean Francaix.
    19 260 0    St.-Mand'e : $b A. Charlin ; $a N[ew] Y[ork] : $b
Distributed by Qualiton Imports, $c p1985.
    20 300      1 sound disc : $b analog, 33 1/3 rpm, stereo. ; $c 12 in.
    21 440  0   Musique francaise
    22 500      The 3rd work is a suite.
    23 511 0    Suzanne Lafaye, soprano, Genevi`eve Macaux, mezzo-soprano,
Paul Derenne, tenor, Andr'e Veissiere, bass (works 2 and 5) ; Gaston
Logerot, double bass (works 2-3) ; Claude and Jean Francaix, pianos
(works 4-5) ; Quatuor Lowenguth (works 1-3).
    24 500      Distributor from label mounted on container.
    25 650  0   Instrumental music.
    26 650  0   Vocal music.
    27 700 10   Lafaye, Suzanne. $w cn
    28 700 10   Macaux, Genevi`eve. $w cn
    29 700 10   Derenne, Paul. $w cn
    30 700 10   Veissiere, Andr'e. $w cn
    31 700 10   Logerot, Gaston. $w cn
    32 700 10   Francaix, Claude. $w cn
    33 700 10   Francaix, Jean, $d 1912- $w cn
    34 700 12   Francaix, Jean, $d 1912- $t Quartets, $m strings. $f 1985.
$w cn
    35 700 12   Francaix, Jean, $d 1912- $t Epigrammes. $f 1985. $w cn
    36 700 12   Francaix, Jean, $d 1912- $t Heure du berger. $f 1985. $w
cn
    37 700 12   Francaix, Jean, $d 1912- $t Danses exotiques. $f 1985. $w
cn
    38 700 12   Francaix, Jean, $d 1912- $t Juv'enalia. $f 1985. $w cn
    39 710 20   Quatuor Lowenguth. $w cn
    40 740 01   Trois epigrammes.
    41 740 01   3 epigrammes.
    42 740 01   Epigrammes.
    43 740 01   Heure du berger.
    44 740 01   Huit danses exotiques.
    45 740 01   8 danses exotiques.
    46 740 01   Danses exotiques.
    47 740 01   Juv'enalia.
```

```
ID:DCLC85754322-R    RTYP:c    ST:p    FRN:    MS:c    EL:        AD:10-04-85
CC:9110  BLT:jm       DCF:a   CSC:    MOD:    SNR:    ATC:       UD:01-01-01
CP:fr    L:fre       FCP:mu  INT:    MEI:1   AMC:
PC:s     PD:1985/            LIT:
RMD:d  OR:u  SPD:b  SND:s  GRV:m  DIM:e  WID:n  TC:n  KD:m  KM:p  KC:1  RC:u
010      85754322/R
028 02   CCPE 1$bA. Charlin
040      $dCStRLIN
045 1    $bd1934$bd1938$bd1947$bd1957
047      su$adf$act
048      sa02$asb01$asc01
048      $bva01$bvb01$bvd01$bvf01$asa02$asb01$asc01$asd01
048      sa02$asb01$asc01$asd01
048      ka01$aka01
048      $bva01$bvb01$bvd01$bvf01$aka01$aka01
050 1    M3.1
050 0    A. Charlin CCPE 1
100 10   Fran_caix, Jean,$d1912-
240 10   Selections
245 00   Quatuor `a cordes ; Trois epigrammes :$bquatre voix mixtes et quintet
         te `a cordes ; L'heure du berger : quatuor `a cordes, contrebasse et pi
         ano ; Huit danses exotiques : pour deux pianos ; Juv_enalia : cantate s
         atirique pour quatre voix mixtes et deux pianos$h[sound recording] /$cJ
         ean Fran_caix.
260 0    St.-Mand_e :$bA. Charlin ;$aN[ew] Y[ork] :$bDistributed by Qualiton I
         mports,$cp1985.
300      1 sound disc :$banalog, 33 1/3 rpm, stereo. ;$c12 in.
440  0   Musique fran_caise
500      The 3rd work is a suite.
511 0    Suzanne Lafaye, soprano, Genevi`eve Macaux, mezzo-soprano, Paul Deren
         ne, tenor, Andr_e Veissiere, bass (works 2 and 5) ; Gaston Logerot, dou
         ble bass (works 2-3) ; Claude and Jean Fran_caix, pianos (works 4-5) ;
         Quatuor Lowenguth (works 1-3).
500      Distributor from label mounted on container.
650  0   Instrumental music.
650  0   Vocal music.
700 10   Lafaye, Suzanne.$4prf
700 10   Macaux, Genevi`eve.$4prf
700 10   Derenne, Paul.$4prf
700 10   Veissiere, Andr_e.$4prf
700 10   Logerot, Gaston.$4prf
700 10   Francaix, Claude.$4prf
700 10   Fran_caix, Jean,$d1912- $4prf
700 12   Fran_caix, Jean,$d1912- $tQuartets,$mstrings.$f1985.
700 12   Fran_caix, Jean,$d1912- $tEpigrammes.$f1985.
700 12   Fran_caix, Jean,$d1912- $tHeure du berger.$f1985.
700 12   Fran_caix, Jean,$d1912- $tDanses exotiques.$f1985.
700 12   Fran_caix, Jean,$d1912- $tJuv_enalia.$f1985.
710 20   Quatuor Lowenguth.$4prf
740 01   Trois epigrammes.
740 01   3 epigrammes.
740 01   Epigrammes.
740 01   Heure du berger.
740 01   Huit danses exotiques.
740 01   8 danses exotiques.
740 01   Danses exotiques.
740 01   Juv_enalia.
```

Domingo, Placido, 1941-
    Placido Domingo sings great love scenes with Renata Scotto, Kiri
Te Kanawa, Ileana Cotrubas [sound recording]. -- New York,
N.Y. : CBS Masterworks, [1984]
      1 sound disc : 33⅓ rpm, stereo. : 12 in.
    CBS Masterworks: M 39030.
    Sung in French and Italian.
    Cover title: Great love scenes.
    Placido Domingo, tenor ; with, variously, Renata Scotto, Kiri
Te Kanawa, Ileana Cotrubas, sopranos ; various orchestras and
conductors.
    English, French, and German translations inserted in container.
    Issued also as cassette.
    Contents: Madama Butterfly. The wedding night : Act 1 /
Puccini (Renata Scotto ; Philharmonia Orchestra ; Lorin Maazel,
conductor) (10:40) -- Adriana Lecouvreur. The lovers' meeting :
Act 1 / Cilea (Renata Scotto ; Philharmonia Orchestra ; James
Levine, conductor) (6:30) -- La rondine. The farewell : Act III /
Puccini (Kiri Te Kanawa ; London Symphony Orchestra ; Lorin
Maazel, conductor) (12:00) -- Manon. Love renewed : Act III,
scene 2 / Massenet (Renata Scotto ; National Philharmonic
Orchestra ; Kurt Herbert Adler, conductor) (8:47) -- Louise. Love's
paradise : Act III, scene I / Charpentier (Ileana Cotrubas ; New
Philharmonia Orchestra ; Georges Pretre, conductor) (6:30) --
Romeo et Juliette. The tragic parting : Act IV, scene I /
Gounod (Renata Scotto ; National Philharmonic Orchestra ; Kurt
Herbert Adler, conductor) (13:30)

    1. Operas--Excerpts. I. Scotto, Renata, 1934-    II. Te Kanawa,
Kiri. III. Cotrubas, Ileana. IV. Title. V. Title: Great love
scenes.
M1505                                  85-750986/R
                                       AACR 2   MARC

    The example shown in these records illustrates the capacity of the MARC format for
lengthy contents notes. In online systems with the capability of searching note fields, each
performance on this anthology is potentially accessible.

```
OCLC: 12916793      Rec stat: c Entrd: 850319          Used: 880915
Type: j Bib lvl: m Lang:  fre Source:   Accomp mat: d
Repr:     Enc lvl:   Ctry: nyu Dat tp: r MEBE: 1
          Mod rec:   Comp:   op Format: n Prts:
Desc: a Int lvl:   LTxt:        Dates: 1984,1976
   1 010      85-750986/R
   2 040      DLC $c DLC $d OCL $d m/c
   3 007      s $b d $c u $d b $e s $f m $g e $h n $i n $j m $k p $l l $m
u
   4 019      10973490 $a 11253812
   5 028 02  M 39030 $b CBS Masterworks
   6 041 0    $d freita $e engfreger $h freita
   7 050 1   M1505
   8 050 0   CBS Masterworks M 39030
   9 090      $b
  10 049      YCLM
  11 100 10  Domingo, Pl'acido, $d 1941- $w cn
  12 245 10  Pl'acido Domingo sings great love scenes with Renata
Scotto, Kiri Te Kanawa, Ileana Cotrubas $h [sound recording].
  13 260 0   New York, N.Y. : $b CBS Masterworks, $c [1984]
  14 300      1 sound disc : $b 33 1/3 rpm, stereo. : $c 12 in.
  15 500      Sung in French and Italian.
  16 500      Cover title: Great love scenes.
  17 511 0   Pl'acido Domingo, tenor ; with, variously, Renata Scotto,
Kiri Te Kanawa, Ileana Cotrubas, sopranos ; various orchestras and
conductors.
  18 500      English, French, and German translations inserted in
container.
  19 500      Issued also as cassette.
  20 505 0   Madama Butterfly. The wedding night : Act 1 / Puccini
(Renata Scotto ; Philharmonia Orchestra ; Lorin Maazel, conductor)
(10:40) -- Adriana Lecouvreur. The lovers' meeting : Act 1 / Cilea
(Renata Scotto ; Philharmonia Orchestra ; James Levine, conductor)
(6:30) -- La rondine. The farewell : Act III / Puccini (Kiri Te Kanawa ;
London Symphony Orchestra ; Lorin Maazel, conductor) (12:00) -- Manon.
Love renewed : Act III, scene 2 / Massenet (Renata Scotto ; National
Philharmonic Orchestra ; Kurt Herbert Adler, conductor) (8:47) --
Louise. Love's paradise : Act III, scene I / Charpentier (Ileana
Cotrubas ; New Phlharmonia Orchestra ; Georges Pr^etre, conductor)
(6:30) -- Romeo et Juliette. The tragic parting : Act IV, scene I /
Gounod (Renata Scotto ; National Philharmonic Orchestra ; Kurt Herbert
Adler, conductor) (13:30).
  21 650  0  Operas $x Excerpts.
  22 700 10  Scotto, Renata, $d 1934- $w cn
  23 700 10  Te Kanawa, Kiri. $w cn
  24 700 10  Cotrubas, Ileana. $w cn
  25 740 01  Great love scenes.
```

```
ID:DCLC85750986-R    RTYP:c    ST:p    FRN:    MS:n      EL:      AD:03-19-85
CC:9110  BLT:jm    DCF:a   CSC:    MOD:    SNR:      ATC:     UD:01-01-01
CP:nyu      L:fre    FCP:op  INT:    MEI:1   AMC:d
PC:r       PD:1984/1976      LIT:
RMD:d  OR:u  SPD:b  SND:s  GRV:m  DIM:e  WID:n  TC:n  KD:m  KM:p  KC:l    RC:u
010       85750986/R
028 02  M 39030$bCBS Masterworks
040       $dCStRLIN
041 0   $dfreita$eengfreger$hfreita
050 1   M1505
050 0   CBS Masterworks M 39030
100 10  Domingo, Pl_acido,$d1941- $4prf
245 10  Pl_acido Domingo sings great love scenes with Renata Scotto, Kiri Te
     Kanawa, Ileana Cotrubas$h[sound recording].
260 0   New York, N.Y. :$bCBS Masterworks,$c[1984]
300       1 sound disc :$b33 1/3 rpm, stereo. :$c12 in.
500       Sung in French and Italian.
500       Cover title: Great love scenes.
511 0   Pl_acido Domingo, tenor ; with, variously, Renata Scotto, Kiri Te Kan
     awa, Ileana Cotrubas, sopranos ; various orchestras and conductors.
500       English, French, and German translations inserted in container.
500       Issued also as cassette.
505 0   Madama Butterfly. The wedding night : Act 1 / Puccini (Renata Scotto
     ; Philharmonia Orchestra ; Lorin Maazel, conductor) (10:40) -- Adriana
     Lecouvreur. The lovers' meeting : Act 1 / Cilea (Renata Scotto ; Philha
     rmonia Orchestra ; James Levine, conductor) (6:30) -- La rondine. The f
     arewell : Act III / Puccini (Kiri Te Kanawa ; London Symphony Orchestra
      ; Lorin Maazel, conductor) (12:00) -- Manon. Love renewed : Act III, s
     cene 2 / Massenet (Renata Scotto ; National Philharmonic Orchestra ; Ku
     rt Herbert Adler, conductor) (8:47) -- Louise. Love's paradise : Act II
     I, scene I / Charpentier (Ileana Cotrubas ; New Phlharmonia Orchestra ;
      Georges Pr^etre, conductor) (6:30) -- Romeo et Juliette. The tragic pa
     rting : Act IV, scene I / Gounod (Renata Scotto ; National Philharmonic
      Orchestra ; Kurt Herbert Adler, conductor) (13:30).
650 0   Operas$xExcerpts.
700 10  Scotto, Renata,$d1934- $4prf
700 10  Te Kanawa, Kiri.$4prf
700 10  Cotrubas, Ileana.$4prf
740 01  Great love scenes.
```

Moore, Hugh.
　　Hello city limits [sound recording] / [performed by] Hugh
Moore ; with Roby Huffman and the Bluegrass Cutups. --
N.Y.C. [i.e. New York City] : Folkways, p1986.
　　1 sound disc : analog, 33⅓ rpm ; 12 in.
　　Folkways: FTS 31108.
　　Hugh Moore, lead vocal, banjo ; Roby Huffman, tenor vocal,
rhythm guitar ; Bluegrass Cutups (vocals, fiddle, mandolin, guitar,
electric bass, pedal steel).
　　Recorded at Star Recording Co., Miller's Creek, N.C., Aug.
1985.
　　Program notes (2 p.) inserted in container.
　　Contents: Hello city limits / John Elgin (2:20) -- Ashes of love /
J. & J. Anglin (2:24) -- The family who prays / Louvin Brothers
(3:20) -- Pain in my heart / B. Osborne & L. Richardson (2:17) --
Let it ride / Hugh Moore (2:28) -- I'll break out again tonight
(3:08) -- Old flames / H. Moffat, P. Sebert (3:36) -- Never again /
Benny Williams (2:07) -- The coo coo bird (2:15) -- Marshals reel /
Hugh Moore (2:30).

　　1. Bluegrass music--1981-　　I. Huffman, Roby.　II. Bluegrass
Cutups.　III. Title.
[M1630.18]　　　　　　　　　　　　　　　　　87-752341/R
　　　　　　　　　　　　　　　　　　　　　AACR 2　MARC

　　The bibliographic records for this recording of bluegrass music demonstrate the versatility of the MARC formats, and their capacity for containing and communicating all bibliographic data. The bibliographic data are not remarkable; which is to say, there is little difference between the way this record reflects the content of the catalog record and the formatting of any of the preceding bibliographic records. Field 008 bytes 18-19 contain a code "bg" for bluegrass, and field 043 contains a code "n-us---" indicating the cultural orientation of the music. Otherwise, these records are just like those illustrated above.

```
OCLC: 16713758      Rec stat: n Entrd: 870629      Used: 870918
Type: j Bib lvl: m Lang:  eng Source:    Accomp mat: g
Repr:     Enc lvl:     Ctry:  nyu Dat tp: p MEBE: 1
          Mod rec:     Comp:  bg Format: n Prts:
Desc: a Int lvl:     LTxt:        Dates: 1986,1985
    1 010       87-752341/R
    2 040       DLC $c DLC
    3 007       s $b d $c u $d b $e u $f m $g e $h n $i n $j m $k p $l l $m
u
    4 028 02    FTS 31108 $b Folkways
    5 033 0     198508-- $b 3903 $c W7
    6 043       n-us---
    7 050 1     M1630.18
    8 050 0     Folkways FTS 31108
    9 090          $b
   10 049       YCLM
   11 100 10    Moore, Hugh. $4 prf
   12 245 10    Hello city limits $h [sound recording] / $c [performed by]
Hugh Moore ; with Roby Huffman and the Bluegrass Cutups.
   13 260 0     N.Y.C. [i.e. New York City] : $b Folkways, $c p1986.
   14 300       1 sound disc : $b analog, 33 1/3 rpm ; $c 12 in.
   15 511 0     Hugh Moore, lead vocal, banjo ; Roby Huffman, tenor vocal,
rhythm guitar ; Bluegrass Cutups (vocals, fiddle, mandolin, guitar,
electric bass, pedal steel).
   16 518       Recorded at Star Recording Co., Miller's Creek, N.C., Aug.
1985.
   17 500       Program notes (2 p.) inserted in container.
   18 505 0     Hello city limits / John Elgin (2:20) -- Ashes of love / J.
& J. Anglin (2:24) -- The family who prays / Louvin Brothers (3:20) --
Pain in my heart / B. Osborne & L. Richardson (2:17) -- Let it ride /
Hugh Moore (2:28) -- I'll break out again tonight (3:08) -- Old flames /
H. Moffat, P. Sebert (3:36) -- Never again / Benny Williams (2:07) --
The coo coo bird (2:15) -- Marshals reel / Hugh Moore (2:30).
   19 650  0    Bluegrass music $y 1981-
   20 700 10    Huffman, Roby. $4 prf
   21 710 20    Bluegrass Cutups. $4 prf
```

```
ID:DCLC87752341-R    RTYP:c    ST:p    FRN:     MS:n     EL:      AD:06-29-87
CC:9110  BLT:jm      DCF:a     CSC:    MOD:     SNR:     ATC:     UD:01-01-01
CP:nyu   L:eng       FCP:bg    INT:    MEI:1    AMC:g
PC:p        PD:1986/1985       LIT:
RMD:d  OR:u  SPD:b  SND:u  GRV:m  DIM:e  WID:n  TC:n  KD:m  KM:p  KC:1  RC:u
010       87752341/R
028 02    FTS 31108$bFolkways
033 0     198508--$b3903$cW7
043       n-us---
050 1     M1630.18
050 0     Folkways FTS 31108
100 10    Moore, Hugh.$4prf
245 10    Hello city limits$h[sound recording] /$c[performed by] Hugh Moore ; w
      ith Roby Huffman and the Bluegrass Cutups.
260 0     N.Y.C. [i.e. New York City] :$bFolkways,$cp1986.
300       1 sound disc :$banalog, 33 1/3 rpm ;$c12 in.
511 0     Hugh Moore, lead vocal, banjo ; Roby Huffman, tenor vocal, rhythm gui
      tar ; Bluegrass Cutups (vocals, fiddle, mandolin, guitar, electric bass
      , pedal steel).
518       Recorded at Star Recording Co., Miller's Creek, N.C., Aug. 1985.
500       Program notes (2 p.) inserted in container.
505 0     Hello city limits / John Elgin (2:20) -- Ashes of love / J. & J. Angl
      in (2:24) -- The family who prays / Louvin Brothers (3:20) -- Pain in m
      y heart / B. Osborne & L. Richardson (2:17) -- Let it ride / Hugh Moore
       (2:28) -- I'll break out again tonight (3:08) -- Old flames / H. Moffa
      t, P. Sebert (3:36) -- Never again / Benny Williams (2:07) -- The coo c
      oo bird (2:15) -- Marshals reel / Hugh Moore (2:30).
650  0    Bluegrass music$y1981-
700 10    Huffman, Roby.$4prf
710 20    Bluegrass Cutups.$4prf
```

# Notes

[1]Garrett Bowles to Walter Gerboth, letter 28 December 1971, in *The MARC Music Format: From Inception to Publication*, by Donald Seibert (Philadelphia, Pa.: Music Library Association, 1982), 25.

[2]Yves LeCompte, "Comment nous utilisons l'electro-mecanographie," *Fontes artis Musicae* 4 (1957): 38-41.

[3]James B. Coover, "Computers, Cataloguing, and Co-operation," *Notes* 25 (1969): 437-46.

[4]Seibert, *MARC Music Format*.

[5]Smiraglia and Papakhian document the scope of the OCLC music database in "Music in the OCLC Online Union Catalog: A Review," *Notes* 38 (1981): 257-74.

[6]Leonore S. Maruyama and Henriette D. Avram, "2. Cataloguing and the Computer," *Fontes artis Musicae* 19 (1972): 165.

[7]Library of Congress. Automated Systems Office, *MARC Formats for Bibliographic Data* (Washington, D.C.: Library of Congress, 1980).

[8]Readers who are unfamiliar with the MARC books format may wish to consult Walt Crawford, *MARC for Library Use: Understanding the USMARC Formats*, Professional Librarian Series (White Plains, N.Y.: Knowledge Industry Publications, c1984).

# Suggested Reading

Coover, J. B. "Computers, Cataloguing, and Co-operation." *Notes* 25 (1969): 437-46.

Crawford, Walt. *MARC for Library Use: Understanding the USMARC Formats.* Professional Librarian Series. White Plains, N.Y.: Knowledge Industry Publications, c1984.

Library of Congress. Automated Systems Office. *MARC Formats for Bibliographic Data.* Washington, D.C.: Library of Congress, 1980.

_____. MARC Development Office. *Music: A MARC Format.* Washington, D.C.: Library of Congress, 1976.

Maruyama, L. S., and H. D. Avram. "Cataloging and the Computer." *Fontes artes Musicae* 19 (1972): 164-71.

Seibert, Donald. *The MARC Format: From Inception to Publication.* MLA Technical Report, No. 13. Philadelphia, Pa.: Music Library Association, 1982.

# 9
# *AUTHORITY CONTROL*

## Introduction

Authority control is the essential process in bibliographic control that creates and maintains the catalog's syndetic structure. It is this characteristic, the connections among headings, that makes collocating devices out of what would otherwise be mere finding lists.

Less broadly, authority control is at the very least the process of controlling access points by recording authorized forms and all variants, and referring from all variant forms. Relationships among access points and the entities they represent may also be expressed and made accessible through authority control. The records derived from this process, called authority records, constitute an authority file. Authority work is the procedural aspect of authority control that encompasses establishing the authorized access points and discovering the variant and related forms. True authority control requires linkage between the headings represented in the authority records and the physical objects represented by the records in the bibliographic file.[1]

Authority control in music is no different from authority control in general. Authority work, by contrast, is both more complex and more commonplace. Musicians' work is not linked to any particular linguistic tradition, therefore a wide variety of forms of names appear on the internationally produced and marketed manifestations of musical works. Further, the widespread use of uniform titles to represent musical works means that much reference work must be engaged in to establish headings, and that the results must be recorded to support future decision making.[2] As a result, music cataloging requires a thorough familiarity with the structure, content, and uses of authority records. This chapter examines some typical music authority records. Examples in this chapter are all from the OCLC online Library of Congress authority file. With the exception of the display format of the fixed field (field 008) these records do not differ from those found in the RLIN online Library of Congress authority file.

## Music Authority Records

Authority records can be made to record headings of any kind, and the decisions made about their structure and use. Components commonly found in authority records are: 1) the authorized heading; 2) *see* references, from variant forms; and 3) *see also* references from related forms. Other components that are useful but less commonly found are: 1) symbols indicating the status of the heading and the rules under which it was devised; and 2) source data that justify decisions made about the form of the heading and its references. Machine-readable Library of Congress authority records have become a de facto standard in U. S. libraries. For a variety of reasons, mostly historical, these records vary in the amount of secondary information they contain.

*NAMES AND UNIFORM TITLES*

The most commonly encountered authority records in music cataloging are name authority records that control the headings for composers and performers, and name/uniform title authority records that control the headings for musical works.

```
ARN: 736571      Rec stat: c      Entrd: 840822          Used: 880310
Type: z          Geo subd: n      Govt agn: _ Lang:      Source:
Roman: _         Subj: a          Series: n   Ser num: n Head: aab
Ref status: a    Upd status: a    Auth status: a         Name: a
Enc lvl: n       Auth/Ref: a      Mod rec:               Rules: c
```

```
1 010      n  82039539
2 040      DLC $c DLC $d DLC
3 100 10   Sessions, Roger, $d 1896-
4 400 10   Sessions, Roger Huntington, $d 1896-
5 670      Centeno, A. The intent of the artist ... 1941.
6 670      His Conversations with Roger Sessions, c1987: $b CIP in
published book (hdg.: Sessions, Roger, 1896-1985)
```

This is an example of a name authority record. This record controls the heading for the composer Roger Sessions. The heading is indicated in the 100 (1xx) field. According to the code "c" in the Rules fixed field (008 byte 39), the heading was established according to *AACR2*. A *see* reference from a fuller form of the name is given in the 400 (4xx) field. Subfield codes within the fields for the headings are the same as in the heading fields of MARC bibliographic records. As source data, field 670 gives a brief citation of a book used to establish this heading.

In the next record, which controls the name heading for the performer Chick Corea, source data consist of descriptions of the location of information about the name and birth date on one of Corea's recordings. The birth date's appearance in the second 670 field probably indicates that it was not known when the heading was established for the recording in the first 670 field. It is LC policy to include dates in *AACR2* headings whenever they are known. This record also includes biographical information in field 678, called the *epitome field*, to distinguish the name in future if necessary.

```
ARN: 626143      Rec stat: c      Entrd: 840821        Used: 850805
Type: z          Geo subd: n      Govt agn: _ Lang:    Source:
Roman: _         Subj: a          Series: n  Ser num: n Head: aab
Ref status: n    Upd status: a    Auth status: a       Name: a
Enc lvl: n       Auth/Ref: a      Mod rec:             Rules: c

  1 010       n  81080890
  2 040       DLC $c DLC $d DLC
  3 100 10    Corea, Chick.
  4 670       His Inner space. [Phonodisc] 1973.
  5 670       Mozart, W. A. Double concerto, KV 365 [SR] p1984: $b label
(Chick Corea) container (b. 1941)
  6 678       Jazz pianist and composer
```

```
ARN: 618994      Rec stat: n      Entrd: 840821        Used: 840821
Type: z          Geo subd: n      Govt agn: _ Lang:    Source:
Roman: _         Subj: a          Series: n  Ser num: n Head: aab
Ref status: a    Upd status: a    Auth status: a       Name: n
Enc lvl: n       Auth/Ref: a      Mod rec:             Rules: c

  1 010       n  81073693
  2 040       DLC $c DLC
  3 110 20    Academy of St. Martin-in-the-Fields.
  4 410 20    Academy of Saint Martin-in-the-Fields $w nna
  5 670       Handel, G. F. $b Twelve concerti grossi, op. 6.
[Phonodisc] 1969.
  6 678       Orchestra
```

This record controls the corporate name heading for the performing group Academy of St. Martin-in-the-Fields. The subfield codes in the 410 field indicate that though this variant is recorded as a *see* reference, no reference will actually appear in the file because the heading in this field is simply a pre-*AACR2* form of heading, not a true variant form of the name.

### Musical Works

The preceding records have controlled name headings. The next two examples illustrate authority records that control the name/uniform title headings for musical works.

```
ARN: 941938      Rec stat: n      Entrd: 840823      Used: 840823
Type: z          Geo subd: n      Govt agn: _ Lang:      Source:
Roman: _         Subj: a          Series: n   Ser num: n Head: aab
Ref status: a    Upd status: a    Auth status: a         Name: a
Enc lvl: n       Auth/Ref: a      Mod rec:               Rules: c
```

```
   1 010       n  83056870
   2 040          DLC $c DLC
   3 100 10       Britten, Benjamin, $d 1913-1976. $t Insect pieces
   4 400 10       Britten, Benjamin, $d 1913-1976. $t 2 insect pieces
   5 400 10       Britten, Benjamin, $d 1913-1976. $t Two insect pieces
   6 670          English music for oboe [SR] 1983? (a.e.) $b label (Two
insect pieces)
```

The record above controls the heading for a single work, Britten's *Insect Pieces*. The entire heading for the work is contained in one 100 field. The author portion appears in the "a" subfield and the title portion in the "t" subfield. According to the source data portion of this record the heading is used as an analytical added entry for the sound recording *English Music for Oboe*. The version of the title on the label of that recording is *Two Insect Pieces*. The *see* references are made to refer users from both the variant title found on the label and a potential variation that might be sought, *Two* represented as a numeral 2.

```
ARN: 707432      Rec stat: c      Entrd: 840822      Used: 880607
Type: z          Geo subd: n      Govt agn: _ Lang:      Source:
Roman: _         Subj: a          Series: n   Ser num: n Head: aab
Ref status: a    Upd status: a    Auth status: a         Name: a
Enc lvl: n       Auth/Ref: a      Mod rec:               Rules: c
```

```
   1 010       n  82010139
   2 040          DLC $c DLC $d DLC
   3 100 10       Schumann, Robert, $d 1810-1856. $t Vocal music. $k
Selections
   4 400 10       Schumann, Robert Alexander, $d 1810-1856. $t Works, $m
vocal. $k Selections $w nnaa
   5 500 10       Schumann, Robert, $d 1810-1856. $t Gesange
   6 500 10       Schumann, Robert, $d 1810-1856. $t Songs
```

This authority record controls a collective uniform title heading. The *see* reference in the second 400 field is from a title proper found on an anthology of Schumann's vocal music to the authorized collective uniform title.

### Series

The final example is an authority record for a music series. Note that the fields following the name heading record LC's decisions about analyzing (full analytics), tracing (traced), and classifying (separately) the individual monographic scores issued in this series.

```
ARN: 8974        Rec stat: n      Entrd: 840817        Used: 840817
Type: z          Geo subd: n      Govt agn: _ Lang:    Source:
Roman: _         Subj: a          Series: a   Ser num: a Head: aaa
Ref status: n    Upd status: a    Auth status: a       Name: n
Enc lvl: n       Auth/Ref: a      Mod rec:             Rules: c
```

```
1 010        n  42009491
2 040        DLC $c DLC
3 130   0    Diletto musicale.
4 642        Nr. 781 $5 DLC
5 643        Wien $b Doblinger.
6 644        f $5 DLC
7 645        t $5 DLC
8 646        s $5 DLC
9 670        Gatti, L. 6 Sonaten fur Violine und Viola, c1980.
```

## SUBJECTS

Authority records are also used to control subject headings. These records indicate additional relationships among terms that are not commonly expressed among headings for either names or works. These include references from broader terms and related terms. An example is the following subject authority record for the heading "Concerti grossi."

```
ARN: 2028078     Rec stat: c      Entrd: 871218        Used: 871218
Type: z          Geo subd: _      Govt agn: _ Lang:    Source:
Roman: _         Subj: a          Series: n   Ser num: n Head: bab
Ref status: a    Upd status: a    Auth status: a       Name: n
Enc lvl: n       Auth/Ref: a      Mod rec:             Rules: n
```

```
1 010        sh 85029628
2 040        DLC $c DLC $d DLC
3 053        M1040 $b M1041 $c Orchestral accompaniment
4 053        M1140 $b M1141 $c String-orchestra accompaniment
5 150   0    Concerti grossi
6 550   0    Concertos $w g
```

# Conclusion

Great potential exists in the realization that authority control can be used for more than tracing *see* references. If authority control were extended to the alphabetic portions of publisher's numbers, tremendous advantage would be gained for the bibliographic control of the output of publishers and record manufacturers.

Even greater potential exists in the understanding that the authority record controls details that describe works as distinct from the description of items. Authority files could be used to link related works, particularly derivative works.

Music librarians have searched for appropriate ways to control access to musical information, such as thematic material represented in notation or in encoded form that could produce notation. This argument has turned on whether the appropriate locus for such work-related information is in the bibliographic record, where it would have to be repeated for every manifestation. If the authority record were truly the locus for all work-related data, even greater capability for online bibliographic control of musical works could be realized in the future.

# Notes

[1]For a thorough treatment of authority control see Robert H. Burger, *Authority Work: The Creation, Use, Maintenance, and Evaluation of Authority Records and Files* (Littleton, Colo.: Libraries Unlimited, 1985).

[2]An indication of the potential variety of forms of music titles is given in Richard P. Smiraglia, "Uniform Titles for Music: An Exercise in Collocating Works." *Cataloging & Classification Quarterly* 9, no. 3 (1989): 97-114.

# Suggested Reading

Burger, Robert H. *Authority Work: The Creation, Use, Maintenance, and Evaluation of Authority Records and Files*. Littleton, Colo.: Libraries Unlimited, 1985.

Taylor, Arlene G. "Authority Control and System Design." In *Policy and Practice in the Bibliographic Control of Nonbook Media*, 64-81. Edited by Sheila S. Intner and Richard P. Smiraglia. Chicago: American Library Association, 1987.

# 10
# *ARRANGEMENT AND FILING*

## Introduction

Many have assumed that filing and catalog arrangement issues were no longer important (or at least were passe) in the online era. However, because of the complexity of music entries it is important for system designers to consider the useful arrangement of entries for musical works, for musical performances, and for descriptions of music materials. This chapter presents a historical overview of filing and arrangement practices in music catalogs, followed by discussion of filing and arrangement issues that remain unresolved at present.

## Codes for Filing Music
## Uniform Titles

Early codes for filing catalog cards did not explicitly mention music materials, yet it is easy to draw a parallel from various approaches to categorical filing to the eventual development of special rules for organizing musical works. It was unquestionably a filing dilemma: the entries for variant manifestations of a given work would *not* collocate under a composer heading. This was the impetus for modifications of title information that eventually lead to the widespread use of uniform titles for musical works.

Cutter's *Rules* included instructions for a classified arrangement of entries under the heading for an author.[1] The arrangement allowed for separate sequences of complete works, selections, single works, and works about the author. This approach, which persisted in music catalogs until the 1980 filing revisions, facilitated a hierarchical approach to finding a particular musical work. If an edition could not be located directly under its own title, it could be sought in a collection. If a Gesamtausgabe were present it was certain to supply a score of the original work. This ability to move from the specific to a more general heading in a known-item search was the chief advantage of classified filing. Other special arrangements were encouraged for voluminous authors, and Cutter recommended a synopsis be supplied at the beginning of the author file when the arrangement was especially complex.

Cutter's filing was word-by-word, and hyphenated terms were treated as separate words. Editions were to be arranged chronologically, earliest first with analytical entries interfiled among the other editions. Translations were arranged immediately following the original, with the name of the language prefixed to the title, in alphabetical order by language. Works about the composer would file at the end in a separate sequence, but criticisms would follow the entries for editions of the work.

The 1942 first edition of the *A.L.A. Rules for Filing Catalog Cards* was published immediately following distribution of the ill-fated 1941 ALA draft catalog code.[2] These filing rules carried Cutter's tradition of categorical, word-by-word filing forward. Alphabetical subarrangements were recommended under the heading for an author, but the classified (or grouped) arrangement continued to be recommended for classic or voluminous authors. There were still no rules especially designed for musical works.

It was at this time, 1941-1942, that the MLA draft cataloging codes for music and sound recordings were being issued in mimeographed format. This draft code contained the first rules for music uniform titles, referred to as "conventional titles." These uniform titles were designed to aid collocation of editions of works, and further, to distinguish among works with similar titles, and to group collected editions in much the same way as Cutter's classified filing. From about 1943 onward uniform titles were used on Library of Congress cataloging for musical works and thereby came to be widely used by music libraries.[3] Rules for ordering conventionalized uniform titles were needed, and were subsequently developed at the Library of Congress.

In 1958 the joint MLA/ALA code for cataloging music and sound recordings included as its final chapter "Filing Rules for Conventional Titles."[4] These were LC's internal rules for filing cards with music uniform titles. The classified arrangement introduced by Cutter was continued. Uniform titles that began with the word *Works* were to be filed at the beginning of a composer's file. This would cause the arrangement of complete works by date (in the rare event that more than one *Gesamtausgabe* were available for a composer), followed by all partial collections, subarranged first by medium of performance and date.

[Works]
[Works, organ]
[Works, piano]
[Works, piano. Selections]
[Works, violin]

Uniform titles beginning with the name of a type of composition were to be interfiled in a single sequence whether the lead term appeared in the singular or the plural.

[Sonata, violin & continuo, no. 1, C major]
[Sonatas, violin & continuo, no. 2-4]
[Sonata, violin & continuo, no. 5, B minor]

Numerals used to indicate the number of instruments or voices were subarranged in numerical order following the alphabetical arrangement of the terms indicating the medium. This was intended to collocate works by medium within a particular genre or form of composition group.

[Quartet, violin, viola, violoncello, double bass ... ]
[Quartet, 2 violins, viola, violoncello ... ]
[Quartet, 4 violins ... ]

Both of these arrangement problems, collocation of forms whether singular or plural and collocation of medium within form despite number, were eventually to be obviated by changes to the rules in *AACR2*.

Punctuation was regarded in filing uniform titles. The filing sequence specified was closing bracket, semicolon, period, parentheses, comma and/or ampersand. This sequence was used to preserve the general-specific hierarchy as well as to cause arrangements to follow original editions, the musical equivalent of the grouping of translations.

[Concertos, harpsichord, op.3]
[Concertos, harpsichord, op.3; arr.]
[Concertos, harpsichord, op. 3. Selections]
[Concerto, harpsichord, op. 3, no. 2, C major]

Uniform titles including terms indicating a manifestation of a work (libretto, piano-vocal score, selections) were to be grouped alphabetically preceding excerpts from a work.

[Carmen. Libretto]
[Carmen. Piano-vocal score]
[Carmen. Selections; arr.]
[Carmen. Suite]

followed by:

[Carmen. Je dis que rien ne m'épouvante]
[Carmen. Fleur que tu m'avais jetée]
[Carmen. Habanera]
[Carmen. Parle-moi de ma mère]

Entries with identical uniform titles (including an italicized general material designation, which was added following the uniform title, thus creating two alphabetical sequences for scores and recordings) were to be subarranged by date of publication. Analytical added entries were thus to be interfiled with main entries to create a single chronological sequence of manifestations of a work. Other composer-uniform title entries (added entries for related works and subject headings) were to be filed following the entries that represented manifestations of the work.

The 1958 rules cover only the classified arrangement of uniform titles for musical works. There is no mention of the arrangement of music subject headings.

The 1961 *Limited Code*, volume 2 of the IAML code, included in its appendix the statement "Arrangement of the Author Catalog."[5] The arrangement suggested here was an even more complex classified arrangement. Works were to be grouped according to genre: theatrical works, vocal works, instrumental works, pedagogical works, and cross references. It was assumed that literary works would be filed in some other catalog, presumably the library's main catalog. Theatrical and pedagogical works were to be subarranged alphabetically by title with translations immediately following the original work, and excerpts arranged alphabetically behind all entries for the complete work. Vocal and instrumental works were to be arranged by form of composition or medium of performance, whichever was more suitable for the given collection.

Undoubtedly this complex suggested arrangement reflects practices in libraries outside North America, where broadly based public service is not a given goal of most libraries. The logic of the approach shows a remarkable understanding of the bibliographic forms that populate music collections but would no doubt seriously confuse all but the most expert users. This suggested arrangement can be seen as a turning point, for from this time on filing rules were to grow ever simpler, reflecting the need to utilize computer-amenable arrangements.

The 1967 publication of *AACR* included an updated version of music rules (see chapter 2), and the 1968 *ALA Rules for Filing Catalog Cards*,[6] second edition, the publication of which was timed to accompany that of *AACR*, also include for the first time rules for filing entries for both music and sound recordings. These rules appear as section B of rule 37, "Non-book Material Arrangement," which also included rules for manuscripts, motion pictures, non-musical sound recordings, and radio and television programs. A preliminary note recognizes the fact that most libraries keep separate catalogs for each nonbook medium, but the general rule is to interfile all entries, with the book entry to be followed by the nonbook should there be otherwise identical manifestations.

With only a few changes the 1968 rules repeat those found in the 1958 joint code. The 1968 rules were characterized by their many options, and this is true for music materials as well. In general a single alphabetical sequence is suggested under the heading for a composer, but an option allows all entries with the uniform title "Works" to be filed first, thus maintaining the classified arrangement. Likewise, a single alphabetical sequence is suggested under the lead term for a musical work, but an option allows the separate arrangement of manifestations of the whole work to precede an alphabetical sequence of excerpts from the work.

The chief departure in the 1968 rules from the 1958 LC provisions is in the subarrangement of identical entries. Subarrangement of identical entries is by title proper for music; identical titles proper are subarranged by date; entries with identical titles and dates are ordered by physical format: score, miniature score, parts. Sound recordings are subarranged by the name of the manufacturer, with further subarrangement alphanumerically by the label number as appropriate.

No further rules for filing music entries appeared. A Music Library Association code was attempted in the 1970s, but this effort seems to have come to nought by the end of the decade.[7] In 1980 the new ALA and LC rules were published.[8] Both of these publications reflect the need to utilize computers to arrange grouped displays of access points, with card arrangement a subsidiary goal. Both sets of rules indicate a single sequence, presumably undisturbed by material types, arranged character-by-character according to a list of characters: spaces, numerals 0-9, letters A-Z. This approach is essentially a word-by-word arrangement. Both codes base their first order of subarrangement on the functions of the access points. The ALA rules have four categories: references for main and added entries, main and added entries, references for subject entries, and subject entries. The LC rules first categorize identical access points as person, place, thing (including topical subjects), or title, then subarrange by function.

LC rules further categorize uniform titles for musical works, grouping identical leading elements by their second elements. These include dates, languages, arranged statements, and form subheadings and excerpt titles interfiled. This grouping will retain the order whole work, translation, arrangement, and parts of a work as in the music rules noted earlier. However, manifestations of the whole work (i.e., vocal scores, or selections) will be interfiled with single excerpts in a departure from the traditional arrangement of musical works. This difference is difficult to explain since content-designation for uniform titles could be used to achieve the categorical arrangement of earlier rules. The ALA rules have no such provisions at all, and uniform titles under identical lead terms will be arranged word-by-word.

Subarrangement of identical access points with the same function, that is, access points for the same manifestation of a work, is by title proper and date in the rules. Optionally, name only added entries, such as those for performers, may be arranged by main entry; thus a performer's recorded repertoire would be arranged by album title and/or composer given the provisions of *AACR2*.

# Problems

## DICTIONARY VERSUS DIVIDED CATALOGS

The first decision to be made in the structure of the music catalog is whether to implement an integrated dictionary catalog including bibliographic records for all kinds of materials, or to establish some sort of divided catalog. This decision is critical because it will determine which kinds of entries will have the potential for collocation in a given file structure.

As noted briefly elsewhere in this book, a variety of catalog structures and formats has been devised for use in music libraries and for music collections of general libraries. It is probably safe to say that integrated dictionary catalogs were rare until very recently. Partially because music and recording collections were often housed apart from book collections, and partially because rules for cataloging music and recordings were nonexistent or too volatile, it was not considered appropriate to integrate cataloging for various types of nonbook materials with that for books. Thus the traditional divided catalog in a music library is divided by format, not by type of entry, and is really a series of material-exclusive dictionary catalogs. A typical academic library arrangement was one catalog for the scores and books, and another for the sound recordings. In many libraries the entries for the books were also filed in a union catalog in the main library, but the entries for the music materials were unique and therefore accessible only in the music library catalog.

Whatever management objective is satisfied by this approach should be viewed in light of Cutter's original objectives for the dictionary catalog, which were, essentially, to show what the library has. Obviously, many types of music library users could benefit from the collocation of variant physical manifestations of the same musical work with its performances as well as analyses and histories of it. Following the implementation of *AACR2* in 1981 and perhaps related to its unified, integrated approach to the construction of bibliographic records for all kinds of materials, many libraries have begun to turn to integrated catalogs. Another impetus in this direction has been the implementation of OPACs, which in their file structure can be made to mimic either integrated or material-exclusive dictionary catalogs.

## MANUFACTURER'S, PLATE, AND PUBLISHER'S NUMBERS

The value of access points based on publisher's name, plate and publisher's numbers, and recording manufacturer's label-name and label and matrix numbers has been discussed elsewhere in this book. Many libraries have maintained separate catalogs of these access points, and they are now commonly indexed in OPACs and online bibliographic networks. Problems arise because the access points, though similar to both corporate names and series titles, are not authority controlled in any way. The lists below indicate some of the potential difficulties in controlling these files.

Boosey & Hawkes B. & H. 20058
Boosey & Hawkes B.&H. 16303
Boosey & Hawkes B. & H. 20231
Hawkes B. & H. 16948
Hawkes B. & H. 16949

These are plate numbers from the music publisher Boosey & Hawkes. Obviously the last two plate numbers are transcribed from printed music issued by the publisher under the name of Hawkes.

Breitkopf & Härtel 6694
Breitkopf & Härtel 8291
Breitkopf & Härtel 8292
Breitkopf & Härtel Wb. 1624
Breitkopf & Härtel Wb. 1656

These plate numbers are transcribed from scores issued by Breitkopf & Härtel. This old and respected German publisher was split into two different entities after the second World War. The numbers with "Wb." are issued from the Wiesbaden (West German) branch.

Should these headings be filed in numerical order, disregarding the change of heading, or entered under a uniform heading? Or should the numbers issued by each named entity be kept separate, following the rule of corporate emanation?

Universal Edition U.E. 15453
Universal Edition U.E. 15477
Universal Edition UE 16968

These Universal Edition plate numbers have been transcribed exactly as they appeared. The slight variation in punctuation of the initialism would result in filing that would not preserve the numerical sequence in systems that treat punctuation as spaces. Should the numbers be transcribed as they appear (as descriptive data), or entered in a uniform fashion (as access points), or both?

EMI His Master's Voice 5E 063-34484
His Master's Voice EALP 1304
His Master's Voice ECSD 2739
His Master's Voice EL 27 0157 1
His Master's Voice LHMV 1006

Similar problems afflict the use of recording manufacturer's label-name and number as access points. In this list we see another example of irregular transcription of the same label-name. (His Master's Voice is a subsidiary of EMI.) We also have evidence of a new wrinkle, however, which is the alphabetical prefix and the structure of the numbers. Should the alphabetical prefixes be regarded? Should the spaces in the numerical portions be regarded?

At present each library that utilizes files of these access points utilizes its own conventions for their transcription and arrangement. In many online files the various numbers are jumbled together as they have been transcribed. The effect of this on searching is that exact matches must be sought for known item searches, and browsing a manufacturer or publisher file (for collection development, for example) may not be possible. A potential solution to these dilemmas is to recognize the utility of these numbers both bibliographically, as transcribed inherent descriptive data, and for retrieval, as structured, precoordinated, and authority controlled access points.

## COMPOSER, PERFORMER INTERFILED

The arrangement of entries under a particular name has an added dimension in the music catalog. Under earlier rules performer entries for sound recordings were always added entries and would therefore file behind the main entries for the same person as a composer. In *AACR2* performer main entry is frequent. In this context a categorical arrangement must be considered if separation of composer and performer entries under the same name is considered desirable. This result can be achieved to some extent by subarranging first by uniform title then by title proper, on the premise that uniform titles will not be present on records where the entry is designated for a performance rather than a composition. Consistent use of MARC relator codes in headings can also be used to achieve this result.

## CLASSIFIED OR ALPHABETICAL ARRANGEMENT OF COMPOSER'S WORK

A variety of approaches to this problem has been attempted, ranging from the simple character-by-character alphabetical approach used with the 1980 ALA rules to the IAML code's suggested categorical arrangement by type of work. Under earlier cataloging rules (e.g., *AACR*) it was considered desirable to keep all anthologies in one sequence so that a user who was unsuccessful in locating a separate edition of a work could then seek that work in an anthology. This result was achieved by using "Works" for complete collections and "Works, piano," "Works, violin," etc., for incomplete collections. Thus all anthologies were collocated under the form heading "Works" and subsequently arranged by medium of performance. Headings established using *AACR2* prefer the phrase headings "Piano music" or "Violin music" for partial collections, thus scattering anthologies by medium. Categorical arrangement would be possible if the separate MARC field tags for these collective uniform titles were used (243). Strictly alphabetical arrangements have been preferred in most online systems, however. Likewise, the manifestations of a work (its arrangements, excerpts, translations, and various scorings, for example) are now usually arranged in a strictly alphabetical sequence.

## GENERIC TITLES VERSUS SUBJECT HEADINGS

The assignment of added entries for titles of musical works with generic titles has always been considered superfluous. It was assumed that the arrangement of bibliographic records under these titles would result in a confused plethora of entries under similar but uncontrolled names of types of composition. Consequently, precoordinated authority controlled subject headings have been preferred to title added entries for all such works, on the premise that the controlled vocabulary of the subject thesaurus would provide better access. This is undoubtedly true in the card catalog, where title and subject headings would have been interfiled to some extent. However, in the online file known-item retrieval (such as searching for a bibliographic record for cataloging) can be enhanced by the use of a specific title proper (such as that on the item in hand).

# Notes

[1]Charles A. Cutter, *Rules for a Dictionary Catalog*, 4th ed., rewritten (Washington, D.C.: Government Printing Office, 1906). Cf. rule "11. Arrangement."

[2]*A.L.A. Rules for Filing Catalog Cards*, prepared by a Special Committee, Sophie K. Hiss, Chairman (Chicago: American Library Association, 1942).

[3]C. Sumner Spalding, "Music Authority Files at the Library of Congress," *Music Cataloging Bulletin* 10, no. 10 (October 1979): 4-6.

[4]Music Library Association, *Code for Cataloging Music and Phonorecords* (Chicago: American Library Association, 1958), iv.

[5]*Limited Code*, Code international de catalogage de la musique, Vol. II (Frankfurt, West Germany; New York: C. F. Peters, 1961), 38-40.

[6]*ALA Rules for Filing Catalog Cards*, 2nd ed., prepared by the ALA Editorial Committee's Subcommittee on the ALA Rules for Filing Catalog Cards, Pauline G. Seely, Chairman and Editor (Chicago: American Library Association, 1968), 218-27.

[7]These curious notices are too numerous to list here. Apparently a subcommittee ascertained that three-quarters of the respondents to a survey used rules based on ALA or LC practice, and set about to compile a set of comparative rules based on those two sources. By 1976 a

preliminary set of rules was in trial use at six unidentified libraries. A 1980 notice of the chairman's new address is the last record of this activity, which apparently succumbed to a lack of interest as libraries moved into online systems and thereby lost their autonomous music catalogs.

[8]Filing Committee, Resources and Technical Services Division, American Library Association, *ALA Filing Rules* (Chicago: American Library Association, 1980); and *Library of Congress Filing Rules*, prepared by John C. Rather and Susan C. Biebel (Washington, D.C.: Library of Congress, 1980).

# Suggested Reading

*Policy and Practice in the Bibliographic Control of Nonbook Media.* Edited by Sheila S. Intner and Richard P. Smiraglia. Chicago: American Library Association for the Resources and Technical Services Division, 1987.

"Symposium on Music in Libraries: Contributed by Various Libraries in the United States." *Library Journal* (August 1915): 563-94.

Weihs, Jean R., Shirley Lewis, and Janet Macdonald. *Nonbook Materials: The Organization of Integrated Collections.* 2nd ed. Ottawa: Canadian Library Association, 1979.

# 11
# SOURCES OF
# MUSIC COPY

The preceding chapters have examined the intellectual issues involved in the bibliographic control of music materials, and specifically the practices known collectively as cataloging and classification. The music librarian who is well versed in these details will be well prepared to perform original cataloging of a wide variety of music materials.

Universal bibliographic control has been a goal of librarians and scholars for centuries. Copy cataloging, or utilizing the fruit of someone else's labor, has long been an option for music librarians. Cooperative cataloging efforts have been undertaken repeatedly in the history of music librarianship and have spawned some notable results. A major impetus for the construction of the multivolume IAML code was to provide unified rules for cooperative music cataloging. The implementation of the MARC Music Format at OCLC in 1976 and the subsequent building of a shared music database by OCLC member libraries is another tribute to the determination of music librarians to provide cooperative sources of bibliographic data.[1] The most recent example of this effort has been the implementation on a national, multinetwork basis of a cooperative retrospective conversion project to make bibliographic data for the nation's music holdings available in machine-readable form.[2]

In this chapter major sources of bibliographic data for music materials, both printed and machine-readable, are examined and issues in the adaptation of copy cataloging are discussed.

## Sources for Copy

Printed catalogs of music collections have long been made available for scholarly uses. It is only since about 1953 that printed union catalogs, most notably the Library of Congress catalogs, were also designed for the use of libraries wishing to adapt the bibliographic records for local use. Machine-readable cataloging, which at first duplicated printed sources but has now largely replaced them, has been available from networks and later the Library of Congress since about 1977.

### PRINTED CATALOGS

#### Library of Congress Catalogs

The 1915 *Library Journal* "Symposium on Music in Libraries" included a detailed contribution from Otto Kinkeldey that described "American Music Catalogs."[3] The printed catalog of the Allen P. Brown collection at the Boston Public Library had appeared between

1910 and 1915. The four-part catalog of the Library of Congress' music holdings prepared by Oscar Sonneck had appeared between 1908 and 1914. These catalogs, together with the 1869 catalog of Joseph Drexel's Philadelphia music collection (since moved to New York Public), were only the beginning of attempts to disseminate widely bibliographic data about North American music holdings. Kinkeldey's article stresses the fact that the Boston and LC catalogs show the results of a "first attempt at a really bibliographical music catalog" as opposed to finding lists published by European libraries.[4] The LC catalog detailed the holdings of dramatic music, orchestral music, early books on music, and opera librettos. It would be nearly four decades before another music catalog would be published at LC.

Some cataloging for music materials, notably collections of ballads, hymnals and other liturgical music, and various popular anthologies, can be located in the *National Union Catalog: Pre-1956 Imprints.* Comprehensive cataloging of music had begun in 1943 and was expanded to include sound recordings in 1953. Beginning in 1953 this cataloging could be found in the series of LC music catalogs, listed below.

> *Library of Congress Catalog: Music and Phonorecords.* Washington, D. C.: Library of Congress, 1954-1972.
>
> Quinquennial cumulations:
>
> > 1953-1957
> > 1958-1962
> > 1963-1967
> > 1968-1972

Volumes in this series included cataloging for music scores and parts, and for all kinds of sound recordings, musical and spoken, but not for books on music. These volumes include only copy produced at the Library of Congress.

Catalog copy for scores during this period was not noticeably different from that for books. Indeed, prior to 1953 cataloging for scores had been included in the *Library of Congress Author Catalog.* The example in figure 11.1 is illustrative. Note that the card number is preceded by the letter-prefix M and is followed by the abbreviation "rev," indicating revised cataloging for a score.

---

**Deprès, Josquin,** *d.* 1521.
₁Missa, De Beata Virgine₁

Missa, De Beata Virgine; zu 4 und 5 Stimmen. Hrsg. von Friedrich Blume. 4. Aufl. Wolfenbüttel, Möseler ₁Vorwort 1936₁

score (40 p.)  26 cm.  (Das Chorwerk, Heft 42)

"Für die vorliegende Herausgabe wurden die Quellen Petrucci 1514, Antiquus 1516 und Petrejus 1539 benutzt."
For 4-5 unspecified voices.

1. Masses—To 1800—Vocal scores.  ɪ. Blume, Friedrich, 1893–
ed.  ɪɪ. Title.  (Series)

M2.C6325  Heft 42                                        M 58–457 rev

Library of Congress        ₁r59b³₁

---

Fig. 11.1. LC card for score, pre-AACR.

However, cataloging for sound recordings continued to evolve rapidly, as reflected in a variety of LC policies for its printed cards. In accordance with revised rules for cataloging sound recordings, LC began to issue "multicarrier" bibliographic records in 1971. A multicarrier card used a single bibliographic description and access points for recordings of the same musical performance, but included multiple physical descriptions of the various formats in which the recording had been issued. The library was expected to line-out the irrelevant description before using the cards in a local catalog. The example in figure 11.2 illustrates this practice. Note, also, that the catalog card contains a classification number in square brackets. These are suggested classification numbers, provided beginning in 1972, for the benefit of libraries using LC cards. LC continues to shelve its recordings by manufacturer's number.

**The New England harmony.** ₁A collection of early American choral music. Phonorecord. Music selected, prepared, and annotated by Alan C. Buechner₁ Folkways Records. ₁1964₁

    disc  FA 2377.  2 s.  12 in.  33⅓ rpm.
    disc  FS 32377.  2 s.  12 in.  33⅓ rpm.  stereophonic.

    Old Sturbridge Singers; members of the Harvard Wind Ensemble; Floyd Corson, conductor.
    "Recorded in the Meeting House at Old Sturbridge Village, Massachusetts, May 1964."
    Introductory note by A. F. Schrader and program notes by Buechner (32 p.) including all music and texts, inserted in slipcase.
    CONTENTS: Billings, W. Jesus wept. Kittery. Judea. David's lament.—Read, D. Mortality. Amity. Russia. Sherburne.—

    (Continued on next card)

                                                    R 67-2914
    rev
    ₁r73c2₁

**The New England harmony.** ₁A collection of early American choral music. Phonorecord₁ (Card 2)
                CONTENTS—Continued.
    Kimball, J. Bradford.—Mason, L. Missionary hymn.—Billings, W. Funeral anthem. Easter anthem.—Blow, J. Welcome song.—Morgan, J. Montgomery.—Hill, U. Berne.—Ingalls, J. Northfield. The young convert.—Edson, L. Greenfield.—French, J. Monmouth.—Swan, T. Rainbow.—Holyoke, S. Sturbridge.—Maxim, A. Portland.—Belcher, S. Plenitude.—Belknap, D. Concord.—Holden, O. Coronation.—Billings, W. Chester.
    1. Hymns, English. 2. Choruses, Sacred (Mixed voices) with instrumental ensemble—To 1800. 3. Choruses, Sacred (Mixed voices), Unaccompanied—To 1800.    I. Billings, William, 1746-1800. Works, vocal. Selections. Phonorecord. 1964. II. Buechner, Alan, comp. III. Corson, Floyd. IV. Old Sturbridge Singers. V. Harvard Wind Ensemble.

    [M2116]                                         R 67-2914
                                rev
    Library of Congress        ₁r73c2₁

Fig. 11.2. Multicarrier LC card.

Note also that by this time the abbreviation "rev" has moved from the card number to the center of the card.

*Library of Congress Catalogs: Music, Books on Music, and Sound Recordings.* Washington, D. C.: Library of Congress, Cataloging Distribution Service, 1973- .

A quinquennial cumulation was issued for 1973-1977, but no cumulation has been issued since. However, the volumes in this series are union catalogs and include cataloging contributed by a group of libraries specially selected by the Music Library Association on the basis of their collection development and cataloging policies. These libraries are the University of Toronto, Stanford University, the University of Chicago, the University of Illinois at Urbana-Champaign, the University of North Carolina, Bowling Green State University, Oberlin College, and Ohio State University.[5] Presumably these libraries follow all published Library of Congress cataloging policies to ensure conformity with the cataloging produced at the Library of Congress. Contributed copy is identifiable by its typed presentation and the location of the contributor's NUC siglum in the lower lefthand corner of each entry. The example in figure 11.3 is contributed copy for a sound recording from the 1973-77 cumulation.

> Mozart, Johann Chrysostom Wolfgang Amadeus,
> 1756-1791.
> [Sinfonia concertante, oboe, clarinet, horn, bassoon
> & orchestra, K.297$^b$ (Anh.9), Eb major] Phonodisc.
> Sinfonia concertante in E-flat major for oboe,
> clarinet, horn and bassoon, K.V. 297$^b$. Diver-
> timento in D major for oboe, 2 horns, 2 violins,
> viola and bass, no.11, K.V. 251. Turnabout TV-S
> 34416. [1973?]
> 2 s. 12 in. 33⅓ rpm. stereophonic.
> Friedrich Milde, oboe; Walter Triebskorn,
> clarinet; Hermann Baumann, horn; Herbert Anton,
> bassoon; Wurttemburg Chamber Orchestra, Heil-
> bronn (in the 1st work); Jörg Faerber, conductor
> (in the 1st work); Hungarian Chamber Orchestra
> (in the 2d); V. Tatrai, conductor (in the 2d)
> Durations listed on slipcase.
> May also be played monophonically.
> Program notes by Siso Gandara on slipcase.
>
> 1. Bassoon, clarinet, horn, oboe with orches-
> tra--To 1800. 2. Suites (Chamber orchestra)--
> To 1800. I. Mozart, Johann Chrysostom Wolfgang
> Amadeus, 1756-1791. Divertimento, K.251, D ma-
> jor. II. Milde, Friedrich. III. Triebskorn, Wal-
> ter. IV. Baumann, Hermann. V. Anton, Herbert.
> VI. Württembergisches Kammerorchester. VII.
> Faerber, Jörg. VIII. Magyar Kamarazenekar.
> IX. Tátrai, Vilmos.
> 00

Fig. 11.3. NUC Contributed Record.

Contributed copy is bumped if LC later catalogs the same item, unless the contributed copy contains analytical added entries and the LC copy does not, in which case both entries will appear. Contributors are not allowed to contribute call numbers. Because most libraries now produce machine-readable cataloging and the Library of Congress will accept contributions only in typed card form, the cooperative program is in jeopardy at present.

There has been no quinquennial cumulation since 1979 and LC has announced no plans to issue one. Many practices have been changed in the intervening years. The following examples from the LC catalogs illustrate the continued evolution of LC copy. Figure 11.4 is cataloging for a score from the 1979 annual cumulation. The rules used are *AACR1* as revised in 1974 to implement ISBD punctuation. Aside from the date implied by the card number, several other differences between this cataloging and cataloging produced according to *AACR2* can be recognized. Note especially the multiple use of the space-colon-space punctuation in the transcription of other title information, the brackets around the copyright date, and the absence of a digit in the specific material designation of the physical description area. Another interesting feature of this card is the use of supplementary classification numbers, given in square brackets under the call number. These represent added entries made in LC's classified music catalog. As a service to the users of its cards, LC included these numbers on cards for scores from 1970 until it closed its classified catalog in 1981.

**Allen, Robert E**        1920–

The Ascension : cantata for Ascensiontide : for mezzo
-soprano solo, chorus of mixed voices, three trumpets, harp,
organ, and timpani / music by Robert E. Allen ; text by
Edwin Markham. — New York : Galleon Press, ₍c1978₎
    score (70 p.) ; 31 cm.
    Duration : ca. 21 min.
    $7.50
    1. Cantatas, Sacred—Scores.  2. Markham, Edwin, 1852–1940—
Musical settings.    I. Title.

M2021.A393A8                                            79–770048
[M1619.5.M257]   [M2068.A6]


Library of Congress        79                              M

Fig. 11.4. *AACR1* revised, score.


*AACR1* rules for cataloging sound recordings were also revised prior to the major
revisions that resulted in *AACR2*, but the results are quite different from the score in the
preceding example. Figures 11.5 and 11.6 comprise the cataloging for a sound recording that
contains two musical works. This form of analysis, which consists of making completely
separate entries for each musical work and linking them with notes, was used by LC and
many music libraries prior to the adoption of *AACR2* in 1981.


**Hoffmeister, Franz Anton,** 1754–1812.
        ₍Concerto, flute, op. 20, no. 6, D major₎  ₍Sound recording₎
    Konzert D-Dur für Flöte und Orchester.    Schwann
VMS 810.  p1970.
        on side 1 of 1 disc.  33⅓ rpm.  stereo.  12 in.  (Meisterhaft ge-
spielt.  Die Flöte)  (Schwann 10 x 10)

        With : Bach, J. C.  Concerto, flute, D major.
        Hans Jürgen Möhring, flute ; Kölner Kammerorchester ; Helmut
Müller-Brühl, conductor.
        Program notes by Carl de Nys in German, English, and French
on container.
        1. Concertos (Flute)      I. Möhring, Hans Jürgen.  II. Müller
-Brühl, Helmut.  III. Kölner Kammerorchester.  IV. Series : Meisterhaft gespielt.  Die Flöte.  ₍Sound recording₎

[M1020]                                               79–761755

Library of Congress        79                              R

Fig. 11.5. AACR1 revised, sound recording analytical entry.

**Bach, Johann Christian,** 1735–1782.
₁Concerto, flute, D major₁  ₁Sound recording₁
Konzert D-Dur für ·Flöte und Orchester.  Schwann
VMS 810.  p1970.
on side 2 of 1 disc.  33⅓ rpm.  stereo.  12 in.  (Meisterhaft gespielt.  Die Flöte)  (Schwann 10 x 10)

With: Hoffmeister, F. A.  Concerto, flute, op. 20, no. 6, D major.
Karl Bernhard Sebon, flute; Kölner Kammerorchester; Helmut
Müller-Brühl, conductor.
Program notes by Carl de Nys in German, English, and French
on container.
1. Concertos (Flute)     I. Sebon, Karl-Bernhard.  II. Müller
-Brühl, Helmut.  III. Kölner Kammerorchester.  IV. Series: Mei-
sterhaft gespielt.  Die Flöte. ₁Sound recording₁

[M1020]                                             79–761756

Library of Congress          79                        R

Fig. 11.6. AACR1 revised, sound recording analytical entry.

Note the physical descriptions that indicate the location of the work on the disc, and the "With" notes that, for each recording, give the composer's heading with forenames abbreviated but the complete uniform title for the other work.

Among various pre-*AACR2* practices illustrated on these cards are the placement of the GMD in the access point instead of the title area, the absence of statements of responsibility, and the transcription of the manufacturer's serial number instead of details of publication. The revised rules for sound recordings are most clearly illustrated by the use of the GMD "sound recording" where "phonorecord" had been used before, and the transcription of the "p" phonogram copyright date.

In 1981 *AACR2* was fully implemented at LC, and in 1985 music cataloging was automated and MARC distribution began. The card in figure 11.7 for a score is produced from a MARC *AACR2* bibliographic record.

**Fouillaud, Patrice.**
Une nuit, j'ai vu énormément d'étoiles : pour orchestre à
cordes et clavecin / Patrice Fouillaud. — ₁Paris₁ : Durand.
c1984.
1 score (35 leaves) ; 36 cm.

For 8 violins, 3 violas, 2 violoncellos, 1 double bass, and harpsichord.
Reproduced from holograph.
Duration: 8:30.

1. String ensembles—Scores.   2. Music—Manuscripts—Facsimiles.   3.
Fouillaud, Patrice—Manuscripts—Facsimiles.     I. Title.   II. Title: 1 nuit, j'ai
vu énormément d'étoiles.

M912.F69N8   1984                               85-753824
                                              AACR 2   MARC

Library of Congress                                    M

Fig. 11.7. AACR2, MARC, score.

The card in figure 11.8, also produced from a MARC *AACR2* bibliographic record, is for a sound recording. Note especially that although the recording contains several musical works, analysis is accomplished through the use of composer-uniform title added entries. The main entry is for the principal performer and the collective title is used in the "unit description," provided according to an option in *AACR2*.

**Gould, Glenn.**
Canadian music in the 20th century ₍sound recording₎. —
Tokyo, Japan : CBS/Sony, ₍between 1983 and 1985₎

1 sound disc : analog, 33 1/3 rpm, mono. ; 12 in.

CBS/Sony: 25AC 1610.
Glenn Gould, piano.
Recorded in New York June 27-28, 1966 (1st work), July 25, 1967 (2nd
work), Aug. 11, 1967 (3rd work).
Includes biography of the performer in Japanese (2 p. ; port.) inserted in
container.
Contents: Fantasy in D minor / Morawetz (16:43) — Fantasia / Anhalt
(11:08) — Variations / Hétu (11:25).

(Continued on next card)

85-754444
AACR 2   MARC
R

**Gould, Glenn.** — Canadian music in the 20th century ₍sound re-
cording₎ ... ₍between 1983 and 1985₎   (Card 2)

1. Piano music.   2. Variations (Piano)   3. Piano music—20th century.   4.
Music—Canada—20th century.     I. Morawetz, Oskar, 1917-           Fanta-
sies, piano, D minor.   1983.   II. Anhalt, István.   Fantasia, piano.   1983.   III.
Hétu, Jacques, 1938-           Variations, piano.   1983.   IV. Title.   V. Title:
Canadian music in the twentieth century.

₍M21₎                                                   85-754444
                                                     AACR 2   MARC

Library of Congress                                                   R

Fig. 11.8. AACR2, MARC, sound recording, unit entry.

## The MLA Catalog

During the years that the LC catalog did not include contributed copy contributions
were nevertheless collected at LC, and this cataloging was compiled, edited, and published
by the Music Library Association in 1973.

> *Music Library Association Catalog of Cards for Printed Music, 1953-1972: A Supple-
> ment to the Library of Congress Catalogs.* Edited by Elizabeth H. Olmsted.
> Totowa, N.J.: Rowman and Littlefield, 1974. 2 vols.

This two-volume set is a valuable bibliographic source but not a particularly reliable source
of accurate original cataloging copy because of a wide variety of local practices represented
in the cataloging. Editors checked LC catalogs to determine whether subsequent LC copy
had appeared. The resulting collection therefore represents unique issues or editions. Entries
from Harvard and the New York Public Library are marked with an asterisk to set them
apart from the others, which are presumably more closely in conformance with LC practice.
No sigla are given so sources are not identified. Call numbers are present in most entries.

## MACHINE-READABLE (MARC) COPY

Despite delays in the development of the music format (see chapter 8) the rise of
cooperative bibliographic networks in the 1970s saw a tremendous explosion of shared music
cataloging. Retrospective conversion efforts beginning in recent years promise to eventually
provide online MARC records for most music materials held in U.S. music libraries.

### Online Computer Library Center, Inc. (OCLC)

OCLC is the largest bibliographic cooperative that includes music materials. Begun in the 1960s as an Ohio college library consortium, OCLC rapidly expanded into an international shared bibliographic network, with over twelve million bibliographic records contributed by nearly 3,000 libraries worldwide. Music use of the system dates to 1970, when a few music libraries began using the books format to enter data for scores. In 1974 members were asked to refrain from this practice pending the implementation of the rapidly developing music format. In September 1976 OCLC's users were invited to begin inputting records for scores and recordings using the new music format. By 1978 music librarians using OCLC had organized into a powerful users' lobby, the Music OCLC Users Group, issuing a newsletter, holding annual conferences, and helping to provide continuing education for online music catalogers. By October 1987, 783,000 music records had been contributed.[6]

OCLC's bibliographic database is called the Online Union Catalog (OLUC), and is used to support cataloging, interlibrary loan, and acquisitions subsystems. Authority control is haphazard, existing only implicitly through the presence of the LC authority records, held separately in OCLC's online authority file. The OLUC employs a unit-record system wherein the first record input (or, when applicable, the LC record) becomes the "master" record. Participating libraries may edit the master record for their own offline use, but the online master record is not altered and local variations are not displayed online. Approximately a dozen well-qualified music libraries have "enhance" capability, which means they are allowed to update or otherwise correct master records. With the exception of this group, bibliographic quality control is dependent on OCLC staff acting on the basis of written reports from member libraries. Another major problem in OCLC is the presence of duplicate records. Duplication is not strictly allowed but neither is it stringently monitored or strictly prohibited. This is illustrated by the examples below.

```
Screen 1 of 3
NO HOLDINGS IN YCL - FOR HOLDINGS ENTER dh DEPRESS DISPLAY RECD SEND
OCLC: 13437732      Rec stat: n Entrd: 851022         Used: 861007
Type: j Bib lvl: m Lang:  N/A Source:   Accomp mat:
Repr:    Enc lvl:   Ctry:  ja Dat tp: q MEBE: 0
         Mod rec:   Comp:  mu Format: n Prts:
Desc: a Int lvl:    LTxt:     Dates: 1983,1985
   1 010      85-754444/R
   2 040      DLC $c DLC $d m/c
   3 007      s $b d $c u $d b $e m $f m $g e $h n $i n $j m $k p $l l $m
u
   4 028 02   25AC 1610 $b CBS/Sony
   5 033 1    19660627 $a 19660628 $b 3804 $c N4
   6 033 0    19670725 $b 3804 $c N4
   7 033 0    19670811 $b 3804 $c N4
   8 043      n-cn---
   9 045 1     $b d1948 $b d1954 $b d1964
  10 047      ft $a vr
  11 048      ka01
  12 050 1    M21
  13 050 0    CBS/Sony 25AC 1610
  14 090       $b
  15 049      YCLM
```

(Screen 2 of 3 and 3 of 3 are on page 186.)

```
Screen 2 of 3
 16 100 10  Gould, Glenn. $w cn
 17 245 10  Canadian music in the 20th century $h [sound recording].
 18 260 0   Tokyo, Japan : $b CBS/Sony, $c [between 1983 and 1985]
 19 300     1 sound disc : $b analog, 33 1/3 rpm, mono. ; $c 12 in.
 20 306     001643 $a 001108 $a 001125
 21 511 0   Glenn Gould, piano.
 22 518     Recorded in New York June 27-28, 1966 (1st work), July 25,
1967 (2nd work), Aug. 11, 1967 (3rd work).
 23 500     Includes biography of the performer in Japanese (2 p. ;
port.) inserted in container.
 24 505 0   Fantasy in D minor / Morawetz (16:43) -- Fantasia / Anhalt
(11:08) -- Variations / H'etu (11:25).
 25 650  0  Piano music.
 26 650  0  Variations (Piano)
 27 650  0  Piano music $y 20th century.
 28 650  0  Music $z Canada $y 20th century.
 29 700 12  Morawetz, Oskar, $d 1917- $t Fantasies, $m piano, $r D
minor. $f 1983. $w cn
 30 700 12  Anhalt, Istv'an. $t Fantasia, $m piano. $f 1983. $w cn

Screen 3 of 3
 31 700 12  H'etu, Jacques, $d 1938- $t Variations, $m piano. $f 1983.
$w cn
 32 740 01  Canadian music in the twentieth century.




Screen 1 of 2
NO HOLDINGS IN YCL - FOR HOLDINGS ENTER dh DEPRESS DISPLAY RECD SEND
OCLC: 11672462     Rec stat: n Entrd: 850208        Used: 850510
Type: j Bib lvl: m Lang:  N/A Source: d Accomp mat:
Repr:    Enc lvl: I Ctry:  ja  Dat tp: q MEBE: 0
         Mod rec:    Comp:  mu  Format: n Prts:
Desc: a Int lvl:    LTxt:      Dates: 1980,1984
  1 010
  2 040     IXA $c IXA $d m/c
  3 007     s $b d $c r $d b $e m $f m $g e $h n $i n
  4 028 01  25AC 1610 $b CBS/Sony
  5 045 1   $b d1948 $b d1954 $b d1964
  6 047     ft $a vr
  7 048     ka01
  8 090      $b
  9 049     YCLM
 10 245 00  Canadian music in the 20th century $h sound recording
 11 260 0   Tokyo, Japan : $b CBS/Sony, $c [198-?]
 12 300     1 sound disc : $b 33 1/3 rpm, mono. ; $c 12 in.
 13 306     001643 $a 001108 $a 001125
 14 511 0   Glenn Gould, piano.
 15 500     Durations: 16:43; 11:08; 11:25.
 16 500     Program notes in Japanese on container.
```

```
Screen 2 of 2
  17 505 0    Fantasy in D minor / Morawetz -- Fantasia / Anhalt --
Variations / H'etu.
  18 650  0  Piano music.
  19 650  0  Variations (Piano)
  20 700 10  Gould, Glenn. $w cn
  21 700 12  Morawetz, Oskar. $t Fantasies, $m piano. $f 198-.
  22 700 12  Anhalt, Istv'an. $t Fantasia, $m piano. $f 198-. $w cn
  23 700 12  H'etu, Jacques, $d 1938- $t Variations, $m piano. $f 198-.
$w cn
```

The member input record was entered several months prior to the LC record. Probably, slightly differing input conventions at LC are responsible for the difference in the transcription of the manufacturer's number in field 028, and different cataloger interpretations have yielded different release dates in field 260. These differences would prevent the online system from replacing the member record with the LC record. Note that both these records are MARC versions of the LC card record illustrated above.

In OCLC's master record system the holding libraries are indicated on a separate display, retrieved with a secondary command. Other features of these records are of interest in copy cataloging. Note the extent of non-cataloging content designation in the fixed length and control fields. Note that in the LC record no bibliographic data are present on the first screen. Both of these records have been mechanically manipulated as indicated by the code "m/c" in field 040. The codes "cn" in $w of the Anhalt added entries indicate that at some point these records were altered to match a new name-authority file record.

### Research Libraries Information Network (RLIN)

RLIN, the shared bibliographic network of the Research Libraries Group, Inc. (RLG), grew from the adoption in 1974 of Stanford University's BALLOTS system.[7] Music implementation in RLIN followed OCLC's by a short interval, with the scores and recordings files becoming accessible in spring 1979.[8] As of March 1988 RLIN statistics indicated 594,532 bibliographic records for scores and sound recordings.[9] Comparisons between the two major networks are complicated by their very different organizational goals and structures. RLG is essentially a research library cooperative with approximately seventy full members. Automated shared cataloging, supported by the RLIN system, is only one of many shared programs of RLG. As a result, RLIN's music database is much smaller than OCLC's, although its scope is intended to address specific needs of research institutions.

Like OCLC, RLIN supports a number of files that in turn support a variety of non-cataloging bibliographic activities. Also like OCLC, RLIN's authority control is only implicit because of the presence alongside the bibliographic files of a copy of the LC authority files. Unlike OCLC, the authority file cannot be accessed from the bibliographic file; the user must log off from the catalog and log on again to check the authority files.

RLIN's search command structure is more sophisticated (including subject term search capability) than OCLC's, making the RLIN music database a more effective bibliographic tool. RLIN maintains format-specific files that help reduce recall in searching. Both networks regularly load LC-MARC tapes including bibliographic records for scores and sound recordings. The example below is RLIN's version of the LC-MARC record seen in OCLC above.

```
ID:DCLC85754444-R    RTYP:c    ST:p    FRN:      MS:n      EL:        AD:10-22-85
CC:9110  BLT:jm       DCF:a    CSC:    MOD:      SNR:      ATC:       UD:01-01-01
CP:ja    L:           FCP:mu   INT:    MEI:0     AMC:
PC:q     PD:1983/1985          LIT:
RMD:d  OR:u  SPD:b  SND:m  GRV:m  DIM:e  WID:n  TC:n  KD:m  KM:p  KC:1  RC:u
010       85754444/R
028 02    25AC 1610$bCBS/Sony
033 1     19660627$a19660628$b3804$cN4
033 0     19670725$b3804$cN4
033 0     19670811$b3804$cN4
040       $dCStRLIN
043       n-cn---
045 1     $bd1948$d1954$bd1964
047       ft$avr
048       ka01
050 1     M21
050 0     CBS/Sony 25AC 1610
100 10    Gould, Glenn.$4prf
245 10    Canadian music in the 20th century$h[sound recording].
260 0     Tokyo, Japan :$bCBS/Sony,$c[between 1983 and 1985]
300       1 sound disc :$banalog, 33 1/3 rpm, mono. ;$c12 in.
306       001643$a001108$a001125
511 0     Glenn Gould, piano.
518       Recorded in New York June 27-28, 1966 (1st work), July 25, 1967 (2nd
          work), Aug. 11, 1967 (3rd work).
500       Includes biography of the performer in Japanese (2 p. ; port.) insert
          ed in container.
505 0     Fantasy in D minor / Morawetz (16:43) -- Fantasia / Anhalt (11:08) --
          Variations / H_etu (11:25).
650  0    Piano music.
650  0    Variations (Piano)
650  0    Piano music$y20th century.
650  0    Music$zCanada$y20th century.
700 12    Morawetz, Oskar,$d1917- $tFantasies,$mpiano,$rD minor.$f1983.
700 12    Anhalt, Istv_an.$tFantasia,$mpiano.$f1983.
700 12    H_etu, Jacques,$d1938- $tVariations,$mpiano.$f1983.
740 01    Canadian music in the twentieth century.
```

A major difference between OCLC and RLIN is that RLIN does not use a master-record system, but allows every member's individual record to reside in the system simultaneously. Using matching algorithms, the RLIN system clusters (that is, stores together) records for the same bibliographic entity to prevent excessive recall in searching. A brief record display, formatted like a catalog card, is encountered in response to a search key. This brief record includes the sigla of the libraries whose own records are clustered. Therefore, it is possible in RLIN to view bibliographic variants as well as variant cataloging interpretations for the same item. For example, a cluster when first located is indicated like this:

```
2) Depr`es, Josquin, d. 1521. [MISSA, PANGE LINGUA] MISSA PANGE LINGUA (Chapel
   Hill : Univ. of N. Carolina Press, c1977.)
NHDG (c-9665 NhD)   NYCX (c-9665 NIC)    PATG (c-9665 PPT)    PAUG (c-9665 PU)
```

On request, a catalog-card-like display may be retrieved that looks like this:

```
Depr`es, Josquin, d. 1521.
  [Missa, Pange lingua]
  Missa Pange lingua / Josquin dez Prez ; an edition, with notes for
performance and commentary by Thomas Warburton. -- Chapel Hill : Univ. of N.
Carolina Press, c1977.
  62 p. ; 29 cm. -- (Early musical masterworks)

  Partial contents: Editing and performing Josquins's Mass.- Text of the mass.-
Score of the mass.- An analytical essay.
  ISBN 0-8078-1296-X

  1. Masses--To 1800. I. Warburton, Thomas, 1940- II. Title. III. Title: Pange
lingua. IV. Series.

  LCCN: 7622703
  ID: NHDG291524301-C          CC: 9665        DCF: i
  CALL: M2011.D33P3 1977
```

In either case, the four symbols at the bottom are the sigla for the libraries whose records form the cluster. In response to the full display command, the first record will be retrieved:

```
ID:NHDG291524301-C  RTYP:c    ST:p    FRN:      MS:n      EL:?       AD:04-25-77
CC:9665  BLT:cm      DCF:i   CSC:d   MOD:      SNR:      ATC:       UD:01-01-01
CP:ncu   L:eng       FCP:ms  INT:    MEI:1     AMC:d
PC:s     PD:0197/            SCO:?   PTS:n     REP:
MMD:     OR:    POL:    DM:     RR:       COL:      EML:     GEN:   BSE:
010      7622703
020      0-8078-1296-X
040      TxFS$cTxFS$dNhD$dCStRLIN
100 10   Depr`es, Josquin,$dd. 1521.
240 10   Missa, Pange lingua
245 10   Missa Pange lingua$c/ Josquin dez Prez ; an edition, with notes for p
         erformance and commentary by Thomas Warburton.
260 0    Chapel Hill :$bUniv. of N. Carolina Press,$cc1977.
300      62 p. ;$c29 cm.
440  0   Early musical masterworks
505 2    Editing and performing Josquins's Mass.- Text of the mass.- Score of
         the mass.- An analytical essay.
650  0   Masses$yTo 1800.
700 11   Warburton, Thomas,$d1940-
740 00   Pange lingua.
```

Unlike OCLC, however, each of the other libraries' records are available for display. For instance, the fourth record may also be retrieved:

```
ID:PAUG2915243-C    RTYP:c    ST:p    FRN:    MS:n    EL:?    AD:04-25-77
CC:9665   BLT:cm       DCF:i    CSC:d   MOD:    SNR:    ATC:    UD:01-01-01
CP:ncu    L:eng        FCP:ms   INT:    MEI:1   AMC:d
PC:s      PD:0197/              SCO:d   PTS:n   REP:
MMD:      OR:    POL:    DM:    RR:    COL:    EML:    GEN:   BSE:
010      7622703
020      0-8078-1296-X
040      TxFS$cTxFS$dPU$dCStRLIN
100 10   Depr`es, Josquin,$dd. 1521.
240 10   Missa, Pange lingua
245 10   Missa Pange lingua$c/ Josquin dez Prez ; an edition, with notes for p
           erformance and commentary by Thomas Warburton.
260 0    Chapel Hill :$bUniv. of N. Carolina Press,$cc1977.
300      62 p. ;$c28 cm.
440 0    Early musical masterworks
505 2    Editing and performing Josquins's Mass.- Text of the mass.- Score of
           the mass.- An analytical essay.
650 0    Masses$yTo 1800.
700 11   Warburton, Thomas,$d1940-
740 00   Pange lingua.
```

Further, local data such as holdings, local call numbers, etc., are not held as part of the bibliographic record as in OCLC's master record system, but are displayed in a holdings record that is attached to each bibliographic record:

```
                                          CIN      OID      FD 07/14/83
CALL M2011.D33$bP3 1977
  VOL
  ANT \FOR MORE INFORMATION SEE AUTHOR CARD\
  INS            EXT
  FNT                               PTH      FSP

  LOC VPL      LCAL
 LVOL
 LANT
 LINS          LEXT
 LHST 01/01/01 N
 LFNT                              LPTH     LFSP
   COP -            MDES
   CCAL
   SHNT $qser ML as
   COP              MDES
   CCAL
   SHNT
```

### Western Library Network (WLN)

WLN, the Western Library Network (originally the Washington [State] Library Network), implemented the music format in early 1984.[10] Though WLN's software is more sophisticated and is designed to serve as the shared online catalog for its member libraries, the scope of the network is limited to libraries in the Pacific Northwest. WLN supports an interactive authority file, comprising all headings used in bibliographic records. Rather than storing each heading in each bibliographic record, each heading is stored only once, in an authority record, with links to the bibliographic records that are used to reassemble the components for display. This promising structure mimics that of a relational database, where the descriptive entities and access entities are stored and manipulated separately according to their characteristics. Unfortunately, as of this writing, the system is used too little for music materials to draw any conclusions about its effectiveness.

# Working with Copy

Shared cataloging, particularly in automated networks, has a seductive quality for librarians. What could be easier than to use someone else's cataloging rather than go the expense of creating your own original copy? However, as noted above, volatility of music cataloging rules, and technological developments in both music material production and library automation, make it difficult to adopt shared copy without expending considerable effort regularizing various aspects of the bibliographic records. A significant factor in this process is the very nature of music collections. As Ruth Watanabe noted in a 1981 review of American music librarianship:

> While the greatest proportion of research in medicine, for example, builds upon the results of the most recent studies and is therefore always forward-looking and immediate in its demands, the greater proportion of musical research builds upon the materials from the past and is apt to be retrospective in purpose and not necessarily immediate in its demands.[11]

Retrospective collection development means that a significant portion of the current cataloging load in a music collection may require use of older bibliographic records. Consequently, music catalogers are required to contend with a large proportion of cataloging produced under earlier rules, utilizing earlier descriptive and input conventions, and in some cases forms of headings no longer authorized.

Many similar management issues require resolution if the music library is to make efficient use of cataloging copy provided from one of the sources described above. Descriptive conventions such as the interpolation of ISBD punctuation are probably of little moment for score cataloging. But important descriptive changes for sound recordings must be carefully considered and procedures for contending with them established. These changes include the changing GMD, the transcription of manufacturer's serial number in an indexed field (028) versus the earlier imprint (262, now obsolete), and unit description versus analysis and linking "with" notes.

Forms of access points for composers, performers, and especially uniform titles changed radically with the implementation of *AACR2*. Careful authority work will be required to make use of earlier copy in a modern catalog using *AACR2* forms. Choice of entry differences are great as well, but may cause less difficulty since it is likely that the same entries would be made regardless of the choice of *main* entry. The scope and structure of *LCSH* continues to change, in particular now that LC is using its own headings internally, so that careful subject authority work is also required to maintain an effective subject catalog.

In all copy cataloging in general, one must contend with other libraries' policies about the use of *LCC:M* or DDC. In particular, since many libraries do not classify recordings, copy catalogers may well need to supply full call numbers for a majority of sound recording copy. LC's switch from analytical cataloging for sound recordings to unit description means that the class numbers formerly assigned for individual musical works will no longer be applicable to the entire recorded performances that now serve as the basis for the bibliographic record. The cataloger must decide whether to continue to collocate recordings on the shelf by prominent musical work, or to begin to build collections in general numbers subarranged by names of performers. For scores, in the many classes where LC does not use cutter numbers to shelve, libraries will have to supply individual cuttering for their own cataloging. Finally, though *LCC:M* has been a very stable classification for music, the approaching introduction of the DDC phoenix schedule will cause great dislocation if it is adopted. If it is not, Dewey libraries will have to provide their own DDC 19 numbers.

Finally, content designation decisions must be made for the library contemplating the introduction of an OPAC. Many libraries disregard fixed length and control fields because they rarely affect card production, but these fields drive the indexing and record manipulation and display functions of online systems, so it is important to make sure adapted records supply essential coded data.

These are the most common pitfalls in the adaptation of copy cataloging for music materials. For detailed guidance in the structure of copy cataloging operations, an excellent sourcebook is Arlene G. Taylor's *Cataloging with Copy*. For a detailed example of an individual library's adaptive policy manual, Judy Weidow's *Music Cataloging Policy in the General Libraries* describes the operations at the University of Texas at Austin. Complete citations for these books appear in the "Suggested Reading" list at the end of this chapter.

# Notes

[1]For a description of this effort see Richard P. Smiraglia and Arsen R. Papakhian, "Music in the OCLC Online Union Catalog: A Review," *Notes* (1981): 257-74.

[2]Cooperative Retrospective Conversion Project," *Music OCLC Users Group Newsletter* 33 (September 1987): 6-7.

[3]Otto Kinkeldey, "American Music Catalogs," *Library Journal* (August 1915): 574-78.

[4]Ibid., 575.

[5]Harvard University is also listed as a contributor, but has never actively participated in the program.

[6]Jay Weitz, "More News from OCLC," *Music OCLC Users Group Newsletter* 34 (January 1988): 5.

[7]Bohdan S. Wynar, *Introduction to Cataloging and Classification*, 7th ed. by Arlene G. Taylor (Littleton, Colo.: Libraries Unlimited, 1985), 537.

[8]Electronic mail communication with Ed Glazier, RLIN, 24 March 1988.

[9]"Statistics as of March 21, 1988," RLIN Log-on screen display.

[10]Telephone conversation with Robert Richart, WLN, 18 August 1988.

[11]Ruth Watanabe, "American Music Libraries and Music Librarianship: An Overview in the Eighties," *Notes* 38 (1981): 246.

# Suggested Reading

*Music OCLC Users Group [MOUG] Newsletter* 1- (October 1977- ).

Taylor, Arlene G. *Cataloging with Copy: A Decision-Maker's Handbook.* 2nd ed. Littleton, Colo.: Libraries Unlimited, 1988.

Weidow, Judy. *Music Cataloging Policy in the General Libraries.* Contributions to Librarianship, No. 8. [Austin, Texas]: The General Libraries, The University of Texas at Austin, 1984.

# GLOSSARY

**AACR 2.** Acronym for *Anglo-American Cataloguing Rules, Second Edition.*

**Aboutness.** Topicality. *See also* Subject analysis.

**Access points.** Points in an index used to retrieve bibliographic items. Usually represented by headings. *See also* Headings.

**Accompaniment.** Instrumental backing for a vocal or instrumental solo.

**Analysis, subject.** *See* Subject analysis.

**ANSCR.** Acronym for Alpha-Numeric System for Classification of Recordings.

**Arrangement, musical.** A specific alteration of the musical content of a work. In particular, a new instrumentation.

**Authority control.** The process of maintaining consistency in the use of unique access points in a bibliographic source.

**Authority records.** The formatted recording of a unique heading used to maintain consistency in the access points of a bibliographic source.

**Authority work.** The act of establishing a unique heading; creating an authority record.

**Bibliographic control.** A communicative process involving the creation, storage, manipulation, and retrieval of bibliographic data.

**Bibliographic description.** In bibliographic control, the process of transcribing inherent bibliographic characteristics from bibliographic items, and providing explanatory annotations.

**Bibliographic items.** Objects embodying recorded knowledge, that are collected in libraries, archives, etc.

**Bibliographic record.** The formatted surrogate for a bibliographic item that includes a complete description and all access points that lead to it.

**Bibliographic source.** A reference tool that provides access to bibliographic items. *See also* Catalog.

**Bibliographic works.** Intellectual entities, communicated through and recorded in bibliographic items.

**Caption title.** In textual bibliography, the title formed from the first words of a work. In music, the title that appears above the first stave of music.

**Catalog.** A systematized bibliographic source, usually alphabetical, that includes descriptions or the bibliographic items and access points leading to the works held in a particular collection(s). *See also* Classified catalogs; Dictionary catalog; Divided catalog; Integrated catalog.

**Chief source of information.** The principal locus of inherent bibliographic data (e.g., a book's title page).

**Chorus score.** The score of a dramatic work that includes only the parts for the chorus.

**Class.** The first and major level of a hierarchical classification. *See also* Division; Subdivision.

**Classified catalog.** A catalog organized according to a notational scheme, usually a topical systematization, rather than alphabetically. *See also* SLACC.

**Close score.** The full score of a choral work with the parts for upper voices combined on one stave and the parts for lower voices combined on a second, vertically coordinated stave.

**Coextensive.** Subject analysis (either verbal or classified) in which the terms used define precisely the complete subject content, but no more than the subject content, of the indexed item.

**Collective title.** The unifying title of an anthology that represents it as a unique bibliographic item.

**Collocating function.** The act of gathering similar access points together in a catalog; the placement, particularly side-by-side, of similar terms.

**Common title.** The title of a work that is consistently found on the majority of its physical manifestations. *See also* Uniform title.

**Condensed score.** A score of a work for large ensemble showing the principal parts, with printed alphabetical instrumental cues.

**Conventional title.** *See* Standardized title.

**Cues.** In printed music, miniature notes or miniature abbreviations of the names of instruments printed in performance parts to indicate the entrance of other instruments.

**DDC.** Acronym for Dewey Decimal Classification.

**Descriptive cataloging.** The process of creating bibliographic descriptions of items, and establishing access points (such as composer/uniform title) based on characteristics of the corresponding intellectual entities.

**Dictionary catalog.** A catalog in which all access points are arranged in a single alphabetical sequence.

**Differentiating function.** The act of uniquely distinguishing access points with shared entry characteristics; the subarrangement of similar access points.

**Distinctive title.** The title of a musical work that includes terms denoting more than type of composition, medium of performance, etc. *See also* Generic title.

**Distinguishing function.** *See* Differentiating function.

**Divided catalog.** A catalog in which more than one alphabetical sequence is employed, usually grouping names and titles in one sequence and subjects in another sequence. In music libraries, divided catalogs are often separate dictionary catalogs for the various formats of music materials (e.g., scores and books, recordings).

**Division.** The second level of a hierarchical classification. *See also* Class; Subdivision.

**Dramatic work.** A musical work employing voices and instruments, such as an opera or an oratorio, with a dramatic plot line.

**Edition.** All copies produced from the same original impression, recording, etc. *See also* Release.

**Edition numbers.** Publisher's numbers used with the name of a publisher's series. *See also* Publisher's (manufacturer's) number.

**Ensemble** (musical). A musical performing group.

**Entries.** *See* Access points.

**Evaluating function.** The act of comparing and selecting the appropriate bibliographic item from a bibliographic source.

**Facet.** In classification, a grouping of phenomena with like characteristics. *See also* Phenomenon.

**Filing title.** The artificial title portion of an access point for a work, used to organize and achieve collocating in a bibliographic source. *See also* Uniform title.

**Full score.** A score of a work for large ensemble, showing all the parts in a vertical correspondence (e.g., an orchestra score).

**Functions of the catalog.** *See* Collocating function; Differentiating function; Evaluating function; Identifying function.

**Generic title.** The title of a musical work that consists solely of the name of one or more types of composition and/or statements of medium of performance, key, and numbering. *See also* Distinctive title.

**Headings.** Unique identifiers, used on bibliographic records, that represent the intellectual entities associated with bibliographic items.

**Holograph.** A musical manuscript in the composer's hand.

**Identifying function.** Utilizing bibliographic description, creating recognizance in bibliographic control.

**Indexing.** The act of creating organized, accessible lists of terms. *See also* Descriptive cataloging; Subject analysis.

**Instrumental/conductor score/part.** A performance part, for a lead instrument such as violin, piano, harpsichord/continuo, that includes cues so as to allow the performer to conduct.

**Integrated catalog.** A catalog that interfiles in a single sequence bibliographic records representing several types of bibliographic formats.

**Isolate.** A specific member of a facet. *See also* Facet.

**Items, Bibliographic.** *See* Bibliographic items.

**Label-name.** The trade name for a series of sound recordings, identified by its use on their labels. Usually associated with a label number. *See also* Label number.

**Label number.** A record manufacturer's serial number, usually associated with a label-name, used to uniquely identify a particular release of a recording. *See also* Publisher's (manufacturer's) number; Label-name.

**LCC:M.** Acronym for *Library of Congress Classification: Class M, Music and Books on Music*.

**LCSH.** Acronym for Library of Congress Subject Headings.

**List title page.** A collective title page (or cover) for a printed musical item that serves as chief source of information for a group of related publications, usually with the applicable bibliographic data underlined.

**MARC.** Acronym for Machine-Readable Cataloging.

**Manufacturer's number.** *See* Publisher's (manufacturer's) number.

**Matrix numbers.** Serial numbers, usually scratched in the ungrooved center portion of a sound disc, that identify a particular impression. *See also* Publisher's (manufacturer's) number.

**Medium of performance.** Instruments and/or voices used to create an instance of musical expression.

**MFBD.** Acronym for *MARC Formats for Bibliographic Data*.

**Miniature score.** A full score, intended for use in study, presented in reduced typeface.

**Music in the popular idiom.** Music in popular forms, often commercial and usually improvisatory (e.g., rock, pop, disco, etc.).

**Music materials.** Printed items, such as scores and parts, and recorded items, such as discs, tapes, cassettes, etc., that convey musical information.

**Musical arrangement.** *See* Arrangement, musical.

**Musical ensemble.** *See* Ensemble (musical).

**Musical part.** *See* Part (musical).

**Musics other than Western art.** Musics derived from cultural influences other than those of Western Europe. Including Western "popular" musics, and all non-Western musics.

**Name, label.** *See* Label-name.

**Number, label.** *See* Label number.

**Number, Publisher's** (manufacturer's). *See* Publisher's (manufacturer's) number.

**Numbers, edition.** *See* Edition numbers.

**Numbers, matrix.** *See* Matrix numbers.

**Numbers, plate.** *See* Plate numbers.

**Numbers, serial.** *See* Publisher's (manufacturer's) number.

**Part** (musical). The music played by one member of an ensemble.

**Passe partout.** *See* List title page.

**Performing medium.** *See* Medium of performance.

**Phenomenon.** A topic, as represented in bibliographic works, that is treated uniquely within a discipline.

**Phoenix.** A portion of a schedule in the Dewey Decimal Classification that has been completely revised without regard to the numerical positions of topics in its predecessor schedule.

**Plate numbers.** Publisher's numbers used to identify a set of printing plates for a musical work. *See also* Publisher's (manufacturer's) number.

**Popular idiom, music in the.** *See* Music in the popular idiom.

**Printed music materials.** Scores (indicating all the parts of an ensemble), parts, and solo music (including microforms of all of the above).

**Publisher's** (manufacturer's) number. Serial number, used to organize a publisher's (manufacturer's, etc.) internal stores, that appears on chief sources of information of music materials.

**Recall.** The proportion of bibliographic records retrieved in response to a search command.

**Recorded music materials.** Sound recordings (e.g., discs, tapes, cassettes, piano rolls, wires, etc.).

**Release.** The copies of a sound recording produced from a single unique master recording. In discography, this term equates with the use of the term *edition* in bibliography. *See also* Edition.

**Relevance.** The proportion of retrieved bibliographic records that is useful to the searcher.

**Retrieval.** The response to a particular search query. More broadly, locating bibliographic items in library collections.

**Score.** The printed or manuscript record of all the parts of an ensemble musical work, displayed vertically. *See also* Part (musical).

**Score, chorus.** *See* Chorus score.

**Score, close.** *See* Close score.

**Score, condensed.** *See* Condensed score.

**Score, full.** *See* Full score.

**Score, miniature.** *See* Miniature score.

**Score, vocal.** *See* Vocal score.

**Score order.** The traditional order of instruments and voices in a full score of a Western art musical work.

**Score/part, instrumental/conductor.** *See* Instrumental/conductor score/part.

**SLACC.** Acronym for Shelf-List as Classified Catalog. *See also* Classified catalog.

**Species.** A genre; musical form; type of composition.

**Standardized title.** The artificially manipulated title portion of an access point in common usage for a work. *See also* Uniform title.

**Subdivision.** The third level of a hierarchical classification. *See also* Class; Division.

**Subject analysis.** In bibliographic control, the process of determining topicality, cultural influence, and the physical and intellectual forms of a work.

**Title, caption.** *See* Caption title.

**Title, collective.** *See* Collective title.

**Title, common.** *See* Common title.

**Title, distinctive.** *See* Distinctive title.

**Title, filing.** *See* Filing title.

**Title, generic.** *See* Generic title.

**Uniform title.** The portion of a unique access point that identifies a work. A uniform title is constructed from the bibliographic title as it has evolved from the title originally assigned to the work. In music, it is derived from the composer's original title. Also referred to as common title, conventional title, filing title, standardized title.

**Unit record.** A bibliographic record used to produce the record independently displayed at each access point in a catalog. *See also* Bibliographic record.

**Vocal score.** The score of a work for voices and large ensemble in which the instrumental accompaniment has been arranged for keyboard.

**Western art music.** Music based on Western European artistic traditions, commonly referred to as "classical" music. *See also* Musics other than Western art.

**Work, dramatic.** *See* Dramatic work.

**Works.** *See* Bibliographic works.

# SELECTED BIBLIOGRAPHY

American Library Association. Committee on Catalog Rules. "Rules for Cataloging of Musical Scores." American Library Association *Bulletin* 14 (1920?): 295-96.

Angell, Richard S. "On the Future of the Library of Congress Classification." In *Classification Research: Proceedings of the Second International Study Conference ...*, 101-12. Edited by Pauline Atherton. Copenhagen: Munksgaard, 1965.

_____. "Printed Cards for Phonorecords: Subject Headings." *Notes* 10 (1952-1953): 198-200.

_____. "Subject Headings." *Notes* 10 (1953): 198-200.

Anker, Ø. "Katalogisering av Musikalier." *Bok og Bibliotek* 6 (1939): 37-43.

"Arrangement and Classification of Sound Recordings." In *Development of Library Collections of Sound Recordings*, 91-104. Edited by F. W. Hoffmann. n.p.: M. Dekker, 1979.

Austin, Derek. *British Catalogue of Music: Code of Practice for the Application of PRECIS.* [London]: British Library, Bibliographic Services Division, 1985. "A British Library internal document, which is not generally available."

Ayer, Clarence W. "Shelf Classification of Music." *Library Journal* 27 (1902): 5-11.

Benton, Rita. "The Nature of Music and Some Implications for the University Music Library." *Fontes artis Musicae* 23 (1976): 53-60.

Berman, Sanford J. "Let There Be Music (But Not Too Soon)." In *The Joy of Cataloging: Essays, Letters, Reviews, and Other Explosions*, 89-91. Phoenix, Ariz.: Oryx Press, 1981.

Birmingham Libraries Cooperative Mechanisation Project (BLCMP). "Study into the Effects of AACR2 on Music MARC Catalogues: Preliminary Report from the BLCMP Music Group." *Brio* 16 (1979): 38-41.

Bishop, William W. "Report of ALA Committee on Catalog Rules: Rules for Cataloging Musical Scores." *ALA Bulletin* 14 (1921?): 295-96.

Bradley, Carol June. *The Dickinson Classification: A Cataloging and Classification Manual for Music: Including a Reprint of the George Sherman Dickinson Classification of Musical Compositions.* Carlisle, Pa.: Carlisle Books, 1968.

_____. "The Dickinson Classification for Music: An Introduction." *Fontes artis Musicae* 19 (1972): 13-22.

_____. *Manual of Music Librarianship*. Ann Arbor, Mich.: Music Library Association, 1966.

_____. "Notes of Some Pioneers: America's First Music Librarians." *Notes* 43 (1986): 272-73.

_____. *Reader in Music Librarianship*. Washington, D.C.: NCR Microcard Books, 1973.

Brown, James Duff. "Cataloguing of Music." *The Library*. Series 1 (1897): 82-84.

Bryant, E. T. *Music Librarianship: A Practical Guide*. London: J. Clarke; New York: Hafner, 1959.

_____. *Music Librarianship: A Practical Guide*. 2nd ed. With the assistance of Guy A. Marco. Metuchen, N.J.: Scarecrow Press, 1985.

Bush, Helen E., and David Judson Haykin. "Music Subject Headings." *Notes* 6 (1948): 39-45.

Buth, Olga. "Scores and Recordings." *Library Trends* 23 (1974): 427-50.

Cazeaux, Isabelle. "Classification and Cataloging." In *Manual of Music Librarianship*. Edited by Carol June Bradley. Ann Arbor, Mich.: Music Library Association, 1966, pp. 30-57.

_____. "The International Code for Cataloguing Music." *Fontes artis Musicae* 10 (1963): 20-29.

Cipolla, Wilma Reid. "Music Subject Headings: A Comparison." *Library Resources & Technical Services* 18 (1974): 387-97.

Clewes, J. P. "Revision of DC 780: The Phoenix Schedule." *Brio* 12 (1975): 7-14.

Coates, Eric James. *The British Catalogue of Music Classification*. Compiled for the Council of the British National Bibliography. London: The Council, 1960.

Coover, J. B. "Computers, Cataloguing, and Co-operation." *Notes* 25 (1969): 437-46.

Cunningham, Virginia. "From Schmidt-Phiseldeck to Zanetti." *Notes* 23 (1967): 449-52.

_____. "Heart of the Music Library." *Music Journal* 11 (1953): 54-57.

_____. "Inside LC's Music Section." *Notes* 25 (1968): 205-8.

_____. "International Code for Cataloging Music." *Notes* 18 (1961): 559-62.

_____. "The Library of Congress Classed Catalog for Music." *Library Resources & Technical Services* 8 (1964): 285.

_____. "Shelflisting Music." *Notes: Supplement for Members* 31 (1961): 11-13.

_____. "Simplified Rules of Cataloging of Music." *Notes: Supplement for Members* 21 (1952): 8-10.

Cutter, Charles Ammi. "Shelf Classification of Music." *Library Journal* 27 (1902): 68-72.

Daily, Jay E. *Cataloging Phonorecordings; Problems and Possibilities.* n.p.: M. Dekker, 1975.

_____. "The Selection, Processing, and Storage of Non-Print Materials: A Critique of the Anglo-American Cataloging Rules as They Relate to Newer Media." *Library Trends* 16 (1967): 283-89.

De Lerma, Dominique-René. "Philosophy and Practice of Phonorecord Classification at Indiana University." *Library Resources & Technical Services* 13 (1969): 86-92.

Dickinson, George Sherman. *Classification of Musical Compositions: A Decimal-Symbol System.* Poughkeepsie, N.Y.: Vassar College, 1938.

Dorfmuller, Kurt. "Form- und Gattungsnamen im Sachkatalog der Musica practica zum Entwurf eines Thesaurus." *Fontes artis Musicae* 28 (1981): 115-29.

Duncan, Barbara. "Review of *Music Subject Headings Used on Printed Catalog Cards of the Library of Congress.*" *Notes* 9 (1952): 607.

Elmer, Minnie. "Classification, Cataloging, Indexing." *Notes: Supplement for Members* 25 (1957): 23-28.

_____. "The Music Catalog as a Reference Tool." *Library Trends* 8 (1960): 529-38.

_____. "Music Cataloging in a Public Library; abridged." *Pacific Northwest Library Association Quarterly* 7 (1942): 40-42.

_____. "Music Cataloging, with an Annotated Bibliography of Useful Reference Sources." Master's thesis, Columbia University, 1946.

Gabbard, Paula Beversdorf. "LCSH and PRECIS in Music: A Comparison." *Library Quarterly* 55 (April 1985): 192-206.

Gaeddert, B. *The Classification and Cataloguing of Sound Recordings: An Annotated Bibliography.* Ann Arbor, Mich.: Music Library Association, 1977.

International Association of Music Libraries. International Cataloging Code Commission. *Code International de Catalogage de la Musique.* Frankfurt, West Germany; New York: C. F. Peters, 1957-1983.

Vol. I. Grasberger, Franz. *Der Autoren-Katalog der Musickdrücke.* 1957.

Vol. II. Federoff, Yvette. *Code restreint.* 1961.

Vol. III. Cunningham, Virginia. *Rules for Full Cataloging.* 1971.

Vol. IV. Gollner, Marie Louise. *Rules for Cataloging Music Manuscripts.* 1975.

Vol. V. Wallon, Simone, and Kurt Dorfmuller. *Le Catalogage des Enregistrements Sonores.* 1983.

Kaufman, Judith. *Library of Congress Subject Headings for Recordings of Western Non-Classical Music.* MLA Technical Reports, No. 14. Philadelphia, Pa.: Music Library Association, 1983.

_____. *Recordings of Non-Western Music: Subject and Added Entry Access.* MLA Technical Reports, No. 5. Ann Arbor, Mich.: Music Library Association, 1977.

Kinkeldey, Otto. "American Music Catalogs." *Library Journal* (August 1915): 574-78.

Köhler, Karl-Heinz. "Grundzüge eines analytischen Systems der Sachkatalogisierung der 'Musica Practica.' " *Zentralblatt für Bibliothekswissenschaft* 71 (1957): 267-80.

Krummel, D. W. *Guide for Dating Early Published Music: A Manual of Bibliographical Practices.* Hackensack, N.J.: J. Boonin, 1974.

_____. "Musical Functions and Bibliographical Forms." *The Library* (5th ser.) 31 (December 1976): 345.

LeCompte, Yves. "Comment nous utilisons l'électro-mecanographie." *Fontes artis Musicae* 4 (1957): 38-41.

Library of Congress. Descriptive Cataloging Division. *Rules for Descriptive Cataloging in the Library of Congress: Phonorecords.* 2nd prelim. ed. Washington, D.C.: Library of Congress, 1964.

_____. *Rules for the Brief Cataloging of Music in the Library of Congress: Exceptions to the Anglo-American Cataloging Rules.* n.p.: Music Library Association, 1970.

Library of Congress. MARC Development Office. *Music: A MARC Format.* Washington, D.C.: Library of Congress, 1976.

Library of Congress. Special Materials Cataloging Division. Music Section. "Music of Ethnic and National Groups." *Music Cataloging Bulletin* 12, no. 5 (1981): 2-4.

Library of Congress. Subject Cataloging Division. *Music Subject Headings Used on Printed Catalog Cards of the Library of Congress.* Washington, D.C.: U.S. Government Printing Office, 1952.

_____. *Classification. Class M. Music and Books on Music.* 2nd ed. with supplementary pages. Washington, D.C.: Library of Congress, 1917; reissued 1968.

_____. *Classification. Class M. Music and Books on Music.* 3rd ed. Washington, D.C.: Library of Congress, 1978.

Look, W. C. *The Classification and Cataloging of Music Scores in Libraries.* Master's dissertation, University of Chicago, 1951.

Maruyama, L. S., and H. D. Avram. "Cataloguing and the Computer." *Fontes artes Musicae* 19 (1972): 164-71.

McColvin, Lionel R., and Harold Reeves. *Music Libraries.* London: Grafton, 1937.

Miller, Karen, and A. Patricia Miller. "Syncopation Automation: An Online Thematic Index." *Information Technology and Libraries* 1 (1982): 270-74.

Music Library Association. American Library Association. Joint Committee. *Code for Cataloging Music and Phonorecords.* Prepared by a Joint Committee of the Music Library Association and the American Library Association, Division of Cataloging and Classification. Chicago: American Library Association, 1958.

Music Library Association. Cataloging and Classification Committee. *S L A C C: The Partial Use of the Shelflist as Classed Catalog.* Donald Seibert, Chairman. MLA Technical Reports, No. 1. Ann Arbor, Mich.: Music Library Association, 1973.

Music Library Association. Cataloging Committee. *Code for Cataloging Music.* Preliminary version issued by chapters. Mimeograph, 1941-1942.

[Chapter 1:] *Music: Entry and Heading.* Reprinted from *A.L.A. Catalog Rules.* Preliminary 2nd American ed. Chicago: American Library Association, 1941.

Chapter 2: *Title.* 1941.

Chapter 3: *Imprint.* February 1942.

Chapter IV: *Collation.* 1942. Chapter V: *Notes.* 1942.

*Code for Cataloging Phonograph Records.* 1942.

Music Library Association. Committee on Classification. "Music Classification." *Notes: Supplement for Members* 15 (1951): 9-15.

___. "Proposed Alternate Scheme for Dewey M780." *Notes: Supplement for Members* 17 (1951): 5-15.

"Music Subject Headings Used on Printed Catalog Cards of the Library of Congress...." *Notes* 9 (1952): 607.

New York. Public Library. Reference Department. *Music Subject Headings Authorized for Use in the Catalogs of the Music Division.* Boston: G. K. Hall, 1959.

Online Computer Library Center, Inc. *Scores Format.* 2nd ed. Dublin, Ohio: OCLC, 1986.

_____. *Sound Recordings Format.* 2nd ed. Dublin, Ohio: OCLC, 1986.

Pethes, Ivan. "The Classification of Music and Literature on Music." *Fontes artis Musicae* 15 (1968): 83-102.

Phillips, Don. "An Expandable Classification Scheme for Phonorecord Libraries." *Library Resources & Technical Services* 13 (1969): 511-15.

Philp, Geraint. "The Proposed Revision of 780 Music and Problems in the Development of Faceted Classification for Music." *Brio* 19 (1982): 1-13.

*Proceedings of the Institute on Library of Congress Music Cataloging Policies and Procedures.* Transcribed and compiled with editorial comments by David Sommerfield. Ann Arbor, Mich.: Music Library Association, 1975. (MLA Technical Reports, No. 3).

*Proposed Revision of 780 Music: Based on Dewey Decimal Classification and Relative Index.* Prepared under the direction of Russell Sweeney and John Clews with assistance from Winton E. Matthews. Albany, N.Y.: Forest Press, 1980.

Redfern, Brian. *Organising Music in Libraries*. London: Bingley, 1966. 2 vol.

_____. *Organising Music in Libraries*. Rev. and rewritten ed. London: Bingley; Hamden, Conn.: Linnet, 1979. 2 vols.

Research Libraries Group, Inc. *MARC Tagging Workbook: Scores*. Stanford, Calif.: RLG, 1980.

*MARC Tagging Workbook: Sound Recordings*. 1980.

*Recordings Field Guide*. 1st ed. 1982.

*Scores Field Guide*. 1st ed. 1982.

Rovelstad, Betsy. "Condensation of the Library of Congress M Classification Schedule." *Notes: Supplement for Members* 34 (1963): 1-34.

Russell, John F. "The Cataloguing of Music." *Library Association Record* 40 (1938): 247-50.

Saheb-Ettaba, Caroline, and Roger B. McFarland. *ANSCR: The Alpha-Numeric System for Classification of Recordings*. Williamsport, Pa.: Bro-Dart, 1969.

Schmidt-Phiseldeck, Kay. "Le Code International de Catalogage." *Fontes artis Musicae* 4 (1957): 26.

_____. "Internationale Kommission für Katalogisierung von Musikalien." *Fontes artis Musicae* 5 (1958): 15-20.

_____. "The Music Cataloguing Committee at Brussels (IAML)." *Fontes artis Musicae* 3 (1956): 31-32.

_____. *Musikkatalogisierung: Ein Beitrag zur Lösung ihrer Probleme*. Leipzig: Breitkopf & Härtel, 1926.

Seibert, Donald. *The MARC Format: From Inception to Publication*. MLA Technical Reports, No. 13. Philadelphia, Pa.: Music Library Association, 1982.

Seibert, Donald, with Charles M. Herrold. "Uniform Titles for Music under AACR2 and Its Predecessors: The Problems and Possibilities of Developing a User-Friendly Reportoire." In *Cataloging Special Materials: Critiques and Innovations*, 133-50. Edited by Sanford Berman. Phoenix, Ariz.: Oryx Press, 1986.

Smiraglia, Richard P. *Cataloging Music: A Manual for Use with AACR2*. 2nd ed. Lake Crystal, Minn.: Soldier Creek Press, 1986.

_____. *Shelflisting Music: Guidelines for Use with Library of Congress Classification: M*. MLA Technical Reports, No. 9. Philadelphia, Pa.: Music Library Association, 1981.

_____. "Uniform Titles for Music: An Exercise in Collocating Works." *Cataloging & Classification Quarterly* 9, no. 3 (1989): 97-114.

Smiraglia, Richard P., with Arsen R. Papakhian. "Music in the OCLC Online Union Catalog: A Review." *Notes* 38 (1981): 257-74.

Sonneck, O. G. "Music." *Rules for a Dictionary Catalog*, 138. By Charles Ammi Cutter. 4th ed., rewritten. Washington, D.C.: U.S. Government Printing Office, 1904.

_____. "Prefatory Note (First Edition)." In *Classification. Class M: Music and Books on Music*. By Library of Congress. Subject Cataloging Division. 2nd ed. with supplementary pages. Washington, D.C.: Library of Congress, 1917; reissued 1968.

_____. "Prefatory Note (Revised Edition)." In *Classification. Class M*, 5.

Spalding, C. Sumner. "Music Authority Files at the Library of Congress." *Music Cataloging Bulletin* 10, no. 10 (October 1979): 4-6.

Sunder, Mary Jane. "Organization of Recorded Sound." *Library Resources & Technical Services* 13 (1969): 93-98.

"Symposium on Music in Libraries: Contributed by Various Libraries in the United States." *Library Journal* (August 1915): 563-94.

Wallace, Ruth, ed. *The Care and Treatment of Music in a Library*. American Library Association, Committee on Cataloging, Contribution, No. 1. Chicago: American Library Association, 1927.

Watanabe, Ruth. "American Music Libraries and Music Librarianship: An Overivew in the Eighties." *Notes* 38 (1981): 239-56.

Weidow, Judy. *Music Cataloging Policy in the General Libraries*. Contributions to Librarianship, No. 8. [Austin, Tex.]: The General Libraries, The University of Texas at Austin, 1984.

Weiss-Reyscher, E. *Anweisung zur Titelaufnahme von Musikalien*. Berlin. Bibliotheksschule. Abteilung für den Dienst an Volksbücherein. Veröffentlichungen 2. Leipzig: Einkaufshaus für Bücherein, 1938.

Weitz, Jay. "More News from OCLC." *Music OCLC Users Group Newsletter* 34 (January 1988): 5.

Young, James Bradford. "A Comparison of PRECIS and Library of Congress Subject Headings for the Retrieval of Printed Music." Computer-generated typescript, Atlanta, Ga., 1986.

# INDEX

An "e" following a page citation indicates the presence of an example; an "i" following a page citation indicates the presence of an illustration.